WORKING PAPERS WITH STUDY GUIDE 1–14

M000289342

College Accounting

Seventh Edition

Douglas J. McQuaig
Wenatchee Valley College

Patricia A. Bille
Highline Community College

Houghton Mifflin Company Boston New York

Senior Accounting Editor: Bonnie Binkert
Associate Sponsoring Editor: Margaret E. Monahan
Editorial Associate: Damaris R. Curran
Project Editor: Elisabeth Kehrer
Senior Production Design Coordinator: Carol Merrigan
Manufacturing Manager: Florence Cadran
Marketing Manager: Melissa Russell

Copyright © 2001 by Houghton Mifflin Company. All rights reserved.

Permission is hereby granted to teachers to reprint or photocopy in classroom quantities the pages or sheets in this work that carry a Houghton Mifflin Company copyright notice. These pages are designed to be reproduced by teachers for use in their classes with accompanying Houghton Mifflin material, provided each copy made shows the copyright notice. Such copies may not be sold and further distribution is expressly prohibited. Except as authorized above, prior written permission must be obtained from Houghton Mifflin Company to reproduce or transmit this work or portions thereof in any other form or by any other electronic or mechanical means, including any information storage or retrieval system, unless expressly permitted by federal copyright law. Address inquiries to College Permissions, Houghton Mifflin Company, 222 Berkeley Street, Boston, MA 02116-3764.

Printed in the U.S.A.

ISBN: 0-618-02288-0

56789-CRS-04 03 02

Contents

PART III THE ACCOUNTING CYCLE FOR A MERCHANDISING BUSINESS: USING SPECIAL JOURNALS

To the Student

As you study *College Accounting*, Seventh Edition, you will find these Working Papers with Study Guide helpful in many different ways. The first part of the book contains the following selections to assist you in your study of accounting:

- Review of T Account Placement and Representative Transactions
- How to Study Accounting
- How to Solve Accounting Problems
- Ten-Key Skills Review
- Introduction to Spreadsheets
- Review of Business Mathematics
- How to Work a Practice Set
- Suggested Abbreviations for Account Titles

Then for each chapter in the textbook, the Working Papers with Study Guide provide the following:

- **Performance Objectives** and **Key Terms**   The Performance Objectives duplicate your textbook. When you begin your study session, read the objectives and try to recall the text explanations. If you do not feel you can fulfill a performance objective, look for the performance objective in the margin of your textbook and review that material before trying to complete your homework assignments. Use the list of key terms to test your recall of vocabulary in the end-of-chapter glossaries. Look in the glossary at the end of the chapter in your textbook to find the definition of any term you do not know. If you still don't understand the term, note the page number in the glossary and look for the term itself in the body of the chapter. Each key term is printed in green type when it is first used and defined. Make sure you understand all the key terms before going on to the next chapter.
- **Study Guide Questions**   After you read each chapter in the textbook, try answering these short questions. They will show how well you have learned the material in the text. Answers are provided at the back of the Working Papers with Study Guide, so you can find out right away whether you are correct. If you missed a few questions, go back to the text and review those areas where your understanding is incomplete. If you have mastered the material, you are ready to go ahead.
- **Demonstration Problem** and **Solution**   Important concepts are illustrated by a self-study problem and its solution. Test yourself by working this sample problem. Next, verify your answer with the solution presented. Also, as you work your homework assignments, you may want to refer to the Demonstration Problem as well as to the text.
- **Accounting forms**   Blank forms are provided for every problem in the textbook. Sometimes information is provided to help you get started. The pages are perforated so that you can tear them out if the instructor asks for them.

In addition, all the information you need to complete the Accounting Cycle Review Problem (following Chapter 5), the Comprehensive Review Problem (following Chapter 14), and the Cumulative Self-Checks is provided in the Working Papers with Study Guide, including the required blank accounting forms. A selection of blank forms is also provided for you to use to solve supplemental problems. If you photocopy these forms as you need them, you shouldn't ever run out of forms.

We hope that the Working Papers with Study Guide will make it easier for you to learn the fundamentals of accounting. Please write to us in care of Houghton Mifflin if you have suggestions about the text or other learning materials in your course.

Good luck in your college accounting class!

Douglas J. McQuaig
Patricia A. Bille

Copyright © by Houghton Mifflin Company. All rights reserved.

Review of T Account Placement and Representative Transactions

PART I
CHAPTERS 2 THROUGH 5

Review of T Account Placement

The following display sums up the placement of T accounts covered in Part I, Chapters 2 through 5, in relation to the fundamental accounting equation. Italicized accounts are contra accounts.

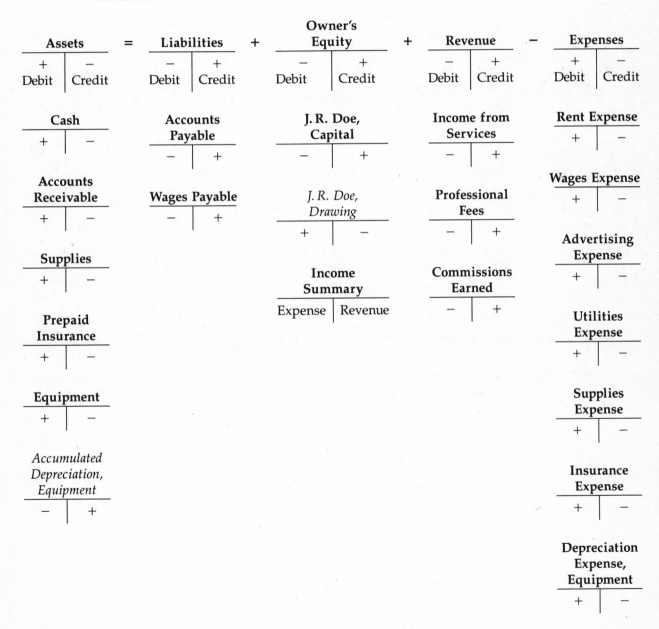

Copyright © by Houghton Mifflin Company. All rights reserved.

Review of Representative Transactions

The following table summarizes the recording of the various transactions described in Part I, Chapters 2–5, and the classification of the accounts involved.

Transaction	Accounts Involved	Class.	Increase or Decrease	Therefore Debit or Credit	Financial Statement
Owner invested cash in business	Cash J.R. Doe, Capital	A OE	I I	Debit Credit	Balance Sheet and Statement of Owner's Equity
Bought equipment for cash	Equipment Cash	A A	I D	Debit Credit	Balance Sheet Balance Sheet
Bought supplies on account	Supplies Accounts Payable	A L	I I	Debit Credit	Balance Sheet Balance Sheet
Bought equipment, paying a down payment with the remainder on account	Equipment Cash Accounts Payable	A A L	I D I	Debit Credit Credit	Balance Sheet Balance Sheet Balance Sheet
Paid premium for insurance policy	Prepaid Insurance Cash	A A	I D	Debit Credit	Balance Sheet Balance Sheet
Paid creditor on account	Accounts Payable Cash	L A	D D	Debit Credit	Balance Sheet Balance Sheet
Sold services for cash	Cash Income from Services	A R	I I	Debit Credit	Balance Sheet Income State.
Paid rent for month	Rent Expense Cash	E A	I D	Debit Credit	Income State. Balance Sheet
Billed customers for services performed	Accounts Receivable Income from Services	A R	I I	Debit Credit	Balance Sheet Income State.
Owner withdrew cash for personal use	J.R. Doe, Drawing Cash	OE A	I D	Debit Credit	Statement of Owner's Equity Balance Sheet

Copyright © by Houghton Mifflin Company. All rights reserved.

Transaction	Accounts Involved	Class.	Increase or Decrease	Therefore Debit or Credit	Financial Statement
Received cash from charge customers to apply on account	Cash Accounts Receivable	A A	I D	Debit Credit	Balance Sheet Balance Sheet
Paid wages to employees	Wages Expense Cash	E A	I D	Debit Credit	Income State. Balance Sheet
Adjusting entry for supplies used	Supplies Expense Supplies	E A	I D	Debit Credit	Income State. Balance Sheet
Adjusting entry for insurance expired	Insurance Expense Prepaid Insurance	E A	I D	Debit Credit	Income State. Balance Sheet
Adjusting entry for depreciation of assets	Depreciation Expense Accumulated Depreciation	E A	I I	Debit Credit	Income State. Balance Sheet
Adjusting entry for accrued wages	Wages Expense Wages Payable	E L	I I	Debit Credit	Income State. Balance Sheet
Closing entry for revenue accounts	Revenue accounts Income Summary	R OE	D —	Debit Credit	Income State. —
Closing entry for expense accounts	Income Summary Expense accounts	OE E	— D	Debit Credit	— Income State.
Closing entry for Income Summary account (Net Income)	Income Summary J. R. Doe, Capital	OE OE	— I	Debit Credit	— Balance Sheet and Statement of Owner's Equity
Closing entry for Drawing account	J. R. Doe, Capital J. R. Doe, Drawing	OE OE	D D	Debit Credit	Balance Sheet and Statement of Owner's Equity

Copyright © by Houghton Mifflin Company. All rights reserved.

Review of T Account Placement

The following sums up the placement of T accounts covered in Part II, Chapters 7 through 9, in relation to the fundamental accounting equation.

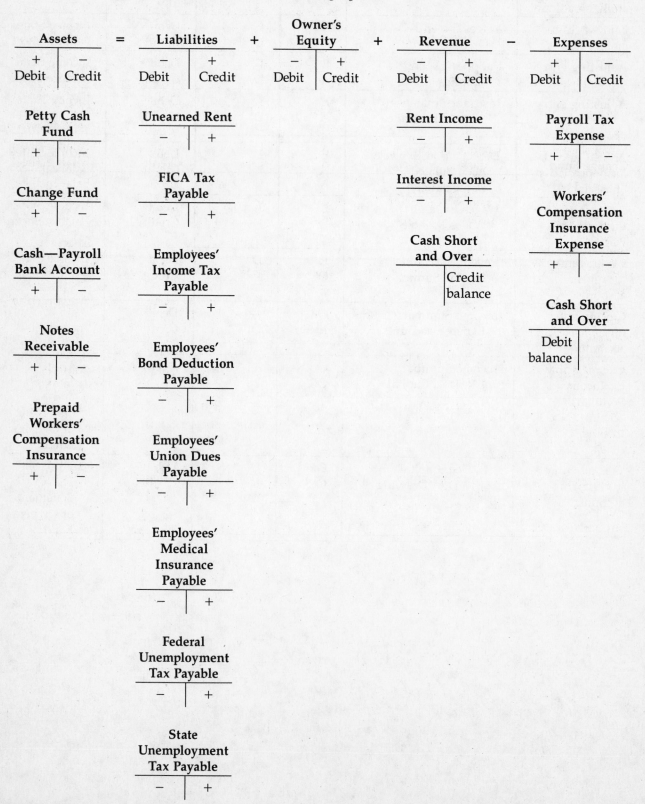

Copyright © by Houghton Mifflin Company. All rights reserved.

Review of Representative Transactions

The following summarizes the recording of transactions covered in Part II, Chapters 7 through 9, along with a classification of the accounts involved.

Transaction	Accounts Involved	Class.	Increase or Decrease	Therefore Debit or Credit	Financial Statement
Established a Petty Cash Fund	Petty Cash Fund Cash	A A	I D	Debit Credit	Balance Sheet Balance Sheet
Reimbursed Petty Cash Fund	Expenses or Assets or Drawing Cash	E A OE A	I D	Debit Debit Debit Credit	Income State. Balance Sheet State. of O.E. Balance Sheet
Established a Change Fund	Change Fund Cash	A A	I D	Debit Credit	Balance Sheet Balance Sheet
Recorded cash sales (amount on cash register tape was larger than cash count)	Cash Cash Short and Over Sales	A E R	I — I	Debit Debit Credit	Balance Sheet Income State. Income State.
Recorded cash sales (amount on cash register tape was less than cash count)	Cash Sales Cash Short and Over	A R R	I I —	Debit Credit Credit	Balance Sheet Income State. Income State.
Recorded service charges on bank account	Miscellaneous Expense Cash	E A	I D	Debit Credit	Income State. Balance Sheet
Recorded NSF check received from customer	Accounts Receivable Cash	A A	I D	Debit Credit	Balance Sheet Balance Sheet
Recorded interest-bearing note receivable collected by our bank	Cash Notes Receivable Interest Income	A A R	I D I	Debit Credit Credit	Balance Sheet Balance Sheet Income State.

Copyright © by Houghton Mifflin Company. All rights reserved.

Transaction	Accounts Involved	Class.	Increase or Decrease	Therefore Debit or Credit	Financial Statement
Recorded the payroll entry from the payroll register	Sales Salary Expense	E	I	Debit	Income State.
	Office Salary Expense	E	I	Debit	Income State.
	FICA Tax Payable	L	I	Credit	Balance Sheet
	Employees' Income Tax Payable	L	I	Credit	Balance Sheet
	Employees' Bond Deduction Payable	L	I	Credit	Balance Sheet
	Employees' Union Dues Payable	L	I	Credit	Balance Sheet
	Salaries Payable	L	I	Credit	Balance Sheet
Issued check payable to Cash to pay payroll	Salaries Payable	L	D	Debit	Balance Sheet
	Cash	A	D	Credit	Balance Sheet
Recorded employer's payroll taxes	Payroll Tax Expense	E	I	Debit	Income State.
	FICA Tax Payable	L	I	Credit	Balance Sheet
	State Unemployment Tax Payable	L	I	Credit	Balance Sheet
	Federal Unemployment Tax Payable	L	I	Credit	Balance Sheet
Recorded deposit of FICA taxes and employees' income tax withheld	Employee's Income Tax Payable	L	D	Debit	Balance Sheet
	FICA Tax Payable	L	D	Debit	Balance Sheet
	Cash	A	D	Credit	Balance Sheet
Recorded deposit of federal unemployment tax	Federal Unemployment Tax Payable	L	D	Debit	Balance Sheet
	Cash	A	D	Credit	Balance Sheet
Paid state unemployment tax	State Unemployment Tax Payable	L	D	Debit	Balance Sheet
	Cash	A	D	Credit	Balance Sheet
Paid for workers' compensation insurance in advance	Prepaid Workers' Compensation Insurance	A	I	Debit	Balance Sheet
	Cash	A	D	Credit	Balance Sheet
Adjusting entry for workers' compensation insurance, assuming an additional amount is owed	Workers' Compensation Insurance Expense	E	I	Debit	Income State.
	Prepaid Workers' Compensation Insurance	A	D	Credit	Balance Sheet
	Workers' Compensation Insurance Payable	L	I	Credit	Balance Sheet
Issued check to transfer cash to the payroll bank account	Cash—Payroll Bank Account	A	I	Debit	Balance Sheet
	Cash	A	D	Credit	Balance Sheet

Copyright © by Houghton Mifflin Company. All rights reserved.

Review of T Account Placement

The following sums up the placement of T accounts covered in Part III, Chapters 10 through 14, in relation to the fundamental accounting equation. Italics indicates those accounts that are treated as deductions from the related accounts above them.

Assets		=	Liabilities		+	Owner's Equity		+	Revenue		−	Expenses	
+	−		−	+		−	+		−	+		+	−
Debit	Credit		Debit	Credit		Debit	Credit		Debit	Credit		Debit	Credit

Merchandise Inventory									Sales			Purchases	
+	−								−	+		+	−

Sales Returns and Allowances

+	−

Purchases Returns and Allowances

−	+

Sales Discount

+	−

Purchases Discount

−	+

Freight In

+	−

Credit Card Expense

+	−

Review of Representative Transactions

The following table summarizes the recording of transactions covered in Part III, Chapters 10 through 14, along with a classification of the accounts involved.

Classifications

	Balance Sheet		Income Statement
CA	Current Assets	S	Revenue from Sales
P & E	Plant and Equipment	CGS	Cost of Goods Sold
CL	Current Liabilities	SE	Selling Expenses
LTL	Long-Term Liabilities	GE	General Expenses
		OI	Other Income
		OE	Other Expenses

Copyright © by Houghton Mifflin Company. All rights reserved.

Transaction	Accounts Involved	Class.	Increase or Decrease	Therefore Debit or Credit	Financial Statement
Sold merchandise on account	Accounts Receivable	CA	I	Debit	Balance Sheet
	Sales	S	I	Credit	Income State.
Sold merchandise on account involving sales tax	Accounts Receivable	CA	I	Debit	Balance Sheet
	Sales	S	I	Credit	Income State.
	Sales Tax Payable	CL	I	Credit	Balance Sheet
Issued credit memo to customer for merchandise returned	Sales Returns and Allowances	S	I	Debit	Income State.
	Accounts Receivable	CA	D	Credit	Balance Sheet
Summarizing entry for the total of sales invoices for sales on account for the month	Accounts Receivable	CA	I	Debit	Balance Sheet
	Sales	S	I	Credit	Income State.
Bought merchandise on account	Purchases	CGS	I	Debit	Income State.
	Accounts Payable	CL	I	Credit	Balance Sheet
Bought merchandise on account with freight prepaid as a convenience to the buyer	Purchases	CGS	I	Debit	Income State.
	Freight In	CGS	I	Debit	Income State.
	Accounts Payable	CL	I	Credit	Balance Sheet
Received credit memo from supplier for merchandise returned	Accounts Payable	CL	D	Debit	Balance Sheet
	Purchases Returns and Allowances	CGS	I	Credit	Income State.
Summarizing entry for the total of purchases of all types of goods on account	Purchases	CGS	I	Debit	Income State.
	Store Supplies	CA	I	Debit	Balance Sheet
	Office Supplies	CA	I	Debit	Balance Sheet
	Store Equipment	P & E	I	Debit	Balance Sheet
	Accounts Payable	CL	I	Credit	Balance Sheet
Paid for transportation charges on incoming merchandise	Freight In	CGS	I	Debit	Income State.
	Cash	CA	D	Credit	Balance Sheet
Sold merchandise, involving sales tax, for cash	Cash	CA	I	Debit	Balance Sheet
	Sales	S	I	Credit	Income State.
	Sales Tax Payable	CL	I	Credit	Balance Sheet

Copyright © by Houghton Mifflin Company. All rights reserved.

Transaction	Accounts Involved	Class.	Increase or Decrease	Therefore Debit or Credit	Financial Statement

Sold merchandise involving a sales tax and the customer used a bank charge card	Cash
	Credit Card Expense
	   Sales
	   Sales Tax Payable
		CA
		SE
		S
		CL
			I
			I
			I
			I
				Debit
				Debit
				Credit
				Credit
					Balance Sheet
					Income State.
					Income State.
					Balance Sheet

Charge customer paid bill within the discount period	Cash Sales Discount Accounts Receivable	CA S CA	I I D	Debit Debit Credit	Balance Sheet Income State. Balance Sheet

Paid invoice for the purchase of merchandise within the discount period	Accounts Payable
	   Cash
	   Purchases Discount
		CL
		CA
		CGS
			D
			D
			I
				Debit
				Credit
				Credit
					Balance Sheet
					Balance Sheet
					Income State.

First adjusting entry for merchandise inventory—periodic	Income Summary
	   Merchandise
	   Inventory
		—
		CA &
		CGS
			—
			D
				Debit
				Credit
					—
					Balance Sheet
					and
					Income State.

Second adjusting entry for merchandise inventory—periodic	Merchandise Inventory Income Summary	CA & CGS —	I —	Debit Credit	Balance Sheet and Income State. —
Adjusting entry for rent earned (Rent Income)	Unearned Rent Rent Income	CL OI	D I	Debit Credit	Balance Sheet Income State.
Reversing entry for adjustment for accrued wages	Wages Payable Wages Expense	CL SE or GE	D D	Debit Credit	Balance Sheet Income State.
Adjusting entry for merchandise inventory—perpetual, if physical count is greater than ledger balance of merchandise inventory	Merchandise Inventory Cost of Goods Sold	CA CGS	I D	Debit Credit	Balance Sheet Income State.
Adjusting entry for merchandise inventory—perpetual, if physical count is less than ledger balance of merchandise inventory	Cost of Goods Sold Merchandise Inventory	CGS CA	I D	Debit Credit	Income State. Balance Sheet

Copyright © by Houghton Mifflin Company. All rights reserved.

How to Study Accounting

Studying is defined as applying oneself to learning.

The purpose of studying accounting is to obtain the textbook and technical knowledge of accounting plus the hands-on experience necessary to succeed in the accounting profession.

Research has shown that the greater your involvement in studying, the more you retain. Retention means how long you are able to remember the concepts and practices. The four groups of study activities are shown from the lowest percentage of retention (about 10%) to the highest level of retention (about 98%):

- Hearing
- Seeing
- Saying
- Doing

Let's also look at why you are studying manual accounting when you hear so much about the use of the computer to complete accounting tasks in business. It is true that computers have become an integral part of accounting. However, you must first know the basics of accounting, the language of the profession, and the flow of the accounting cycle before you can effectively enlist the aid of a computer. A computer is only a tool to perform routine accounting tasks and print the results more quickly and attractively.

Now, let's begin our journey learning manual accounting. To do so, we shall work our way through the hierarchy of retention.

Hearing alone will only take you to the lowest level of retention. This means that if the only activity you enlist in your learning process is listening, you will retain very little. However, this does not mean that listening is not important as a learning tool. There are several things you can do in the area of listening.

Attend class equipped with paper and pencil to **take notes.** Use a tape recorder if this fits your needs and the instructor agrees. Also, take your textbook to class to refer to as the presentation progresses.

Be prepared to listen to questions asked and answers given, as well as classroom discussion.

The second level of retention adds **seeing** to hearing to increase the amount you remember. Two resources are critical to this level: your instructor and your textbook.

First, **observe your instructor** carefully. Take note when he or she makes references to textbook examples, shows illustrations on handouts, distributes material on transparencies or overhead projections, or shows examples drawn in chalkboard presentations.

Second, **know your textbook** and what it contains, how it is structured, and where you can find various tools.

So far, we have looked at only half of the retention hierarchy. Hearing allows you to retain the least. Hearing and seeing together increase your chances for retention. However, if you add saying or **verbal participation** at the third level, you will significantly increase what you remember. There are several ways in which you can strengthen your learning by hearing the sound of your own voice speaking about the subject.

Copyright © by Houghton Mifflin Company. All rights reserved.

Ask questions. Sometimes you may feel confused and feel unable to formulate a question. Don't let that stop you. Try to avoid the sweeping negative statement, "I just don't get this." Narrow your question to the place your understanding went off the track.

Volunteer answers. Be an active and enthusiastic learner!

Participate in classroom discussions. You may be surprised how your own life experiences have prepared you for this course in accounting. You have owned things, owed money, bought items, sold things, incurred expenses, and earned an income. You may have filled out a W-4 form when you went to work for an employer, and received a W-2 form from the employer at the end of a calendar year. You may have had a checking account. Each of the activities mentioned are ones that you will experience in accounting. Your experience is valuable—share it in class. Use your personal experiences to visualize accounting tasks. See how each task fits into the accounting cycle. The **discussion questions** at the end of each chapter provide material to spark conversations and support discussions.

Study with a partner or group. It will serve not only as a way to get acquainted, but it will also provide you with support. The give and take of studying as a team will help both of you learn. You both win because your voice is a powerful tool for teaching others as well as strengthening your own learning.

Finally, outside of class, **talk to yourself.** Yes, talk to yourself! For example, study glossary terms aloud, reread your notes aloud, talk your way through an accounting transaction. Let your brain hear you. You will decrease your journalizing and posting errors considerably with this technique. Don't be bashful. It will be much easier for you to speak up in class as the terminology becomes more familiar.

Let's add the last retention builder to the hierarchy—**doing.** So far, we have investigated

- hearing only
- hearing plus seeing
- hearing plus seeing plus saying

and now,

- hearing plus seeing plus saying plus **doing.**

You may have heard it said that accounting is best learned through the end of a pencil. In other words, you can read and listen all you wish, but until you actually do it, it does not become yours. An analogy might be one of studying to become a surgeon or an auto mechanic by only reading and hearing about your profession—until you try it, you do not have a working knowledge of the subject. Therefore, let me suggest that you thoughtfully and conscientiously complete all assignments your instructor makes whether they are questions, exercises, or problems.

Accounting is like a pyramid. What you learn in each new chapter builds on knowledge from previous chapters. If the base of the pyramid is not firmly in place, your accounting skills will be weak.

To summarize, in looking at "How to Study Accounting," you have seen that you need to put into force all levels of action to give yourself the highest level of retention—hearing plus seeing plus saying plus doing. You have also seen how important it is that you know your textbook—how it is structured and where to find the things you need.

Copyright © by Houghton Mifflin Company. All rights reserved.

How to Solve Accounting Problems

Solving means to find or provide a satisfactory answer or explanation for a problem. A solution to a problem, whether in accounting or in any other discipline, involves more than just "getting the answer." This is what most of us search for, but other preliminary steps lead to the final solution.

Before you can solve any problem, you need to understand accounting fundamentals and strategies for solving problems. First, we will look at these fundamentals, then we will review problem-solving strategies.

The **fundamental accounting equation** (Assets = Liabilities + Owner's Equity) is the basis for **double-entry accounting. Assets** are things owned. **Liabilities** are amounts owed to creditors. **Owner's equity** is the financial interest of the owner in the company.

We can think of owner's equity as an umbrella that covers the **Capital account.** The Capital account increases with investments and revenues, and decreases with withdrawals by the owner and expenses incurred.

Revenues, expenses, and the **Drawing account** are considered temporary owner's equity accounts, or nominal accounts. They are open for the accounting period to keep track of changes to owner's equity due to revenue earned and expenses incurred. At the end of the accounting period, they are closed out and the difference between the revenue and expenses is transferred to the Capital account. A net profit increases Capital, and a net loss decreases it.

Our expanded fundamental accounting equation now reads:

$$\text{Assets} = \text{Liabilities} + \text{Owner's Equity} + \text{Revenue} - \text{Expenses}$$

Both sides of any equation must balance.

The equation elements or classifications are broken down into subdivisions called **accounts.** Each account can be represented by a **T account**—a visualization of the information presented in a formal ledger account. The T account provides a structure to demonstrate the rules of **debit** and **credit.** It has two sides, a left side called the debit side and a right side called the credit side. You must clear your mind of your emotional attachment to the term credit. A credit is neither good nor bad, plus nor minus. Increases can be shown by debits or credits, depending on which account is involved.

The first accounting rule is that **debits must equal credits** in any entry.

Another rule is that the **normal balance** of an account is the plus side, which can be either the debit or credit side.

The problems at the end of the chapter provide the opportunity to apply the fundamentals that you have learned. Now let's look at some basic problem-solving techniques.

Scan the entire problem to get an overview of what is involved and what is expected. Most of the problem sets in your textbook have three sections that you must read carefully.

The first section includes a list of learning objectives, a problem number, and information about the problem and the business.

There is a list of transactions or other information providing the basis for solving the problem.

There are step-by-step instructions to guide you through the problem.

Read and follow each instruction carefully. Do them in order and do not skip any. Write down any questions you have, and remember to ask your instructor to clarify them.

Most of the problems in your book include **narrative transactions**—sentences describing the transaction. The secret for solving this kind of problem

Copyright © by Houghton Mifflin Company. All rights reserved.

is finding and understanding **key words.** Here are some translations of some of the more common words you will encounter in the problems:

Paid means cash going out, cash decreased.

Invested may mean cash was invested by the owner, but an investment can also mean another asset besides cash, such as personal equipment, one's law library, or other assets which are then given a fair market value.

Received cash means cash coming in, cash increased.

Bought means purchased something with cash or maybe on account or with a promissory note. In either of the latter two cases a promise has been made to pay cash at a later date agreed upon by both parties.

Received and paid a bill is the same as paid. Cash went out, cash decreased.

Received a bill, without any reference to paying means cash is not paid out at this time. The bill has been put away for payment at a later date.

Billed customers for services means no cash was received, but customers have promised to pay us after they receive the bill. (The **accrual basis** of accounting allows us to book revenue when earned and expenses when incurred, the opposite of the cash basis most people use for their personal accounting.)

Another way of looking at key words in transactions is to group phrases which you can expect to see together in certain types of transactions. Here are some words and phrases that you might encounter in a problem involving a customer:

Issued a credit memo	*Sales Returns and Allowances*
Sales	*Accounts Receivable*
Sold	*Accounts Receivable Ledger*
Sales Discount	

You will not see these customer-related key phrases mixed with phrases involving vendors and suppliers.

Here are some words and phrases associated with vendors and suppliers:

Received a credit memo	*Purchases Returns and Allowances*
Purchases	*Accounts Payable*
Purchases Discount	*Accounts Payable Ledger*

We have just looked at key words in transactions described in sentences, but in real-world situations, transactions are primarily generated by **source documents.** A source document is a piece of paper that evidences a transaction—some change in the financial condition of the business—for example an invoice or a check. However, most of the problems in your book are based on sentences describing transactions. Whether the transaction is generated by a sentence or a document, analyze the transaction to decide what accounts are debited and credited. The steps taken to analyze a transaction are:

1. Which accounts are involved?
2. Where do the accounts fall in the fundamental accounting equation: Assets, Liabilities, Owner's Equity, Revenues, or Expenses?
3. Are the accounts increased or decreased?
4. Which accounts are debited and which accounts are credited?
5. Do total debits equal total credits?

These steps work for every transaction, no matter how complex. Analyzing each transaction using these steps is critical to your success in accounting.

In summary, you need a firm base in accounting fundamentals before you begin to journalize transactions. You need to understand the fundamental accounting equation, the rules of debiting and crediting, and how to analyze each transaction based on these rules. Next you must understand the problem posed. Scan the problem, and then read it carefully. Follow, in order, the specific instructions listed at the end of each problem.

If you follow these rules and steps, your accounting experience will be more successful and satisfying. Try them—they work.

Copyright © by Houghton Mifflin Company. All rights reserved.

Keyboard arrangement:

Finger/thumb locations

Index	Middle	Ring
7	8	9
4	5	6
1	2	3
0	00	decimal
Thumb	Thumb	Thumb

Home Row →
5 may be more deeply recessed than other keys or be marked by a bump

Finger used	Number keys
Index	7 4 1
Middle	8 5 2
Ring	9 6 3
Thumb	0's decimal

Steps to complete each addition problem:
a. Clear the machine by pressing the total bar.
b. Use the correct fingers to enter each digit, keep your eyes on the copy, and move steadily.
c. Tap the plus (+) key after each entry.
d. When all entries are made, tap the total bar and check your answer.

10-Key Skill Review Problems

Practice 1, 2, and 3

1.	2.	3.
31	21	32
22	32	13
12	11	11
13	23	22
32	31	21
110	118	99

Practice 4, 5, and 6

4.	5.	6.
44	55	66
45	56	65
64	65	46
66	44	45
55	54	44
274	274	266

Practice 7, 8, and 9

7.	8.	9.
78	89	77
88	87	89
79	79	78
89	78	87
98	99	98
432	432	429

Practice Index Finger

10.	11.	12.
11	47	44
44	74	71
77	17	17
71	14	11
41	77	14
244	229	157

Practice Middle Finger

13.	14.	15.
22	58	82
55	85	58
88	52	25
28	25	85
25	28	22
218	248	272

Practice Ring Finger

16.	17.	18.
33	36	39
66	39	36
99	93	93
96	69	63
63	63	93
357	300	324

Copyright © by Houghton Mifflin Company. All rights reserved.

INTRODUCTION TO SPREADSHEETS

Definition: A type of computer application software made up of rows and columns that lets users perform calculations electronically rather than writing on a paper spreadsheet.

Purpose: A spreadsheet is an essential business tool because users can quickly recalculate computations after a change in a value. This feature enables users to engage in "what if" sessions; that is, try out different numbers, let the spreadsheet recalculate, and then consider the new results.

Example: Think of a spreadsheet as columnar working paper with rows displayed on a screen.

Appearance: In addition to the powerful capability of spreadsheets to calculate and recalculate instantly, the appearance of the spreadsheet information can be enhanced with borders, shading, different sizes and shapes of print, as well as charts and graphs to illustrate the data.

Illustration: This generic spreadsheet includes the major areas of most spreadsheets.

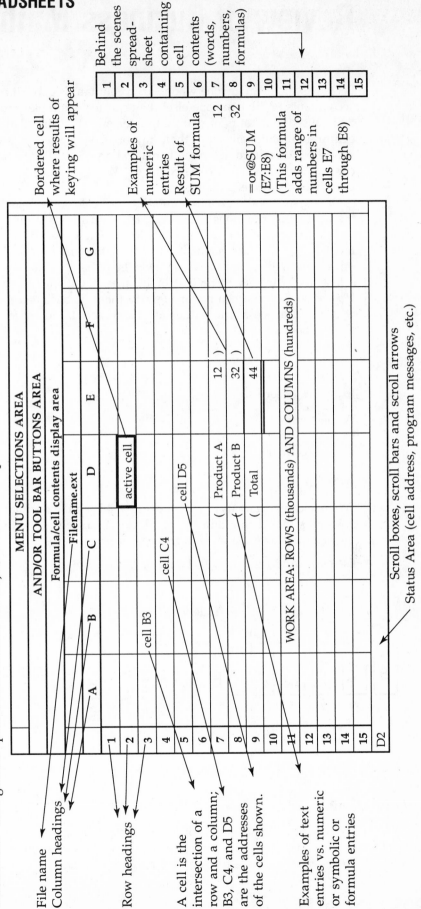

Copyright © by Houghton Mifflin Company. All rights reserved.

Review of Business Mathematics

People assume that anyone who is an accountant is good at mathematics. But accountants are like anyone else; they can make simple errors in arithmetic that cause them hours of searching later on. The thing that slows down the beginning accountant more than any other single factor is not being really sure about certain common mathematical processes. For example, how do you convert from fractions to percentages? What do you do with the decimal point when you are dividing?

Of course, we all agree that an electronic calculator capable of performing the arithmetic functions is an invaluable aid in accounting. However, even with a calculator, you still need to know what to divide by what, what to multiply by what, and so forth. The calculator will do only what you tell it to do, so you will always need a knowledge of basic business mathematics.

The following short review of business mathematics, which has items labeled so that you can better identify them, is designed to help you recall what you learned about mathematics long ago. In other words, it's a mathematical booster shot.

DECIMALS

Examples of terms:

Whole number   12
Decimal   .62
Mixed decimal   4.15

Addition

When adding decimals or mixed decimals, keep the decimal points lined up, one under the other. Fill in any blank places to the right with zeros so that all the addends have the same number of decimal places.

Example   Add 4.2, 16.53, .004, and 322.

$$
\left.
\begin{array}{r}
4.200 \\
16.530 \\
.004 \\
+\ 322.000
\end{array}
\right\} \text{Addends}
$$
$$
\overline{342.734}
$$

Example   Add 16.02, 4.035, 40, and .06.

$$
\begin{array}{r}
16.020 \\
4.035 \\
40.000 \\
+\quad .060 \\
\hline
60.115
\end{array}
$$

Subtraction

When subtracting decimals or mixed decimals, keep the decimal points lined up, one under the other. Fill in any blank places to the right with zeros so that all the numbers have the same number of decimal places.

Copyright © by Houghton Mifflin Company. All rights reserved.

Example   5.378 minus .8421.

$$
\begin{array}{rl}
5.3780 & \text{Minuend} \\
-\ \ \underline{.8421} & \text{Subtrahend} \\
4.5359 &
\end{array}
$$

Example   624.1 minus 16.003.

$$
\begin{array}{r}
624.100 \\
-\ \ \underline{16.003} \\
608.097
\end{array}
$$

Multiplication

When multiplying decimals or mixed decimals, find the position of the decimal point in the product (answer) by adding the number of decimal places in the multiplicand (number to be multiplied) and in the multiplier (number of times to multiply), and count off the same number of places from right to left in the product.

Example   Multiply .62 by .4.

$$
\begin{array}{rl}
.62 & \text{Multiplicand} \\
\times\ \ \ \underline{.4} & \text{Multiplier} \\
.248 & \text{Product}
\end{array}
$$

Example   Multiply 626.231 by 2.87.

$$
\begin{array}{r}
626.231 \\
\times\ 2.87 \\
\hline
43\,83617 \\
500\,9848 \\
1\,252\,462 \\
\hline
1{,}797.28297
\end{array}
$$

When the number of decimal places required is greater than the number of places in the product, add as many zeros to the left of the product as necessary.

Example   Multiply .049 by .02.

$$
\begin{array}{r}
.049 \\
\times\ \ \ .02 \\
\hline
.00098
\end{array}
$$

Example   Multiply .26 by .0091.

$$
\begin{array}{r}
.26 \\
\times\ \ \ .0091 \\
\hline
26 \\
234 \\
\hline
.002366
\end{array}
$$

Division

When the divisor (dividing number) is a whole number and the dividend (number to be divided) is a mixed decimal, place the decimal point in the quotient (answer) directly above the decimal point in the dividend.

Copyright © by Houghton Mifflin Company. All rights reserved.

Example   Divide 172.64 by 4.

$$
\begin{array}{r}
43.16 \quad \text{Quotient} \\
\text{Divisor} \quad 4\overline{)172.64} \quad \text{Dividend} \\
\underline{16} \\
12 \\
\underline{12} \\
6 \\
\underline{4} \\
24 \\
\underline{24}
\end{array}
$$

Example   Divide 6.39 by 15.

$$
\begin{array}{r}
.426 \\
15\overline{)6.390} \\
\underline{6\,0} \\
39 \\
\underline{30} \\
90 \\
\underline{90}
\end{array}
$$

When the divisor is a decimal, move the decimal point in the divisor as many places to the right as necessary to make the divisor a whole number, and move the decimal point in the dividend to the right also, the same number of places.

Example   Divide 14.406 by .007.

$$
\begin{array}{r}
2\,058. \\
.007\overline{)14.406} \\
\underline{14} \\
40 \\
\underline{35} \\
56 \\
\underline{56}
\end{array}
$$

Example   Divide 8.3927 by .943.

$$
\begin{array}{r}
8.9 \\
.943\overline{)8.3927} \\
7\,544 \\
8487 \\
8487
\end{array}
$$

FRACTIONS

Examples of terms:

Numerator $\longrightarrow$ 6
Denominator $\longrightarrow$ 39
Proper fraction: 8/9
Improper fraction: 13/6
Mixed number: $2\frac{3}{8}$
Like fractions: 2/5, 3/5, 4/5
Unlike fractions: 1/2, 1/4, 5/6

Addition

To add like fractions, add their numerators.

Copyright © by Houghton Mifflin Company. All rights reserved.

Example Add 1/5 and 3/5.

$$\begin{array}{r} 1/5 \\ + \, 3/5 \\ \hline 4/5 \end{array}$$

To add unlike fractions, you must convert them to like fractions. First, find the least common denominator (the smallest number that is exactly divisible by each denominator).

Next, divide the least common denominator by the denominator of each original fraction. Then multiply both the numerator and the denominator of each original fraction by this number. Add the numerators of the like fractions and, if necessary, reduce the sum to lowest terms.

Example Add 3/4 and 2/3. The least common denominator is 12.

$$4\overline{)12}^{\,3} \qquad \frac{3}{4} = \frac{3 \times 3}{4 \times 3} = \frac{9}{12}$$

$$3\overline{)12}^{\,4} \qquad \frac{2}{3} = \frac{2 \times 4}{3 \times 4} = + \frac{8}{12}$$

$$\frac{17}{12} = 1\frac{5}{12}$$

Example Add 1/3, 1/6, and 3/8. The least common denominator is 24.

$$3\overline{)24}^{\,8} \qquad \frac{1}{3} = \frac{1 \times 8}{3 \times 8} = \frac{8}{24}$$

$$6\overline{)24}^{\,4} \qquad \frac{1}{6} = \frac{1 \times 4}{6 \times 4} = \frac{4}{24}$$

$$8\overline{)24}^{\,3} \qquad \frac{3}{8} = \frac{3 \times 3}{8 \times 3} = + \frac{9}{24}$$

$$\frac{21}{24} = \frac{7}{8}$$

Subtraction

To subtract like fractions, subtract their numerators.

Example 7/8 minus 3/8.

$$\begin{array}{r} 7/8 \\ - \, 3/8 \\ \hline 4/8 = 1/2 \end{array}$$

To subtract unlike fractions, you must convert them to like fractions. First, find the least common denominator and divide it by the denominator of each original fraction. Then multiply both the numerator and the denominator of each original fraction by this number and subtract. When subtracting mixed numbers, change each mixed number to an improper like fraction.

Example 8/9 minus 5/12. The common denominator is 36.

$$9\overline{)36}^{\,4} \qquad \frac{8}{9} = \frac{8 \times 4}{9 \times 4} = \frac{32}{36}$$

$$12\overline{)36}^{\,3} \qquad \frac{5}{12} = \frac{5 \times 3}{12 \times 3} = - \frac{15}{36}$$

$$\frac{17}{36}$$

Copyright © by Houghton Mifflin Company. All rights reserved.

Example   4 1/6 minus 2 3/8. The common denominator is 24.

$$6\overline{)24} \quad 4\frac{1}{6} = \frac{25 \times 4}{6 \times 4} = \frac{100}{24}$$

$$8\overline{)24} \quad 2\frac{3}{8} = \frac{19 \times 3}{8 \times 3} = -\frac{57}{24}$$

$$\frac{43}{24} = 1\frac{19}{24}$$

Multiplication

When multiplying fractions, first simplify by canceling (dividing one numerator and one denominator, regardless of their positions, by the same number). Next multiply the numerators, multiply the denominators, and reduce the results to the lowest terms.

Example   5/16 × 1/5 × 9/8.

$$\frac{\overset{1}{\cancel{5}}}{16} \times \frac{1}{\underset{1}{\cancel{5}}} \times \frac{9}{8} = \frac{1 \times 1 \times 9}{16 \times 1 \times 8} = \frac{9}{128}$$

Example   140 × 4/25 × 5/18.

$$\frac{\overset{14}{\cancel{\overset{28}{\cancel{140}}}}}{1} \times \frac{4}{\underset{\underset{1}{\cancel{5}}}{\cancel{25}}} \times \frac{\overset{1}{\cancel{5}}}{\underset{9}{\cancel{18}}} = \frac{14 \times 4 \times 1}{1 \times 1 \times 9} = \frac{56}{9} = 6\frac{2}{9}$$

Division

When dividing fractions, invert the divisor (turn the fraction upside down) and multiply.

Example   Divide 7/16 by 3/4.

$$\frac{7}{16} \div \frac{3}{4} = \frac{7}{\underset{4}{\cancel{16}}} \times \frac{\overset{1}{\cancel{4}}}{3} = \frac{7 \times 1}{4 \times 3} = \frac{7}{12}$$

Example   Divide 36 by 2/3.

$$36 \div \frac{2}{3} = \frac{\overset{18}{\cancel{36}}}{1} \times \frac{3}{\underset{1}{\cancel{2}}} = 54$$

Changing a Fraction to a Decimal

Divide the numerator by the denominator.

Example   Change 7/8 to a decimal.

```
   .875
8)7.000
   6 4
   ───
    60
    56
    ──
    40
    40
    ──
```

Copyright © by Houghton Mifflin Company. All rights reserved.

Example Change 146/42 to a decimal.

$$\frac{146}{42} = \frac{146 \div 2}{42 \div 2} = \frac{73}{21}$$

$$
\begin{array}{r}
3.476+ \\
21\overline{)73.000} \\
63 \\
\overline{10\,0} \\
8\,4 \\
\overline{1\,60} \\
1\,47 \\
\overline{130} \\
126 \\
\overline{4}
\end{array}
$$

Changing a Decimal to a Fraction

Draw a line under the decimal. Write a 1 immediately below the decimal point and a 0 below each number in the decimal. Then drop the decimal point. Reduce to lowest terms.

Example Change .72 to a fraction.

$$.72 = \frac{72}{100} = \frac{72 \div 4}{100 \div 4} = \frac{18}{25}$$

Example Change .8125 to a fraction.

$$.8125 = \frac{8125}{10,000} = \frac{8125 \div 625}{10,000 \div 625} = \frac{13}{16}$$

Common Decimal Equivalents

The following equivalents are rounded off at the fourth decimal place.

$\frac{1}{2} = .5$	$\frac{1}{6} = .1667$	$\frac{1}{10} = .1$
$\frac{1}{3} = .3333$	$\frac{1}{7} = .1429$	$\frac{1}{11} = .0909$
$\frac{2}{3} = .6667$	$\frac{1}{8} = .125$	$\frac{1}{12} = .0833$
$\frac{1}{4} = .25$	$\frac{3}{8} = .375$	$\frac{1}{15} = .0667$
$\frac{3}{4} = .75$	$\frac{5}{8} = .625$	$\frac{1}{16} = .0625$
$\frac{1}{5} = .2$	$\frac{7}{8} = .875$	$\frac{1}{20} = .05$
$\frac{3}{5} = .6$	$\frac{1}{9} = .1111$	$\frac{1}{25} = .04$

PERCENTAGES

Percentages are fractions that have 100 for their denominators.

Changing a Percentage to a Decimal

Drop the percent sign and move the decimal point two places to the left. If the percentage consists of only one digit, add a 0 to the left of the digit.

Copyright © by Houghton Mifflin Company. All rights reserved.

Example   Change 36 percent to a decimal.

$$36\% = 36. = .36$$

Example   Change 5.85 percent to a decimal.

$$5.85\% = 05.85 = .0585$$

Changing a Decimal to a Percentage

Move the decimal point two places to the right and add the percent sign.

Example   Change .48 to a percentage.

$$.48 = .48 = 48\%$$

Example   Change 1.495 to a percentage.

$$1.495 = 1.495 = 149.5\%$$

Changing a Percentage to a Fraction

Drop the percent sign, make a fraction with the percentage as numerator and 100 as denominator, and reduce to lowest terms.

Example   Change 25 percent to a fraction.

$$25\% = \frac{25}{100} = \frac{25 \div 25}{100 \div 25} = \frac{1}{4}$$

Example   Change 31.5% to a fraction.

$$31.5\% = \frac{31.5}{100} = \frac{315}{1,000} = \frac{315 \div 5}{1,000 \div 5} = \frac{63}{200}$$

Changing a Fraction to a Percentage

Reduce to lowest terms. Divide the numerator by the denominator and move the decimal point two places to the right and add the percent sign.

Example   Change 5/8 to a percentage.

$$.625 = .625 = 62.5\%$$

$$
\begin{array}{r}
.625 \\
8\overline{)5.000} \\
\underline{4\,8} \\
20 \\
\underline{16} \\
40 \\
\underline{40} \\
\end{array}
$$

Example   Change 46/8 to a percentage.

$$\frac{46}{8} = \frac{46 \div 2}{8 \div 2} = \frac{23}{4}$$

$$5.75 = 5.75 = 575\%$$

$$
\begin{array}{r}
5.75 \\
4\overline{)23.00} \\
\underline{20} \\
3\,0 \\
\underline{2\,8} \\
20 \\
\underline{20} \\
\end{array}
$$

Copyright © by Houghton Mifflin Company. All rights reserved.

Finding the Ratio of . . . to . . .

This is the same thing as finding the percentage that one thing is of another. Write the "of..." amount in the numerator and the "to..." amount in the denominator. Reduce to lowest terms and divide the numerator by the denominator. Put a colon and the number 1 to the right of the answer.

Example Find the ratio of current assets ($69,000) to current liabilities ($27,000).

$$\frac{69,000}{27,000} = \frac{69,000 \div 3,000}{27,000 \div 3,000} = \frac{23}{9}$$

$$\begin{array}{r} 2.555 = 2.555 \text{ or } 2.56 = 2.56:1 \\ 9\overline{)23.000} \\ \underline{18} \\ 5\,0 \\ \underline{4\,5} \\ 50 \\ \underline{45} \\ 50 \\ \underline{45} \\ 5 \end{array}$$

Example Find the ratio of salesroom floor space (6,000 square feet) to office floor space (900 square feet).

$$\frac{6,000}{900} = \frac{6,000 \div 300}{900 \div 300} = \frac{20}{3}$$

$$\begin{array}{r} 6.666 = 6.666 \text{ or } 6.67 = 6.67:1 \\ 3\overline{)20.000} \\ \underline{18} \\ 2\,0 \\ \underline{1\,8} \\ 20 \\ \underline{18} \\ 20 \\ \underline{18} \\ 2 \end{array}$$

Finding the Percentage of Increase or Decrease

Divide the amount of the change by the base (starting figure). Change the decimal to a percentage.

Example Moore's income increased from $12,000 to $15,000. Find the percentage of increase.

Amount of change = 15,000 − 12,000 = 3,000

$$\begin{array}{r} .25 \qquad = .25 = 25\% \\ 12,000\overline{)3,000.00} \\ \underline{2\,400\,0} \\ 600\,00 \\ \underline{600\,00} \end{array}$$

Copyright © by Houghton Mifflin Company. All rights reserved.

Example Arnold's grade-point average decreased from 3.6 to 3.1. Find the percentage of decrease.

Amount of change = 3.6 − 3.1 = .5

$$
= .1388 \text{ or } .139 = 13.9\%
$$

$$
\begin{array}{r}
.1388 \\
3.6\overline{)5.0000} \\
\underline{3\ 6} \\
1\ 40 \\
\underline{1\ 08} \\
320 \\
\underline{288} \\
320 \\
\underline{288} \\
32
\end{array}
$$

ROUNDING OFF

If the last number in a decimal is 5 or greater, drop it and add one to the next number on the left. If the last number in a decimal is less than 5, drop it and let the other number stay the same.

Example Round off to two decimal places.

1.825 = 1.83

Example Round off to three decimal places.

.6923 = .692

Copyright © by Houghton Mifflin Company. All rights reserved.

How to Work a Practice Set

A practice set is a packet of accounting materials involving one business. Its purpose is to give you the opportunity to practice on a hypothetical company's accounting records, using what you have learned from the text and presentations by your instructor.

The advantages of completing a practice set during your accounting education are:

1. You are working for the same company.
2. You are able to maintain the continuity of the accounting cycle.
3. The materials are designed to simulate the records you will see on an accounting job.
4. The practice set may provide source documents to generate transactions to bridge the gap between textbook materials and real-world experiences.
5. It is rewarding to see your studying of text topics come together in a complete picture.
6. Completing the practice set is an excellent review of accounting.

Whatever practice set or sets your instructor chooses for you, here are some tips for working a practice set.

You will be most confident and successful if you first open the practice set, find the introduction, and answer the following questions:

- Where is the business located?
- What is the owner's name?
- Is it a sole proprietorship, a partnership, or a corporation?
- Does the company sell services, products, or both?
- What is your job title?
- What are your duties?
- Where do your duties fall in the accounting cycle, or will you be involved in the entire cycle?
- What is the length of the fiscal period?
- Are the books on the accrual basis?
- What date are you beginning work?
- In what format are the directions? In narrative form or in memos written to you?
- Are the transactions in narrative form or will source documents generate the transactions?
- Are there check figures?
- What is required by the practice set? That is, what is the story behind the set—recording, finding errors, organizing? What is it trying to emphasize?
- What subjects does it cover?
- Is it manual or computerized?
- How long is it expected to take?
- Are you expected to file paperwork? Are there checkpoints where you must submit work?

Now it is time to begin the practice set. Follow these steps throughout the practice set to help ensure a more pleasant and rewarding experience:

- Read the instructions carefully, sometimes more than once. As you read, circle or highlight important words or phrases. Use this same technique when reading documents as you analyze the transaction generated by the document.

Copyright © by Houghton Mifflin Company. All rights reserved.

- Check off each instruction as you complete it. In the case of documents, initial each document as it is journalized.
- List questions that occur to you, and take them to class to get answers.
- Write words and numbers clearly; this will avoid some errors. Remember, this is an opportunity to show your best work.
- Follow the rules of accounting precisely—the step-by-step procedures you learned during the prior weeks in class will save you time.
- Talk yourself through the analysis, journalizing, and posting of amounts.
- Maintain an awareness of where you are in the accounting cycle.

SUGGESTED ABBREVIATIONS FOR ACCOUNT TITLES IN CHAPTERS 1–14

Because traditional accounting methods have called for the use of full account titles in journal entries and financial statements, the text and solutions keep abbreviations to a minimum. However, computerized accounting programs and working papers present significant space constraints, and students' handwriting differs considerably in size. As a result, many instructors have requested a list of suggested abbreviations for account titles. Please bear in mind that there is no standard list of abbreviations; these are suggestions only. Account titles that are not included in this list are generally short enough to be written out in full.

Accounts Payable	Accts. Pay. or A/P
Accounts Receivable	Accts. Rec. or A/R
Accumulated Depreciation, Equipment	Accum. Deprec., Equip.
Depreciation Expense, Equipment	Deprec. Exp., Equip.
N. L. Clark, Capital	N. L. Clark, Cap.
N. L. Clark, Drawing	N. L. Clark, Draw.
Employees' Bond Deduction Payable	Empl. Bond Ded. Pay.
Employees' Federal Income Tax Payable	Empl. Fed. Inc. Tax Pay.
Employees' Medical Insurance Payable	Empl. Med. Ins. Pay.
Employees' Union Dues Payable	Empl. Union Dues Pay.
Federal Unemployment Tax Payable	Fed. Unemp. Tax Pay.
FICA Tax Payable	FICA Tax Pay.
Interest Expense	Int. Exp.
Interest Income	Int. Inc.
Interest Payable	Int. Pay.
Merchandise Inventory	Merch. Inv.
Miscellaneous General Expense	Misc. Gen. Exp.
Miscellaneous Selling Expense	Misc. Sell. Exp.
Notes Payable	Notes Pay.
Notes Receivable	Notes Rec.
Prepaid Insurance, Workers' Compensation	Prepaid Ins., Workers' Comp.
Purchases Discount	Purch. Disct.
Purchases Returns and Allowances	Purch. Ret. and Allow.
Sales Commissions	Sales Comm. Exp.
Sales Discount	Sales Disct.
Sales Returns and Allowances	Sales Ret. and Allow.
State Unemployment Tax Payable	State Unemp. Tax Pay.
Workers' Compensation Insurance Expense	Workers' Comp. Ins. Exp.

Copyright © by Houghton Mifflin Company. All rights reserved.

Introduction

PERFORMANCE OBJECTIVES

After you have completed this introduction, you will be able to do the following:

1. Define *accounting*.
2. Explain the importance of accounting information.
3. Describe the various career opportunities in accounting.

KEY TERMS

Accountant
Accounting
Economic unit
Generally Accepted Accounting Principles (GAAP)
Paraprofessional Accountant
Transaction

<table>
<tr><td>1</td><td>

Asset, Liability, Owner's Equity, Revenue, and Expense Accounts

</td></tr>
</table>

PERFORMANCE OBJECTIVES

After you have completed this chapter, you will be able to do the following:

1. Define and identify *asset*, *liability*, and *owner's equity* accounts.
2. Record a group of business transactions, in column form, involving changes in assets, liabilities, and owner's equity.
3. Define and identify *revenue* and *expense* accounts.
4. Record a group of business transactions, in column form, involving all five elements of the fundamental accounting equation.

KEY TERMS

Accounts
Accounts Payable
Accounts Receivable
Assets
Business entity
Capital
Chart of accounts
Creditor
Double-entry accounting

Equity
Expenses
Fundamental accounting equation
Liabilities
Owner's equity
Revenues
Separate entity concept
Sole proprietorship
Withdrawal

Copyright © by Houghton Mifflin Company. All rights reserved.

STUDY GUIDE QUESTIONS

PART 1   True/False

For each of the following statements, circle T if the statement is true and F if the statement is false.

T   F   1. The term *owner's equity* means the owner's investment.

T   F   2. When an asset is purchased for cash, the owner's equity account is decreased.

T   F   3. People who loan money to a company are considered the company's debtors.

T   F   4. A business entity is considered an economic unit.

T   F   5. Equipment and supplies are considered assets.

T   F   6. Expenses have the effect of decreasing owner's equity.

T   F   7. The amounts owed by charge customers are recorded in the Accounts Receivable account.

T   F   8. Withdrawals by the owner decrease owner's equity.

T   F   9. When a business receives a payment from a charge customer, the revenue account is not affected.

T   F   10. An accountant keeps a separate record for each asset, liability, owner's equity, revenue, and expense account.

PART 2   Completion—Language of Business

Complete each of the following statements by writing the appropriate words in the spaces provided.

1. A one-owner business is called a(n) _____ .
2. Debts owed by a business are called _____ .
3. A person or business to whom money is owed is called a(n) _____ .
4. The categories listed under the classifications Assets, Liabilities, Owner's Equity, Revenue, and Expenses are called _____ .
5. An event affecting a business that can be expressed in terms of money and that must be recorded in the accounting records is called a(n) _____ .
6. The owner's investment or equity in an enterprise is called _____ .
7. The equation expressing the relationship of assets, liabilities, and owner's equity is called the _____ .
8. The _____ is the official list of account titles to be used to record the transactions of a business.
9. A financial interest in or claim to an asset is called _____ .
10. _____ represents the amount a business earns by providing or performing a service for a customer.
11. If the owner takes cash out of the business each month, this is called a(n) _____ .
12. The account used to record the amounts owed by charge customers is _____ .
13. _____ are the costs related to the earning of revenue.

Copyright © by Houghton Mifflin Company. All rights reserved.

PART 3 Classifying Accounts

The office of financial consultant M. A. Dailey has the following accounts:

Income from Services   Wages Expense
Office Equipment   Mortgage Payable
Supplies   Land
Accounts Payable   M. A. Dailey, Capital
Building   Prepaid Insurance
Cash   Neon Sign
Rent Expense   M. A. Dailey, Drawing

List each account under the appropriate heading.

Assets   **Owner's Equity**

_____   _____
_____   _____
_____
_____   **Revenue**
_____
_____   _____
_____
_____   **Expenses**

Liabilities

_____   _____
_____   _____
_____

PART 4 Analyzing Transactions

Here are some typical transactions of Myers Insect Control Service. For each transaction, indicate the increase (+) or the decrease (−) in Assets (A), Liabilities (L), Owner's Equity (OE), Revenue (R), or Expenses (E) by placing the appropriate sign(s) in the appropriate column(s). The first transaction is given as an example.

	A	L	OE	R	E
0. *Example:* Owner invested cash	+		+		
1. Payment of rent					
2. Sales of services for cash					
3. Investment of equipment by owner					
4. Payment of insurance premium for two years					
5. Payment of wages					
6. Sales of services on account					
7. Withdrawal of cash by owner					
8. Purchase of supplies on account					
9. Collection from charge customer previously billed					
10. Payment made to creditor on account					

Copyright © by Houghton Mifflin Company. All rights reserved.

3

DEMONSTRATION PROBLEM

During November of this year, James Chin opened an accounting practice called James Chin, CPA. The following transactions were completed during the first month:

a. Deposited $13,500 in a bank account in the name of James Chin, CPA.
b. Paid rent for the month, $1,600 (Rent Expense).
c. Bought office equipment, including a computer and a printer, for $9,500 from Bingham Company. Paid $6,700 in cash, with the balance due in thirty days.
d. Purchased office supplies and announcements for $970 from City Stationers. Payment is due in thirty days.
e. Billed clients $5,500 for services rendered (Client Fees).
f. Paid $1,450 salary to secretary/assistant for the month.
g. Paid telephone bill of $210 (Telephone Expense).
h. Received cash from clients previously billed on account, $2,450.
i. Paid Bingham Company $970 to apply on account.
j. Paid $275 for continuing education course (Miscellaneous Expense).
k. Chin withdrew $2,200 for personal use.

Instructions

1. Record the transactions and the balance after each transaction, using the following headings:

Assets	= Liabilities +	Owner's Equity
Cash + Accts. Rec. + Supp. + Equip.	Accounts Payable	J. Chin, + Revenue − Expenses Capital

2. Demonstrate that the total of one side of the equation equals the total of the other side of the equation.

Copyright © by Houghton Mifflin Company. All rights reserved.

SOLUTION

	Cash +	Accts. Rec. +	Supp. +	Equip. =	Accounts Payable +	J. Chin, Capital +	Revenue −	Expenses
(a)	+13,500					+13,500		
(b)	−1,600							+1,600 (Rent Expense)
Bal.	11,900 +	+	+	=	+	13,500 +	−	1,600
(c)	−6,700			+9,500	+2,800			
Bal.	5,200 +	+	+	9,500 =	2,800 +	13,500 +	−	1,600
(d)			+970		+970			
Bal.	5,200 +	+	970 +	9,500 =	3,770 +	13,500 +	−	1,600
(e)		+5,500					+5,500 (Client Fees)	
Bal.	5,200 +	5,500 +	970 +	9,500 =	3,770 +	13,500 +	5,500 −	1,600
(f)	−1,450							+1,450 (Salary Expense)
Bal.	3,750 +	5,500 +	970 +	9,500 =	3,770 +	13,500 +	5,500 −	3,050
(g)	−210							+210 (Telephone Expense)
Bal.	3,540 +	5,500 +	970 +	9,500 =	3,770 +	13,500 +	5,500 −	3,260
(h)	+2,450	−2,450						
Bal.	5,990 +	3,050 +	970 +	9,500 =	3,770 +	13,500 +	5,500 −	3,260
(i)	−970				−970			
Bal.	5,020 +	3,050 +	970 +	9,500 =	2,800 +	13,500 +	5,500 −	3,260
(j)	−275							+275 (Miscellaneous Expense)
Bal.	4,745 +	3,050 +	970 +	9,500 =	2,800 +	13,500 +	5,500 −	3,535
(k)	−2,200					−2,200 (Drawing)		
Bal.	2,545 +	3,050 +	970 +	9,500 =	2,800 +	11,300 +	5,500 −	3,535

Left Side of Equals Sign		Right Side of Equals Sign	
Cash	$ 2,545	Accounts Payable	$ 2,800
Accts. Rec.	3,050	J. Chin, Capital	11,300
Supplies	970	Revenue	5,500
Equip.	9,500		$19,600
	$16,065	Expenses	− 3,535
			$16,065

Copyright © by Houghton Mifflin Company. All rights reserved.

PROBLEM 1-1A or 1-1B

	Assets				Liabilities		Owner's Equity			
	Cash	+	Office Supplies	+	Office Equipment	=	Accounts Payable	+	Capital	+ Revenue − Expenses

(a)
(b)

Bal.

(c)

Bal.

(d)

Bal.

(e)

Bal.

(f)

Bal.

(g)

Bal.

(h)

Bal.

(i)

Bal.

(j)

Bal.

(k)

Bal.

6

Copyright © by Houghton Mifflin Company. All rights reserved.

PROBLEM 1-1A or 1-1B (concluded)

Left Side of Equals Sign		Right Side of Equals Sign	
	Amount		Amount
Cash		Accounts Payable	
Office Supplies		, Capital	
Office Equipment	_____	Revenue	_____
	=====	Subtotal	
		Expenses	
			_____
			=====

Copyright © by Houghton Mifflin Company. All rights reserved.

PROBLEM 1-2A or 1-2B

	Assets				Liabilities		Owner's Equity		
	Cash	+ Supplies	+ Professional Equipment	+ Office Equipment	=	Accounts Payable	+	Capital	+ Revenue − Expenses
(a)									
(b)									
Bal.	+	+	+	+	=	+	+	+ −
(c)									
Bal.	+	+	+	+	=	+	+	+ −
(d)									
Bal.	+	+	+	+	=	+	+	+ −
(e)									
Bal.	+	+	+	+	=	+	+	+ −
(f)									
Bal.	+	+	+	+	=	+	+	+ −
(g)									
Bal.	+	+	+	+	=	+	+	+ −
(h)									
Bal.	+	+	+	+	=	+	+	+ −
(i)									
Bal.	+	+	+	+	=	+	+	+ −
(j)									
Bal.	+	+	+	+	=	+	+	+ −
(k)									
Bal.	+	+	+	+	=	+	+	+ −

8

Copyright © by Houghton Mifflin Company. All rights reserved.

PROBLEM 1-2A or 1-2B (concluded)

Left Side of Equals Sign	Amount	Right Side of Equals Sign	Amount
Cash		Accounts Payable	
Supplies		, Capital	
Professional Equipment		Revenue	_____
Office Equipment	_____	Subtotal	
	=====	Expenses	_____
			=====

Copyright © by Houghton Mifflin Company. All rights reserved.

PROBLEM 1-3A or 1-3B

	Assets					=	Liabilities	+	Owner's Equity		
	Cash + Office Supplies + Prepaid Insurance + Office Equipment + Library					=	Accounts Payable	+	Capital + Revenue − Expenses		
(a)											
(b)											
Bal.	+	+	+	+	+	=	+	+	+	+	−
(c)											
Bal.	+	+	+	+	+	=	+	+	+	+	−
(d)											
Bal.	+	+	+	+	+	=	+	+	+	+	−
(e)											
Bal.	+	+	+	+	+	=	+	+	+	+	−
(f)											
Bal.	+	+	+	+	+	=	+	+	+	+	−
(g)											
Bal.	+	+	+	+	+	=	+	+	+	+	−
(h)											
Bal.	+	+	+	+	+	=	+	+	+	+	−
(i)											
Bal.	+	+	+	+	+	=	+	+	+	+	−
(j)											
Bal.	+	+	+	+	+	=	+	+	+	+	−
(k)											
Bal.	+	+	+	+	+	=	+	+	+	+	−
(l)											
Bal.	+	+	+	+	+	=	+	+	+	+	−
(m)											
Bal.	+	+	+	+	+	=	+	+	+	+	−

Copyright © by Houghton Mifflin Company. All rights reserved.

PROBLEM 1-3A or 1-3B (concluded)

Left Side of Equals Sign		Right Side of Equals Sign	
	Amount		**Amount**
Cash		Accounts Payable	
Office Supplies		, Capital	
Prepaid Insurance		Revenue	
Office Equipment		Subtotal	
Library	_____	Expenses	_____
	========		========

Copyright © by Houghton Mifflin Company. All rights reserved.

PROBLEM 1-4A or 1-4B

	Assets					=	Liabilities	+	Owner's Equity		
	Cash + Accounts + Supplies + Prepaid + Truck + Equipment					=	Accounts Payable	+	Capital + Revenue − Expenses		
	Receivable		Insurance								
(a)											
(b)											
Bal.											
(c)											
Bal.											
(d)											
Bal.											
(e)											
Bal.											
(f)											
Bal.											
(g)											
Bal.											
(h)											
Bal.											
(i)											
Bal.											
(j)											
Bal.											
(k)											
Bal.											
(l)											
Bal.											
(m)											
Bal.											

Copyright © by Houghton Mifflin Company. All rights reserved.

PROBLEM 1-4A or 1-4B (concluded)

Left Side of Equals Sign		Right Side of Equals Sign	
	Amount		**Amount**
Cash		Accounts Payable	
Accounts Receivable		_____ , Capital	
Supplies		Revenue	
Prepaid Insurance		Subtotal	
Truck		Expenses	
Equipment			

Copyright © by Houghton Mifflin Company. All rights reserved.

T Accounts, Debits and Credits, Trial Balance, and Financial Statements

PERFORMANCE OBJECTIVES

1. Determine balances of T accounts having entries recorded on both sides of the accounts.
2. Present the fundamental accounting equation with the T account form, and label the plus and minus sides.
3. Present the fundamental accounting equation with the T account form, and label the debit and credit sides.
4. Record directly in T accounts a group of business transactions involving changes in asset, liability, owner's equity, revenue, and expense accounts for a service business.
5. Prepare a trial balance.
6. Prepare (a) an income statement, (b) a statement of owner's equity, and (c) a balance sheet.
7. Prepare (a) an income statement involving more than one revenue account and a net loss, and (b) a statement of owner's equity with an additional investment and either a net income or a net loss.
8. Recognize the effect of transpositions and slides on account balances.

KEY TERMS

Balance sheet
Compound entry
Credit
Debit
Fair market value
Financial position
Financial statement
Footings
Income statement

Net income
Net loss
Normal balance
Report form
Slide
Statement of owner's equity
T account form
Transposition
Trial balance

STUDY GUIDE QUESTIONS

PART 1   True/False

For each of the following statements, circle T if the statement is true and F if the statement is false.

T   F   1. Expenses have the effect of decreasing owner's equity.

T   F   2. A summary of assets, liabilities, and owner's equity shows the financial position of an economic unit.

T   F   3. The third line in the heading of a balance sheet indicates one specific date.

T   F   4. The amounts owed by charge customers are recorded in the Accounts Payable account.

T   F   5. The net income for a given financial period is found in both the income statement and the balance sheet.

T   F   6. To prepare the financial statements for a business, you should prepare the balance sheet first, followed by the income statement, and then the statement of owner's equity.

Copyright © by Houghton Mifflin Company. All rights reserved.

T F 7. The net income is the connecting link between the income statement and the statement of owner's equity.

T F 8. An income statement is prepared at the end of the financial period to show the results of operations.

T F 9. When a business receives a payment from a charge customer, the revenue account is not affected.

T F 10. If the owner withdraws more than the amount of the net income, there will be a decrease in owner's equity.

PART 2 Completion—Language of Business

Complete each of the following statements by writing the appropriate word(s) in the spaces provided.

1. The left-hand side of any account is the _____ side.
2. The small, penciled-in figures used to record the totals of each side of a T account are called _____ .
3. If the digits are switched around when you record a number, the error is called a(n) _____ .
4. The device used to prove that the total of all the debit balances equals the total of all the credit balances is called a(n) _____ .
5. A(n) _____ is used to record a transaction that has more than one debit and/or more than one credit.
6. The right-hand side of any account is called the _____ side.

PART 3 Accounting Entries

The following transactions were completed by C. R. Hendricks, Physical Therapist. Using appropriate account titles, record the transactions in pairs of T accounts, and show plus and minus signs with each T account. List accounts to be debited in the left-hand T account column and accounts to be credited in the right-hand T account column.

	Utilities Expense		Cash	
	+	−	+	−
0. *Example:* Paid electric bill, $92.	(0) 92			(0) 92
a. Bought professional equipment on account, $760.				
b. Billed patients for services performed, $764.				
c. Paid rent for the month, $950.				
d. Bought supplies on account, $410.				
e. Paid telephone bill, $76.				

Copyright © by Houghton Mifflin Company. All rights reserved.

f. Collected $610 from patients
    previously billed.

g. Paid creditors on account, $500.

h. Paid salary of assistant, $990.

i. Bought office equipment for
    cash, $342.

j. Returned $200 of supplies bought
    previously on credit in **d** and
    received a reduction in the bill.

Copyright © by Houghton Mifflin Company. All rights reserved.

DEMONSTRATION PROBLEM

Dr. Christy Russo maintains an office for the practice of veterinary medicine. The account balances as of September 1 are given below. All are normal balances.

Assets		Revenue	
Cash	$ 2,459	Professional Fees	$72,118
Accounts Receivable	18,120	**Expenses**	
Supplies	840	Salary Expense	14,380
Prepaid Insurance	980	Rent Expense	10,320
Automobile	20,650	Automobile Expense	859
Furniture and Equipment	5,963	Utilities Expense	1,213
Liabilities			
Accounts Payable	1,590		
Owner's Equity			
C. Russo, Capital	42,076		
C. Russo, Drawing	40,000		

The following transactions occurred during September of this year:

a. Paid rent for the month, $1,290.
b. Paid $1,800 for one year's coverage of liability insurance.
c. Bought medical equipment on account from Bennett Surgical Supply, $849, paying $200 down with the balance due in thirty days.
d. Billed patients for services performed, $9,015.
e. Paid employee salaries, $1,797.
f. Received and paid gas and electric bill, $112.
g. Received cash from patients previously billed, $11,060.
h. Received bill for gasoline for car, used only in the professional practice, from Garza Fuel Company, $116.
i. Paid creditors on account, $1,590.
j. Dr. Russo withdrew cash for personal use, $5,000.

Instructions

1. Correctly place plus and minus signs under each T account and label the sides of the T accounts as either debit or credit in the fundamental accounting equation. Record the account balances as of September 1.
2. Record the September transactions in the T accounts. Key each transaction to the letter that identifies the transaction.
3. Foot the columns.
4. Prepare a trial balance dated September 30.
5. Prepare an income statement for month ended September 30, 20—.
6. Prepare a statement of owner's equity for month ended September 30, 20—.
7. Prepare a balance sheet as of September 30.

Copyright © by Houghton Mifflin Company. All rights reserved.

SOLUTION

Assets	=	Liabilities	+	Owner's Equity	+	Revenue	–	Expenses
+ −		− +		− +		− +		+ −
Debit Credit		Debit Credit		Debit Credit		Debit Credit		Debit Credit

Cash

+	−
Bal. 2,459	(a) 1,290
(g) 11,060	(b) 1,800
13,519	(c) 200
	(e) 1,797
	(f) 112
	(i) 1,590
	(j) 5,000
	11,789
Bal. 1,730	

Accounts Receivable

+	−
Bal. 18,120	(g) 11,060
(d) 9,015	
27,135	
Bal. 16,075	

Supplies

+	−
Bal. 840	

Prepaid Insurance

+	−
Bal. 980	
(b) 1,800	
Bal. 2,780	

Automobile

+	−
Bal. 20,650	

Furniture and Equipment

+	−
Bal. 5,963	
(c) 849	
Bal. 6,812	

Accounts Payable

−	+
(i) 1,590	Bal. 1,590
	(c) 649
	(h) 116
	2,355
	Bal. 765

C. Russo, Capital

−	+
	Bal. 42,076

C. Russo, Drawing

+	−
Bal. 40,000	
(j) 5,000	
Bal. 45,000	

Professional Fees

−	+
	Bal. 72,118
	(d) 9,015
	Bal. 81,133

Salary Expense

+	−
Bal. 14,380	
(e) 1,797	
Bal. 16,177	

Rent Expense

+	−
Bal. 10,320	
(a) 1,290	
Bal. 11,610	

Automobile Expense

+	−
Bal. 859	
(h) 116	
Bal. 975	

Utilities Expense

+	−
Bal. 1,213	
(f) 112	
Bal. 1,325	

Dr. Christy Russo
Trial Balance
September 30, 20—

ACCOUNT NAME	DEBIT	CREDIT
Cash	1 7 3 0 00	
Accounts Receivable	16 0 7 5 00	
Supplies	8 4 0 00	
Prepaid Insurance	2 7 8 0 00	
Automobile	20 6 5 0 00	
Furniture and Equipment	6 8 1 2 00	
Accounts Payable		7 6 5 00
C. Russo, Capital		42 0 7 6 00
C. Russo, Drawing	45 0 0 0 00	
Professional Fees		81 1 3 3 00
Salary Expense	16 1 7 7 00	
Rent Expense	11 6 1 0 00	
Automobile Expense	9 7 5 00	
Utilities Expense	1 3 2 5 00	
	123 9 7 4 00	123 9 7 4 00

18

Copyright © by Houghton Mifflin Company. All rights reserved.

SOLUTION (continued)

Dr. Christy Russo

Income Statement

For Quarter Ended September 30, 20—

Revenue:			
Professional Fees			$81 1 3 3 00
Expenses:			
Salary Expense	$16 1 7 7 00		
Rent Expense	11 6 1 0 00		
Automobile Expense	9 7 5 00		
Utilities Expense	1 3 2 5 00		
Total Expenses		30 0 8 7 00	
Net Income		$51 0 4 6 00	

Dr. Christy Russo

Statement of Owner's Equity

For Quarter Ended September 30, 20—

C. Russo, Capital, September 1, 20—			$42 0 7 6 00
Net Income for September	$51 0 4 6 00		
Less Withdrawals for September	45 0 0 0 00		
Increase in Capital			6 0 4 6 00
C. Russo, Capital, September 30, 20—			$48 1 2 2 00

Copyright © by Houghton Mifflin Company. All rights reserved.

SOLUTION (concluded)

Dr. Christy Russo

Balance Sheet

September 30, 20—

Assets											
Cash	$	1	7	3	0	00					
Accounts Receivable		16	0	7	5	00					
Supplies				8	4	0	00				
Prepaid Insurance		2	7	8	0	00					
Automobile		20	6	5	0	00					
Furniture and Equipment		6	8	1	2	00					
							$48	8	8	7	00
Liabilities											
Accounts Payable							$	7	6	5	00
Owner's Equity											
C. Russo, Capital							48	1	2	2	00
							$48	8	8	7	00

Copyright © by Houghton Mifflin Company. All rights reserved.

PROBLEM 2-1A or 2-1B

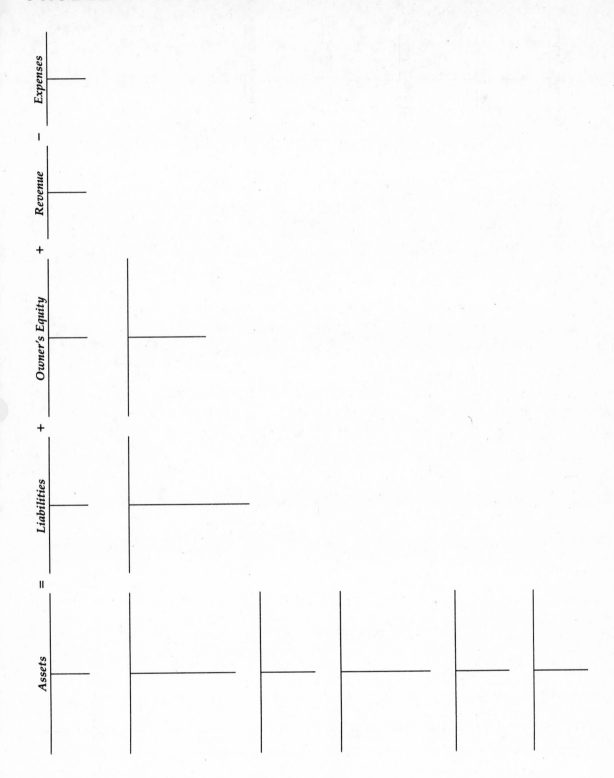

Copyright © by Houghton Mifflin Company. All rights reserved.

PROBLEM 2-2A or 2-2B

Assets = Liabilities + Owner's Equity + Revenue − Expenses

Expenses

Advertising Expense

Rent Expense

Utilities Expense

Wages Expense

Miscellaneous Expense

Revenue

Income from Services

Owner's Equity

Capital

Drawing

Liabilities

Accounts Payable

Assets

Cash

Supplies

Computer Software

Office Equipment

Electric Sign

22

Copyright © by Houghton Mifflin Company. All rights reserved.

PROBLEM 2-2A or 2-2B (concluded)

ACCOUNT NAME	DEBIT	CREDIT

Copyright © by Houghton Mifflin Company. All rights reserved.

PROBLEM 2-3A or 2-3B

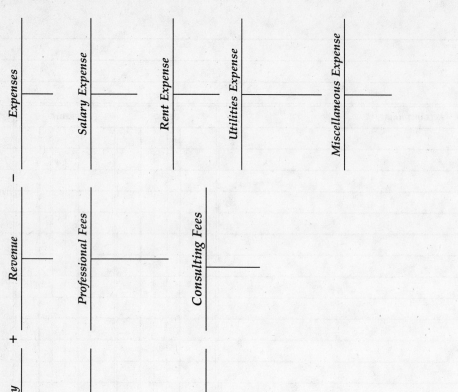

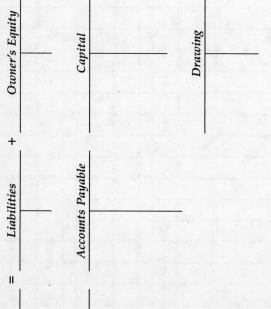

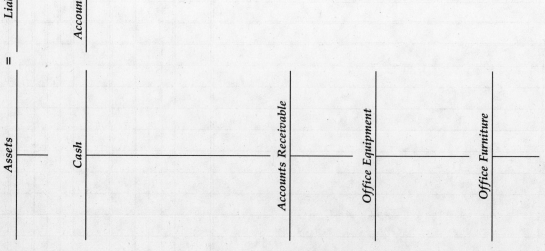

Copyright © by Houghton Mifflin Company. All rights reserved.

PROBLEM 2-3A or 2-3B (continued)

ACCOUNT NAME	DEBIT	CREDIT

Copyright © by Houghton Mifflin Company. All rights reserved.

PROBLEM 2-3A or 2-3B (continued)

Copyright © by Houghton Mifflin Company. All rights reserved.

PROBLEM 2-3A or 2-3B (concluded)

Copyright © by Houghton Mifflin Company. All rights reserved.

PROBLEM 2-4A or 2-4B

Cash	Accounts Payable	Laundry Revenue

	, Capital	Wages Expense

	, Drawing	Rent Expense

Supplies		Utilities Expense

Prepaid Insurance		Miscellaneous Expense

Equipment

Furniture and Fixtures

   Copyright © by Houghton Mifflin Company. All rights reserved.

PROBLEM 2-4A or 2-4B (continued)

ACCOUNT NAME	DEBIT	CREDIT

Copyright © by Houghton Mifflin Company. All rights reserved.

PROBLEM 2-4A or 2-4B (concluded)

Copyright © by Houghton Mifflin Company. All rights reserved.

3

The General Journal and the General Ledger

PERFORMANCE OBJECTIVES

1. Record a group of transactions pertaining to a service enterprise in a two-column general journal.
2. Post entries from a two-column general journal to general ledger accounts.
3. Prepare a trial balance from the ledger accounts.
4. Correct entries using the ruling method.
5. Correct entries using the correcting entry method.

KEY TERMS

Account numbers
Cost principle
Cross-reference
General ledger
Journal

Journalizing
Ledger account
Posting
Source documents
Two-column general journal

STUDY GUIDE QUESTIONS

PART 1   True/False

For each of the following statements, circle T if the statement is true and F if the statement is false.

T F 1. The credit part of a journal entry always comes first.

T F 2. Dollar signs are required in all journal entries.

T F 3. A transaction must be posted before it is journalized.

T F 4. In a journal entry, if two accounts are debited, two accounts must be credited.

T F 5. The first step in the posting process is to write the date of the transaction.

T F 6. In the presentation of a general journal in the text, the title of the account credited is indented approximately one-half inch.

T F 7. A number in the Post. Ref. column in the ledger account indicates that the balance has been recorded in the trial balance.

T F 8. Failure to post an entire transaction from the journal to the ledger will show up in the trial balance.

T F 9. Having a running balance is an advantage of a four-column ledger account form.

T F 10. A trial balance is prepared directly from the journal.

PART 2 Completion—Language of Business

Complete each of the following statements by writing the appropriate words in the spaces provided.

1. A loose-leaf binder containing the accounts of a business is called a(n) _____ _____ .

2. The process of transferring information from the journal to the ledger is called _____ _____ .

3. Business papers that serve as evidence that a transaction took place are called _____ _____ .

4. The _____ states that the purchase of an asset should be recorded at the agreed amount of the transaction.

5. The process of recording a business transaction in a book of original entry is called _____ .

6. A cross-reference exists when the journal page number is recorded in the Post. Ref. column of the ledger and the ledger account number is recorded in the _____ _____ .

7. The accounts in the ledger are listed according to _____ .

PART 3 Completing a Journal Entry

Here are a partially completed journal entry and the Cash ledger account. Complete the entry, including the explanation, using the data given. The entry represents the first entry on page 33 and occurred during October of the current year.

GENERAL JOURNAL

PAGE _____

	DATE		DESCRIPTION	POST. REF.	DEBIT	CREDIT	
1	20—						1
2	Oct.	29	Cash		1 1 0 0 00		2
3			Accounts Receivable	113			3
4			Income from Services	411		1 7 0 0 00	4
5							5
6							6
7							7
8							8

GENERAL LEDGER

ACCOUNT _Cash_   ACCOUNT NO. _111_

DATE		ITEM	POST. REF.	DEBIT	CREDIT	BALANCE DEBIT	BALANCE CREDIT
20—							
Oct.	6		30	6 0 0 00		3 5 0 0 00	
	6		30		7 0 0 00	2 8 0 0 00	
	12		32	1 1 0 0 00		3 9 0 0 00	
	14		32		4 0 0 00	3 5 0 0 00	
	27		32		2 0 0 00	3 3 0 0 00	
	29		33	1 1 0 0 00		4 4 0 0 00	

Copyright © by Houghton Mifflin Company. All rights reserved.

1. What is the missing amount in the journal entry? _____
2. What is the total cash received during October? _____
3. What is the total cash paid out during October? _____
4. The journal entry is an example of a(n) _____ journal entry.

DEMONSTRATION PROBLEM

C. P. Morris, a fitness enthusiast, buys an existing exercise center, Body Firm, with the following chart of accounts:

Assets
111 Cash
113 Supplies
124 Land
126 Building
128 Equipment

Liabilities
221 Accounts Payable
223 Mortgage Payable

Owner's Equity
311 C. P. Morris, Capital
312 C. P. Morris, Drawing

Revenue
411 Income from Services

Expenses
511 Wages Expense
512 Utilities Expense
513 Advertising Expense
514 Repair Expense
519 Miscellaneous Expense

Apr. 16 Morris deposited $100,000 in a bank account for the purpose of buying Body Firm.
17 Bought the assets of Body Firm for a total price of $188,000. The assets include supplies, $750; equipment, $27,250; building, $96,000; and land, $64,000. Made a down payment of $89,000 and signed a mortgage note for the remainder.
17 Bought additional equipment from Fitness Supply Co. on account for $3,550, paying $710 down, with balance due in thirty days.
29 Celebrated the grand opening of Body Firm. Advertising expenses were paid in cash for the following:

Advertising in newspaper	$314
Announcements mailed to local residences	85
Postage	125
Balloons, ribbons, flowers	126
Food and refreshments	58

30 Received fees for daily use of the facilities, $1,152.
30 Paid wages for the period April 17 through April 30, $833.
30 Received and paid electric bill, $129.
30 Received and paid repair bill, $96.
30 Morris withdrew $600 for personal use.

Instructions

1. Record the transactions in the general journal.
2. Post the transactions in the general ledger.
3. Prepare a trial balance as of April 30.

Copyright © by Houghton Mifflin Company. All rights reserved.

SOLUTION

GENERAL JOURNAL

	DATE		DESCRIPTION	POST. REF.	DEBIT	CREDIT	
1	20—						1
2	Apr.	16	Cash	111	100 0 0 0 00		2
3			C. P. Morris, Capital	311		100 0 0 0 00	3
4			Invested cash in the business.				4
5							5
6		17	Supplies	113	7 5 0 00		6
7			Equipment	128	27 2 5 0 00		7
8			Building	126	96 0 0 0 00		8
9			Land	124	64 0 0 0 00		9
10			Cash	111		89 0 0 0 00	10
11			Mortgage Payable	223		99 0 0 0 00	11
12			Bought Body Firm.				12
13							13
14		17	Equipment	128	3 5 5 0 00		14
15			Cash	111		7 1 0 00	15
16			Accounts Payable	221		2 8 4 0 00	16
17			Bought equipment on account from				17
18			Fitness Supply Co., with balance				18
19			due in 30 days.				19
20							20
21		29	Advertising Expense	513	7 0 8 00		21
22			Cash	111		7 0 8 00	22
23			Grand opening expenses.				23
24							24
25		30	Cash	111	1 1 5 2 00		25
26			Income from Services	411		1 1 5 2 00	26
27			Received fees.				27
28							28
29		30	Wages Expense	511	8 3 3 00		29
30			Cash	111		8 3 3 00	30
31			Paid wages for period April 17				31
32			through April 30.				32
33							33
34		30	Utilities Expense	512	1 2 9 00		34
35			Cash	111		1 2 9 00	35
36			Paid electric bill.				36
37							37
38		30	Repair Expense	514	9 6 00		38
39			Cash	111		9 6 00	39
40			Paid repair bill.				40
41							41
42		30	C. P. Morris, Drawing	312	6 0 0 00		42
43			Cash	111		6 0 0 00	43
44			Withdrawal for personal use.				44
45							45
46							46
47							47

Copyright © by Houghton Mifflin Company. All rights reserved.

SOLUTION (continued)

GENERAL LEDGER

ACCOUNT _Cash_   ACCOUNT NO. _111_

DATE	ITEM	POST. REF.	DEBIT	CREDIT	BALANCE DEBIT	BALANCE CREDIT
20—						
Apr. 16		1	100 000 00		100 000 00	
17		1		89 000 00	11 000 00	
17		1		710 00	10 290 00	
29		1		708 00	9 582 00	
30		1	1 152 00		10 734 00	
30		1		833 00	9 901 00	
30		1		129 00	9 772 00	
30		1		96 00	9 676 00	
30		1		600 00	9 076 00	

ACCOUNT _Supplies_   ACCOUNT NO. _113_

DATE	ITEM	POST. REF.	DEBIT	CREDIT	BALANCE DEBIT	BALANCE CREDIT
20—						
Apr. 17		1	750 00		750 00	

ACCOUNT _Land_   ACCOUNT NO. _124_

DATE	ITEM	POST. REF.	DEBIT	CREDIT	BALANCE DEBIT	BALANCE CREDIT
20—						
Apr. 17		1	64 000 00		64 000 00	

ACCOUNT _Building_   ACCOUNT NO. _126_

DATE	ITEM	POST. REF.	DEBIT	CREDIT	BALANCE DEBIT	BALANCE CREDIT
20—						
Apr. 17		1	96 000 00		96 000 00	

Copyright © by Houghton Mifflin Company. All rights reserved.

SOLUTION (continued)

ACCOUNT _Equipment_ ACCOUNT NO. _128_

DATE		ITEM	POST. REF.	DEBIT	CREDIT	BALANCE DEBIT	BALANCE CREDIT
20—							
Apr.	17		1	27 2 5 0 00		27 2 5 0 00	
	17		1	3 5 5 0 00		30 8 0 0 00	

ACCOUNT _Accounts Payable_ ACCOUNT NO. _221_

DATE		ITEM	POST. REF.	DEBIT	CREDIT	BALANCE DEBIT	BALANCE CREDIT
20—							
Apr.	17		1		2 8 4 0 00		2 8 4 0 00

ACCOUNT _Mortgage Payable_ ACCOUNT NO. _223_

DATE		ITEM	POST. REF.	DEBIT	CREDIT	BALANCE DEBIT	BALANCE CREDIT
20—							
Apr.	17		1		99 0 0 0 00		99 0 0 0 00

ACCOUNT _C. P. Morris, Capital_ ACCOUNT NO. _311_

DATE		ITEM	POST. REF.	DEBIT	CREDIT	BALANCE DEBIT	BALANCE CREDIT
20—							
Apr.	16		1		100 0 0 0 00		100 0 0 0 00

ACCOUNT _C. P. Morris, Drawing_ ACCOUNT NO. _312_

DATE		ITEM	POST. REF.	DEBIT	CREDIT	BALANCE DEBIT	BALANCE CREDIT
20—							
Apr.	30		1	6 0 0 00		6 0 0 00	

Copyright © by Houghton Mifflin Company. All rights reserved.

SOLUTION (continued)

ACCOUNT _Income from Services_ ACCOUNT NO. _411_

DATE		ITEM	POST. REF.	DEBIT	CREDIT	BALANCE DEBIT	BALANCE CREDIT
20—							
Apr.	30		1		1 1 5 2 00		1 1 5 2 00

ACCOUNT _Wages Expense_ ACCOUNT NO. _511_

DATE		ITEM	POST. REF.	DEBIT	CREDIT	BALANCE DEBIT	BALANCE CREDIT
20—							
Apr.	30		1	8 3 3 00		8 3 3 00	

ACCOUNT _Utilities Expense_ ACCOUNT NO. _512_

DATE		ITEM	POST. REF.	DEBIT	CREDIT	BALANCE DEBIT	BALANCE CREDIT
20—							
Apr.	30		1	1 2 9 00		1 2 9 00	

ACCOUNT _Advertising Expense_ ACCOUNT NO. _513_

DATE		ITEM	POST. REF.	DEBIT	CREDIT	BALANCE DEBIT	BALANCE CREDIT
20—							
Apr.	29		1	7 0 8 00		7 0 8 00	

ACCOUNT _Repair Expense_ ACCOUNT NO. _514_

DATE		ITEM	POST. REF.	DEBIT	CREDIT	BALANCE DEBIT	BALANCE CREDIT
20—							
Apr.	30		1	9 6 00		9 6 00	

Copyright © by Houghton Mifflin Company. All rights reserved.

SOLUTION (concluded)

ACCOUNT __Miscellaneous Expense__ ACCOUNT NO. __519__

DATE	ITEM	POST. REF.	DEBIT	CREDIT	BALANCE DEBIT	BALANCE CREDIT

Body Firm
Trial Balance
April 30, 20—

ACCOUNT NAME	DEBIT	CREDIT
Cash	9 0 7 6 00	
Supplies	7 5 0 00	
Land	64 0 0 0 00	
Building	96 0 0 0 00	
Equipment	30 8 0 0 00	
Accounts Payable		2 8 4 0 00
Mortgage Payable		99 0 0 0 00
C. P. Morris, Capital		100 0 0 0 00
C. P. Morris, Drawing	6 0 0 00	
Income from Services		1 1 5 2 00
Wages Expense	8 3 3 00	
Utilities Expense	1 2 9 00	
Advertising Expense	7 0 8 00	
Repair Expense	9 6 00	
	202 9 9 2 00	202 9 9 2 00

Copyright © by Houghton Mifflin Company. All rights reserved.

PROBLEM 3-1A or 3-1B

GENERAL JOURNAL

PAGE _____

	DATE	DESCRIPTION	POST. REF.	DEBIT	CREDIT	
1						1
2						2
3						3
4						4
5						5
6						6
7						7
8						8
9						9
10						10
11						11
12						12
13						13
14						14
15						15
16						16
17						17
18						18
19						19
20						20
21						21
22						22
23						23
24						24
25						25
26						26
27						27
28						28
29						29
30						30
31						31
32						32
33						33
34						34
35						35
36						36
37						37

Copyright © by Houghton Mifflin Company. All rights reserved.

PROBLEM 3-1A or 3-1B (continued)

GENERAL JOURNAL

PAGE _____

	DATE		DESCRIPTION	POST. REF.	DEBIT	CREDIT	
1							1
2							2
3							3
4							4
5							5
6							6
7							7
8							8
9							9
10							10
11							11
12							12
13							13
14							14
15							15
16							16
17							17
18							18
19							19
20							20
21							21
22							22
23							23
24							24
25							25
26							26
27							27
28							28
29							29
30							30
31							31
32							32
33							33
34							34
35							35
36							36
37							37

Copyright © by Houghton Mifflin Company. All rights reserved.

NAME _____ DATE _____ CLASS _____

PROBLEM 3-1A or 3-1B (concluded)

GENERAL JOURNAL   PAGE _____

	DATE	DESCRIPTION	POST. REF.	DEBIT	CREDIT	
1						1
2						2
3						3
4						4
5						5
6						6
7						7
8						8
9						9
10						10
11						11
12						12
13						13
14						14
15						15
16						16
17						17
18						18
19						19
20						20
21						21
22						22
23						23
24						24
25						25
26						26
27						27
28						28
29						29
30						30
31						31
32						32
33						33
34						34
35						35
36						36
37						37

Copyright © by Houghton Mifflin Company. All rights reserved.

PROBLEM 3-2A

GENERAL JOURNAL

	DATE		DESCRIPTION	POST. REF.	DEBIT	CREDIT	
1	20—						1
2	Aug.	1	Rent Expense		1 0 0 0 00		2
3			Cash			1 0 0 0 00	3
4			Paid rent for August, Ck. No. 145.				4
5							5
6		5	Cash		2 7 00		6
7			Accounts Receivable			2 7 00	7
8			Bob's Deli, on account, Inv. 316.				8
9							9
10		8	Cash		3 2 4 1 00		10
11			Income from Services			3 2 4 1 00	11
12			Week of August 1.				12
13							13
14		10	Accounts Payable		5 1 2 00		14
15			Cash			5 1 2 00	15
16			Paid Osborne Equipment Co.,				16
17			on account, Ck. No. 146.				17
18							18
19		15	Cash		3 1 6 4 00		19
20			Income from Services			3 1 6 4 00	20
21			Week of August 8.				21
22							22
23		16	Wages Expense		1 2 8 6 00		23
24			Cash			1 2 8 6 00	24
25			Wages, August 1–15, Ck. No. 147.				25
26							26
27		18	Accounts Receivable		8 4 0 00		27
28			Income from Services			8 4 0 00	28
29			Metro Transit, for services				29
30			rendered, Inv. No. 317.				30
31							31
32		20	Supplies		8 5 0 00		32
33			Accounts Payable			8 5 0 00	33
34			Bought supplies from Office				34
35			Supply Company, Inv. 6165.				35
36							36
37							37

Copyright © by Houghton Mifflin Company. All rights reserved.

PROBLEM 3-2A (continued)

GENERAL JOURNAL   PAGE ___6___

	DATE		DESCRIPTION	POST. REF.	DEBIT	CREDIT	
1	20—						1
2	Aug.	22	Cash		3 0 2 0 00		2
3			Income from Services			3 0 2 0 00	3
4			Week of August 15.				4
5							5
6		24	Utilities Expense		3 2 0 00		6
7			Cash			3 2 0 00	7
8			Paid utilities bill, Ck. 148.				8
9							9
10		25	Accounts Payable		5 0 0 00		10
11			Cash			5 0 0 00	11
12			Office Supply Co. on account,				12
13			Ck. No. 149.				13
14							14
15		29	Cash		2 0 6 7 00		15
16			Income from Services			2 0 6 7 00	16
17			Week of August 22.				17
18							18
19		31	Wages Expense		1 2 9 2 00		19
20			Cash			1 2 9 2 00	20
21			Wages, August 16–31,				21
22			Ck. No. 150.				22
23							23
24		31	Cash		3 0 0 00		24
25			Accounts Receivable			3 0 0 00	25
26			Metro Transit, on account,				26
27			Inv. No. 317.				27
28							28
29		31	Advertising Expense		5 6 8 00		29
30			Accounts Payable			5 6 8 00	30
31			Received advertising bill from				31
32			Community News, Inv. D1694.				32
33							33
34		31	W. Howell, Drawing		1 8 5 0 00		34
35			Cash			1 8 5 0 00	35
36			Withdrawal for personal use,				36
37			Ck. No. 151.				37

Copyright © by Houghton Mifflin Company. All rights reserved.

PROBLEM 3-2A (continued)

GENERAL LEDGER

ACCOUNT __Cash__   ACCOUNT NO. __111__

DATE		ITEM	POST. REF.	DEBIT	CREDIT	BALANCE DEBIT	BALANCE CREDIT
20—							
July	31	Balance	✓			24 1 1 3 00	

ACCOUNT __Accounts Receivable__   ACCOUNT NO. __113__

DATE		ITEM	POST. REF.	DEBIT	CREDIT	BALANCE DEBIT	BALANCE CREDIT
20—							
July	31	Balance	✓			1 5 0 00	

ACCOUNT __Supplies__   ACCOUNT NO. __115__

DATE		ITEM	POST. REF.	DEBIT	CREDIT	BALANCE DEBIT	BALANCE CREDIT
20—							
July	31	Balance	✓			3 2 0 00	

Copyright © by Houghton Mifflin Company. All rights reserved.

PROBLEM 3-2A (continued)

ACCOUNT _Prepaid Insurance_   ACCOUNT NO. _117_

DATE		ITEM	POST. REF.	DEBIT	CREDIT	BALANCE	
						DEBIT	CREDIT
20—							
July	31	Balance	✓			8 40 00	

ACCOUNT _Equipment_   ACCOUNT NO. _124_

DATE		ITEM	POST. REF.	DEBIT	CREDIT	BALANCE	
						DEBIT	CREDIT
20—							
July	31	Balance	✓			18 9 50 00	

ACCOUNT _Accounts Payable_   ACCOUNT NO. _221_

DATE		ITEM	POST. REF.	DEBIT	CREDIT	BALANCE	
						DEBIT	CREDIT
20—							
July	31	Balance	✓				4 2 36 00

ACCOUNT _, Capital_   ACCOUNT NO. _311_

DATE		ITEM	POST. REF.	DEBIT	CREDIT	BALANCE	
						DEBIT	CREDIT
20—							
July	31	Balance	✓				42 0 00 00

ACCOUNT _, Drawing_   ACCOUNT NO. _312_

DATE		ITEM	POST. REF.	DEBIT	CREDIT	BALANCE	
						DEBIT	CREDIT
20—							
July	31	Balance	✓			4 5 00 00	

Copyright © by Houghton Mifflin Company. All rights reserved.

PROBLEM 3-2A (continued)

ACCOUNT _Income from Services_   ACCOUNT NO. _411_

DATE		ITEM	POST. REF.	DEBIT	CREDIT	BALANCE DEBIT	BALANCE CREDIT
20—							
July	31	Balance	✓				6 8 0 0 00

ACCOUNT _Wages Expense_   ACCOUNT NO. _511_

DATE		ITEM	POST. REF.	DEBIT	CREDIT	BALANCE DEBIT	BALANCE CREDIT
20—							
July	31	Balance	✓			2 3 9 5 00	

ACCOUNT _Rent Expense_   ACCOUNT NO. _512_

DATE		ITEM	POST. REF.	DEBIT	CREDIT	BALANCE DEBIT	BALANCE CREDIT
20—							
July	31	Balance	✓			9 0 0 00	

Copyright © by Houghton Mifflin Company. All rights reserved.

PROBLEM 3-2A (continued)

ACCOUNT **Advertising Expense** _____ ACCOUNT NO. 513

DATE		ITEM	POST. REF.	DEBIT	CREDIT	BALANCE	
						DEBIT	CREDIT
20—							
July	31	Balance	√			487 00	

ACCOUNT **Utilities Expense** _____ ACCOUNT NO. 514

DATE		ITEM	POST. REF.	DEBIT	CREDIT	BALANCE	
						DEBIT	CREDIT
20—							
July	31	Balance	√			381 00	

ACCOUNT NAME	DEBIT	CREDIT

Copyright © by Houghton Mifflin Company. All rights reserved.

PROBLEM 3-2A (continued)

Copyright © by Houghton Mifflin Company. All rights reserved.

NAME _____ DATE _____ CLASS _____

PROBLEM 3-2A (concluded)

Copyright © by Houghton Mifflin Company. All rights reserved.

NAME _____ DATE _____ CLASS _____

PROBLEM 3-2B

GENERAL JOURNAL   PAGE ___4___

	DATE		DESCRIPTION	POST. REF.	DEBIT	CREDIT	
1	20—						1
2	May	1	Rent Expense		8 50 00		2
3			Cash			8 50 00	3
4			Paid rent for May, Ck. No. 148.				4
5							5
6		5	Cash		9 88 00		6
7			Accounts Receivable			9 88 00	7
8			Tay Company, on account, Inv.				8
9			No. 125.				9
10							10
11		7	Cash		1 5 48 00		11
12			Income from Services			1 5 48 00	12
13			Week of May 1.				13
14							14
15		8	Accounts Payable		3 46 00		15
16			Cash			3 46 00	16
17			Paid Tiffany Equipment Co.,				17
18			on account, Ck. No. 149.				18
19							19
20		14	Cash		1 6 55 00		20
21			Income from Services			1 6 55 00	21
22			Week of May 8.				22
23							23
24		15	Wages Expense		8 46 00		24
25			Cash			8 46 00	25
26			Paid wages, March 25–April 15,				26
27			Ck. No. 150.				27
28							28
29		17	Accounts Receivable		1 2 75 00		29
30			Income from Services			1 2 75 00	30
31			Le Company on account, Inv.				31
32			No. 126.				32
33							33
34		18	Supplies		3 64 00		34
35			Accounts Payable			3 64 00	35
36			Supplies on account from Vega				36
37			Company, Inv. 3160.				37

50

Copyright © by Houghton Mifflin Company. All rights reserved.

PROBLEM 3-2B (continued)

GENERAL JOURNAL

PAGE ___5___

	DATE		DESCRIPTION	POST. REF.	DEBIT	CREDIT	
1	20—						1
2	May	21	Cash		1 6 7 9 00		2
3			Income from Services			1 6 7 9 00	3
4			Week of May 15.				4
5							5
6		23	Utilities Expense		4 3 5 00		6
7			Cash			4 3 5 00	7
8			Paid telephone bill, Ck. No. 151.				8
9							9
10		25	Accounts Payable		2 6 0 00		10
11			Cash			2 6 0 00	11
12			Paid Vega Supply Company on				12
13			account, Inv. 3160.				13
14							14
15		31	Wages Expense		1 2 7 6 00		15
16			Cash			1 2 7 6 00	16
17			Paid wages, May 16–May 31.				17
18							18
19		31	Cash		1 8 2 0 00		19
20			Income from Services			1 8 2 0 00	20
21			Week of May 22.				21
22							22
23		31	Cash		2 5 0 00		23
24			Accounts Receivable			2 5 0 00	24
25			Le Company on account, Inv.				25
26			No. 126.				26
27							27
28		31	Advertising Expense		5 6 0 00		28
29			Accounts Payable			5 6 0 00	29
30			Received advertising bill from				30
31			Community News, Inv. 316.				31
32							32
33		31	T. Singh, Drawing		1 2 0 0 00		33
34			Cash			1 2 0 0 00	34
35			Withdrawal for personal use.				35
36							36
37							37

Copyright © by Houghton Mifflin Company. All rights reserved.

PROBLEM 3-2B (continued)

GENERAL LEDGER

ACCOUNT _Cash_   ACCOUNT NO. _111_

DATE		ITEM	POST. REF.	DEBIT	CREDIT	BALANCE	
						DEBIT	CREDIT
20—							
Apr.	30	Balance	✓			12 9 8 0 00	

ACCOUNT _Accounts Receivable_   ACCOUNT NO. _113_

DATE		ITEM	POST. REF.	DEBIT	CREDIT	BALANCE	
						DEBIT	CREDIT
20—							
Apr.	30	Balance	✓			1 5 6 0 00	

ACCOUNT _Supplies_   ACCOUNT NO. _115_

DATE		ITEM	POST. REF.	DEBIT	CREDIT	BALANCE	
						DEBIT	CREDIT
20—							
Apr.	30	Balance	✓			1 8 0 00	

Copyright © by Houghton Mifflin Company. All rights reserved.

PROBLEM 3-2B (continued)

ACCOUNT *Prepaid Insurance*   ACCOUNT NO. **117**

DATE	ITEM	POST. REF.	DEBIT	CREDIT	BALANCE DEBIT	BALANCE CREDIT
20—						
Apr. 30	Balance	√			4 6 0 00	

ACCOUNT *Equipment*   ACCOUNT NO. **124**

DATE	ITEM	POST. REF.	DEBIT	CREDIT	BALANCE DEBIT	BALANCE CREDIT
20—						
Apr. 30	Balance	√			8 5 0 0 00	

ACCOUNT *Accounts Payable*   ACCOUNT NO. **221**

DATE	ITEM	POST. REF.	DEBIT	CREDIT	BALANCE DEBIT	BALANCE CREDIT
20—						
Apr. 30	Balance	√				2 0 8 0 00

ACCOUNT *, Capital*   ACCOUNT NO. **311**

DATE	ITEM	POST. REF.	DEBIT	CREDIT	BALANCE DEBIT	BALANCE CREDIT
20—						
Apr. 30	Balance	√				21 5 7 2 00

Copyright © by Houghton Mifflin Company. All rights reserved.

PROBLEM 3-2B (continued)

ACCOUNT _____ , *Drawing* _____ ACCOUNT NO. ___ 312

DATE		ITEM	POST. REF.	DEBIT	CREDIT	BALANCE DEBIT	BALANCE CREDIT
20—							
Apr.	30	Balance	✓			1 5 0 0 00	

ACCOUNT ___ *Income from Services* _____ ACCOUNT NO. ___ 411

DATE		ITEM	POST. REF.	DEBIT	CREDIT	BALANCE DEBIT	BALANCE CREDIT
20—							
Apr.	30	Balance	✓				4 2 3 6 00

ACCOUNT ___ *Wages Expense* _____ ACCOUNT NO. ___ 511

DATE		ITEM	POST. REF.	DEBIT	CREDIT	BALANCE DEBIT	BALANCE CREDIT
20—							
Apr.	30	Balance	✓			1 0 5 0 00	

ACCOUNT ___ *Rent Expense* _____ ACCOUNT NO. ___ 512

DATE		ITEM	POST. REF.	DEBIT	CREDIT	BALANCE DEBIT	BALANCE CREDIT
20—							
Apr.	30	Balance	✓			8 5 0 00	

54

Copyright © by Houghton Mifflin Company. All rights reserved.

PROBLEM 3-2B (continued)

ACCOUNT *Advertising Expense*   ACCOUNT NO. **513**

DATE		ITEM	POST. REF.	DEBIT	CREDIT	BALANCE DEBIT	BALANCE CREDIT
20—							
Apr.	30	Balance	√			4 2 3 00	

ACCOUNT *Utilities Expense*   ACCOUNT NO. **514**

DATE		ITEM	POST. REF.	DEBIT	CREDIT	BALANCE DEBIT	BALANCE CREDIT
20—							
Apr.	30	Balance	√			3 8 5 00	

ACCOUNT NAME	DEBIT	CREDIT

Copyright © by Houghton Mifflin Company. All rights reserved.

PROBLEM 3-2B (continued)

Copyright © by Houghton Mifflin Company. All rights reserved.

NAME _____ DATE _____ CLASS _____

PROBLEM 3-2B (concluded)

Copyright © by Houghton Mifflin Company. All rights reserved.

PROBLEM 3-3A

GENERAL JOURNAL

	DATE		DESCRIPTION	POST. REF.	DEBIT	CREDIT	
1							1
2							2
3							3
4							4
5							5
6							6
7							7
8							8
9							9
10							10
11							11
12							12
13							13
14							14
15							15
16							16
17							17
18							18
19							19
20							20
21							21
22							22
23							23
24							24
25							25
26							26
27							27
28							28
29							29
30							30
31							31
32							32
33							33
34							34
35							35
36							36
37							37

Copyright © by Houghton Mifflin Company. All rights reserved.

PROBLEM 3-3A (continued)

GENERAL JOURNAL

PAGE _____

	DATE		DESCRIPTION	POST. REF.	DEBIT	CREDIT	
1							1
2							2
3							3
4							4
5							5
6							6
7							7
8							8
9							9
10							10
11							11
12							12
13							13
14							14
15							15
16							16
17							17
18							18
19							19
20							20
21							21
22							22
23							23
24							24
25							25
26							26
27							27
28							28
29							29
30							30
31							31
32							32
33							33
34							34
35							35
36							36
37							37

Copyright © by Houghton Mifflin Company. All rights reserved.

PROBLEM 3-3A (continued)

GENERAL LEDGER

ACCOUNT _Cash_ _____ ACCOUNT NO. _111_

DATE		ITEM	POST. REF.	DEBIT	CREDIT	BALANCE	
						DEBIT	CREDIT
20—							
June	30	Balance	√			25 312 00	

ACCOUNT _Accounts Receivable_ _____ ACCOUNT NO. _113_

DATE		ITEM	POST. REF.	DEBIT	CREDIT	BALANCE	
						DEBIT	CREDIT
20—							
June	30	Balance	√			5 60 00	

ACCOUNT _Supplies_ _____ ACCOUNT NO. _115_

DATE		ITEM	POST. REF.	DEBIT	CREDIT	BALANCE	
						DEBIT	CREDIT
20—							
June	30	Balance	√			2 80 00	

ACCOUNT _Prepaid Insurance_ _____ ACCOUNT NO. _117_

DATE		ITEM	POST. REF.	DEBIT	CREDIT	BALANCE	
						DEBIT	CREDIT
20—							
June	30	Balance	√			4 50 00	

60

Copyright © by Houghton Mifflin Company. All rights reserved.

PROBLEM 3-3A (continued)

ACCOUNT __Equipment_____ ACCOUNT NO. __124__

DATE		ITEM	POST. REF.	DEBIT	CREDIT	BALANCE DEBIT	BALANCE CREDIT
20—							
June	30	Balance	√			16 5 0 0 00	

ACCOUNT __Accounts Payable_____ ACCOUNT NO. __221__

DATE		ITEM	POST. REF.	DEBIT	CREDIT	BALANCE DEBIT	BALANCE CREDIT
20—							
June	30	Balance	√				2 9 7 6 00

ACCOUNT _____ , Capital_____ ACCOUNT NO. __311__

DATE		ITEM	POST. REF.	DEBIT	CREDIT	BALANCE DEBIT	BALANCE CREDIT
20—							
June	30	Balance	√				40 1 2 6 00

ACCOUNT _____ , Drawing_____ ACCOUNT NO. __312__

DATE		ITEM	POST. REF.	DEBIT	CREDIT	BALANCE DEBIT	BALANCE CREDIT

ACCOUNT __Professional Fees_____ ACCOUNT NO. __411__

DATE		ITEM	POST. REF.	DEBIT	CREDIT	BALANCE DEBIT	BALANCE CREDIT

Copyright © by Houghton Mifflin Company. All rights reserved.

PROBLEM 3-3A (continued)

ACCOUNT *Salary Expense*   ACCOUNT NO. *511*

DATE	ITEM	POST. REF.	DEBIT	CREDIT	BALANCE	
					DEBIT	CREDIT

ACCOUNT *Rent Expense*   ACCOUNT NO. *512*

DATE	ITEM	POST. REF.	DEBIT	CREDIT	BALANCE	
					DEBIT	CREDIT

ACCOUNT *Laboratory Expense*   ACCOUNT NO. *513*

DATE	ITEM	POST. REF.	DEBIT	CREDIT	BALANCE	
					DEBIT	CREDIT

ACCOUNT *Utilities Expense*   ACCOUNT NO. *514*

DATE	ITEM	POST. REF.	DEBIT	CREDIT	BALANCE	
					DEBIT	CREDIT

Copyright © by Houghton Mifflin Company. All rights reserved.

NAME _____ DATE _____ CLASS _____

PROBLEM 3-3A (concluded)

ACCOUNT NAME	DEBIT	CREDIT

Copyright © by Houghton Mifflin Company. All rights reserved.

PROBLEM 3-3B

GENERAL JOURNAL

PAGE _____

	DATE	DESCRIPTION	POST. REF.	DEBIT	CREDIT	
1						1
2						2
3						3
4						4
5						5
6						6
7						7
8						8
9						9
10						10
11						11
12						12
13						13
14						14
15						15
16						16
17						17
18						18
19						19
20						20
21						21
22						22
23						23
24						24
25						25
26						26
27						27
28						28
29						29
30						30
31						31
32						32
33						33
34						34
35						35
36						36
37						37

Copyright © by Houghton Mifflin Company. All rights reserved.

NAME _____ DATE _____ CLASS _____

PROBLEM 3-3B (continued)

GENERAL JOURNAL   PAGE _____

	DATE	DESCRIPTION	POST. REF.	DEBIT	CREDIT	
1						1
2						2
3						3
4						4
5						5
6						6
7						7
8						8
9						9
10						10
11						11
12						12
13						13
14						14
15						15
16						16
17						17
18						18
19						19
20						20
21						21
22						22
23						23
24						24
25						25
26						26
27						27
28						28
29						29
30						30
31						31
32						32
33						33
34						34
35						35
36						36
37						37

Copyright © by Houghton Mifflin Company. All rights reserved.

PROBLEM 3-3B (continued)

GENERAL LEDGER

ACCOUNT *Cash* _____ ACCOUNT NO. *111*

DATE		ITEM	POST. REF.	DEBIT	CREDIT	BALANCE	
						DEBIT	CREDIT
20—							
June	30	Balance	✓			4 5 6 8 00	

ACCOUNT *Accounts Receivable* _____ ACCOUNT NO. *113*

DATE		ITEM	POST. REF.	DEBIT	CREDIT	BALANCE	
						DEBIT	CREDIT
20—							
June	30	Balance	✓			3 0 4 5 00	

ACCOUNT *Supplies* _____ ACCOUNT NO. *115*

DATE		ITEM	POST. REF.	DEBIT	CREDIT	BALANCE	
						DEBIT	CREDIT
20—							
June	30	Balance	✓			1 5 6 00	

ACCOUNT *Prepaid Insurance* _____ ACCOUNT NO. *117*

DATE		ITEM	POST. REF.	DEBIT	CREDIT	BALANCE	
						DEBIT	CREDIT
20—							
June	30	Balance	✓			2 1 8 5 00	

Copyright © by Houghton Mifflin Company. All rights reserved.

PROBLEM 3-3B (continued)

ACCOUNT *Equipment*   ACCOUNT NO. __124__

DATE		ITEM	POST. REF.	DEBIT	CREDIT	BALANCE	
						DEBIT	CREDIT
20—							
June	30	Balance	√			16 850 00	

ACCOUNT *Accounts Payable*   ACCOUNT NO. __221__

DATE		ITEM	POST. REF.	DEBIT	CREDIT	BALANCE	
						DEBIT	CREDIT
20—							
June	30	Balance	√				2 804 00

ACCOUNT _____ *, Capital*   ACCOUNT NO. __311__

DATE		ITEM	POST. REF.	DEBIT	CREDIT	BALANCE	
						DEBIT	CREDIT
20—							
June	30	Balance	√				24 000 00

ACCOUNT _____ *, Drawing*   ACCOUNT NO. __312__

DATE		ITEM	POST. REF.	DEBIT	CREDIT	BALANCE	
						DEBIT	CREDIT

ACCOUNT *Professional Fees*   ACCOUNT NO. __411__

DATE		ITEM	POST. REF.	DEBIT	CREDIT	BALANCE	
						DEBIT	CREDIT

Copyright © by Houghton Mifflin Company. All rights reserved.

PROBLEM 3-3B (continued)

ACCOUNT *Salary Expense*   ACCOUNT NO. *511*

DATE	ITEM	POST. REF.	DEBIT	CREDIT	BALANCE	
					DEBIT	CREDIT

ACCOUNT *Rent Expense*   ACCOUNT NO. *512*

DATE	ITEM	POST. REF.	DEBIT	CREDIT	BALANCE	
					DEBIT	CREDIT

ACCOUNT *Laboratory Expense*   ACCOUNT NO. *513*

DATE	ITEM	POST. REF.	DEBIT	CREDIT	BALANCE	
					DEBIT	CREDIT

ACCOUNT *Utilities Expense*   ACCOUNT NO. *514*

DATE	ITEM	POST. REF.	DEBIT	CREDIT	BALANCE	
					DEBIT	CREDIT

Copyright © by Houghton Mifflin Company. All rights reserved.

PROBLEM 3-3B (concluded)

ACCOUNT NAME	DEBIT	CREDIT

Copyright © by Houghton Mifflin Company. All rights reserved.

NAME _____ DATE _____ CLASS _____

PROBLEM 3-4A or 3-4B

GENERAL JOURNAL

PAGE _____

	DATE	DESCRIPTION	POST. REF.	DEBIT	CREDIT	
1						1
2						2
3						3
4						4
5						5
6						6
7						7
8						8
9						9
10						10
11						11
12						12
13						13
14						14
15						15
16						16
17						17
18						18
19						19
20						20
21						21
22						22
23						23
24						24
25						25
26						26
27						27
28						28
29						29
30						30
31						31
32						32
33						33
34						34
35						35
36						36
37						37

70

Copyright © by Houghton Mifflin Company. All rights reserved.

NAME _____ DATE _____ CLASS _____

PROBLEM 3-4A or 3-4B (continued)

GENERAL JOURNAL   PAGE _____

	DATE		DESCRIPTION	POST. REF.	DEBIT	CREDIT	
1							1
2							2
3							3
4							4
5							5
6							6
7							7
8							8
9							9
10							10
11							11
12							12
13							13
14							14
15							15
16							16
17							17
18							18
19							19
20							20
21							21
22							22
23							23
24							24
25							25
26							26
27							27
28							28
29							29
30							30
31							31
32							32
33							33
34							34
35							35
36							36
37							37

Copyright © by Houghton Mifflin Company. All rights reserved.

PROBLEM 3-4A or 3-4B (continued)

GENERAL JOURNAL

PAGE _____

	DATE		DESCRIPTION	POST. REF.	DEBIT	CREDIT	
1							1
2							2
3							3
4							4
5							5
6							6
7							7
8							8
9							9
10							10
11							11
12							12
13							13
14							14
15							15
16							16
17							17
18							18
19							19
20							20
21							21
22							22
23							23
24							24
25							25
26							26
27							27
28							28
29							29
30							30
31							31
32							32
33							33
34							34
35							35
36							36
37							37

Copyright © by Houghton Mifflin Company. All rights reserved.

PROBLEM 3-4A or 3-4B (continued)

GENERAL LEDGER

ACCOUNT _Cash_ _____ ACCOUNT NO. _111_

DATE	ITEM	POST. REF.	DEBIT	CREDIT	BALANCE	
					DEBIT	CREDIT

ACCOUNT _Accounts Receivable_ _____ ACCOUNT NO. _113_

DATE	ITEM	POST. REF.	DEBIT	CREDIT	BALANCE	
					DEBIT	CREDIT

ACCOUNT _Supplies_ _____ ACCOUNT NO. _115_

DATE	ITEM	POST. REF.	DEBIT	CREDIT	BALANCE	
					DEBIT	CREDIT

ACCOUNT _Prepaid Insurance_ _____ ACCOUNT NO. _117_

DATE	ITEM	POST. REF.	DEBIT	CREDIT	BALANCE	
					DEBIT	CREDIT

Copyright © by Houghton Mifflin Company. All rights reserved.

PROBLEM 3-4A or 3-4B (continued)

ACCOUNT _*Equipment*_____ ACCOUNT NO. _124_

DATE		ITEM	POST. REF.	DEBIT	CREDIT	BALANCE	
						DEBIT	CREDIT

ACCOUNT _*Accounts Payable*_____ ACCOUNT NO. _221_

DATE		ITEM	POST. REF.	DEBIT	CREDIT	BALANCE	
						DEBIT	CREDIT

ACCOUNT _____, *Capital*_____ ACCOUNT NO. _311_

DATE		ITEM	POST. REF.	DEBIT	CREDIT	BALANCE	
						DEBIT	CREDIT

ACCOUNT _____, *Drawing*_____ ACCOUNT NO. _312_

DATE		ITEM	POST. REF.	DEBIT	CREDIT	BALANCE	
						DEBIT	CREDIT

Copyright © by Houghton Mifflin Company. All rights reserved.

PROBLEM 3-4A or 3-4B (continued)

ACCOUNT _Landscaping Income_ _____ ACCOUNT NO. _411_

DATE	ITEM	POST. REF.	DEBIT	CREDIT	BALANCE	
					DEBIT	CREDIT

ACCOUNT _Salary Expense_ _____ ACCOUNT NO. _511_

DATE	ITEM	POST. REF.	DEBIT	CREDIT	BALANCE	
					DEBIT	CREDIT

ACCOUNT _Rent Expense_ _____ ACCOUNT NO. _512_

DATE	ITEM	POST. REF.	DEBIT	CREDIT	BALANCE	
					DEBIT	CREDIT

ACCOUNT _Gas and Oil Expense_ _____ ACCOUNT NO. _513_

DATE	ITEM	POST. REF.	DEBIT	CREDIT	BALANCE	
					DEBIT	CREDIT

ACCOUNT _Utilities Expense_ _____ ACCOUNT NO. _514_

DATE	ITEM	POST. REF.	DEBIT	CREDIT	BALANCE	
					DEBIT	CREDIT

Copyright © by Houghton Mifflin Company. All rights reserved.

PROBLEM 3-4A or 3-4B (concluded)

ACCOUNT NAME	DEBIT	CREDIT

Copyright © by Houghton Mifflin Company. All rights reserved.

CUMULATIVE SELF-CHECK: Chapters 1–3

Part II:

1.
GENERAL JOURNAL

PAGE _____

	DATE		DESCRIPTION	POST. REF.	DEBIT	CREDIT	
1							1
2							2
3							3
4							4
5							5
6							6
7							7
8							8
9							9
10							10
11							11
12							12
13							13
14							14
15							15
16							16
17							17
18							18
19							19
20							20
21							21
22							22
23							23
24							24
25							25
26							26
27							27
28							28
29							29
30							30
31							31
32							32
33							33
34							34
35							35
36							36
37							37

Copyright © by Houghton Mifflin Company. All rights reserved.

Assets = Liabilities + Owner's Equity + Revenue - Expenses

2, 3, 4.

Copyright © by Houghton Mifflin Company. All rights reserved.

CUMULATIVE SELF-CHECK (continued)

5.

ACCOUNT NAME	DEBIT	CREDIT

6.

Copyright © by Houghton Mifflin Company. All rights reserved.

CUMULATIVE SELF-CHECK (concluded)

7.

	ACCOUNT NAME	DEBIT	CREDIT

8.

		DEBIT	CREDIT

Copyright © by Houghton Mifflin Company. All rights reserved.

┌─────────┐
│   │
│   4   │
│   │
└─────────┘

4 | Adjusting Entries and the Work Sheet

PERFORMANCE OBJECTIVES

1. Define *fiscal period* and *fiscal year*.
2. List the classifications of the accounts that occupy each column of a ten-column work sheet.
3. Complete a work sheet for a service enterprise, involving adjustments for supplies used, expired insurance, depreciation, and accrued wages.
4. Prepare an income statement, a statement of owner's equity, and a balance sheet for a service business directly from the work sheet.
5. Journalize and post the adjusting entries.
6. Prepare an income statement and a balance sheet for a business with more than one revenue account and more than one accumulated depreciation account.

KEY TERMS

Accounting cycle	Depreciation
Accrual	Fiscal period
Accrued wages	Fiscal year
Adjusting entry	Matching principle
Adjustments	Mixed accounts
Book value or carrying value	Straight-line depreciation
Contra account	Work sheet

STUDY GUIDE QUESTIONS

PART 1   True/False

For each of the following statements, circle T if the statement is true and F if the statement is false.

T F 1. Adjusting entries recorded on a work sheet must also be journalized.

T F 2. The book value of an asset is always equal to the asset's true market value.

T F 3. Each adjusting entry involves both an income statement account and a balance sheet account.

T F 4. The purpose of a work sheet is to enable the accountant to prepare the financial statements.

T F 5. The cost of supplies used will appear in the Adjustments Debit column, the Adjusted Trial Balance Debit column, and the Income Statement Debit column.

T F 6. The purpose of adjustments is to correct account amounts that are incorrect.

T F 7. The purpose of depreciating an asset is to spread out the cost of the asset over its useful life.

T F 8. The normal balance of Accumulated Depreciation, Equipment, is on the debit side.

Copyright © by Houghton Mifflin Company. All rights reserved.

T   F   9. If the total of the Income Statement Debit column is larger than the total of the Income Statement Credit column, the company must have a net loss.

T   F   10. The Drawing account is recorded on a work sheet in the Trial Balance Debit column, the Adjusted Trial Balance Debit column, and the Income Statement Debit column.

PART 2   Completion—Language of Business

Complete each of the following statements by writing the appropriate words in the spaces provided.

1. The cost of an asset less the accumulated depreciation is called the _____ _____ .

2. The time span that covers a company's accounting cycle is called its _____ _____ .

3. Since the plus and minus signs on Accumulated Depreciation, Equipment, are the opposite of the signs on Equipment, the Accumulated Depreciation, Equipment, account is called a(n) _____ account.

4. Internal transactions that are used to bring the ledger accounts up to date are called __ _____ .

5. The amount of unpaid wages owed to employees for the time between the last payday and the end of the fiscal period is called _____ .

6. The _____ represents the steps in the accounting process that are completed during the fiscal period.

7. The Prepaid Insurance and Supplies accounts are called _____ because their balances that appear in the Trial Balance column consist partly of income statement amounts and partly of balance sheet amounts.

8. The _____ requires that the expenses of one period must be related to the revenue of the same period.

9. The term representing loss in usefulness of assets is _____ .

PART 3   Adjusting Entries

Record the adjusting entries directly in the T accounts, and label the other account.

1. Insurance expired, $510.

Prepaid Insurance

Bal.	950		

2. Supplies inventory, $580.

Supplies

Bal.	1,100		

3. Additional depreciation, $2,500.

Accumulated Depreciation, Equipment

		Bal.	7,500

4. Accrued wages, $470.

Wages Expense

Bal.	8,100		

Copyright © by Houghton Mifflin Company. All rights reserved.

PART 4   Analyzing the Work Sheet

Carry the balances forward from the Trial Balance columns to the appropriate column. The first two accounts are provided as examples.

Account Name	Trial Balance		Adjustments		Adj. Trial Balance		Income Statement		Balance Sheet	
	Debit	Credit	Debit	Credit	Debit	Credit	Debit	Credit	Debit	Credit
0. Equipment	X				X				X	
0. Supplies Expense			X		X		X			
1. Cash	X									
2. C. Tumi, Capital		X								
3. Advertising Expense	X									
4. Accounts Receivable	X									
5. Wages Expense	X									
6. Accumulated Depreciation, Equipment		X								
7. Wages Payable										
8. Supplies	X									
9. C. Tumi, Drawing	X									
10. Service Revenue		X								

DEMONSTRATION PROBLEM

The general ledger of Best Carpenters contains the following account balances for the year ended December 31.

Cash	$ 2,560	H. Best, Drawing	$60,000
Accounts Receivable	7,428	Income from Services	89,845
Supplies	1,218	Wages Expense	21,500
Prepaid Insurance	960	Rent Expense	4,800
Equipment	4,270	Advertising Expense	1,216
Accumulated Depreciation,		Utilities Expense	1,344
Equipment	1,230	Insurance Expense	0
Truck	21,550	Supplies Expense	0
Accumulated Depreciation, Truck	4,310	Depreciation Expense, Equipment	0
Accounts Payable	426	Depreciation Expense, Truck	0
Wages Payable	0	Miscellaneous Expense	279
H. Best, Capital	31,314		

Since the firm has been in operation for longer than a year, Accumulated Depreciation, Equipment, and Accumulated Depreciation, Truck, have balances that should be included in the trial balance.

Copyright © by Houghton Mifflin Company. All rights reserved.

DEMONSTRATION PROBLEM (continued)

Data for the year-end adjustments are as follows:

a. Wages accrued at December 31, $448.
b. Insurance expired during the year, $768.
c. Inventory of supplies at December 31, $679.
d. Depreciation of equipment during the year, $854.
e. Depreciation of truck during the year, $4,310.

Instructions

Complete the work sheet for the year.

SOLUTION

Best Carpenters
Work Sheet
For Year Ended December 31, 20—

	ACCOUNT NAME	TRIAL BALANCE DEBIT	TRIAL BALANCE CREDIT	ADJUSTMENTS DEBIT	ADJUSTMENTS CREDIT
1	Cash	2 5 6 0 00			
2	Accounts Receivable	7 4 2 8 00			
3	Supplies	1 2 1 8 00			(c) 5 3 9 00
4	Prepaid Insurance	9 6 0 00			(b) 7 6 8 00
5	Equipment	4 2 7 0 00			
6	Accumulated Depreciation, Equipment		1 2 3 0 00		(d) 8 5 4 00
7	Truck	21 5 5 0 00			
8	Accumulated Depreciation, Truck		4 3 1 0 00		(e) 4 3 1 0 00
9	Accounts Payable		4 2 6 00		
10	H. Best, Capital		31 3 1 4 00		
11	H. Best, Drawing	6 0 0 0 00			
12	Income from Services		89 8 4 5 00		
13	Wages Expense	21 5 0 0 00		(a) 4 4 8 00	
14	Rent Expense	4 8 0 0 00			
15	Advertising Expense	1 2 1 6 00			
16	Utilities Expense	1 3 4 4 00			
17	Miscellaneous Expense	2 7 9 00			
18		127 1 2 5 00	127 1 2 5 00		
19	Wages Payable				(a) 4 4 8 00
20	Insurance Expense			(b) 7 6 8 00	
21	Supplies Expense			(c) 5 3 9 00	
22	Depreciation Expense, Equipment			(d) 8 5 4 00	
23	Depreciation Expense, Truck			(e) 4 3 1 0 00	
24				6 9 1 9 00	6 9 1 9 00
25	Net Income				
26					
27					
28					
29					
30					
31					
32					
33					
34					
35					
36					
37					

Copyright © by Houghton Mifflin Company. All rights reserved.

ADJUSTED TRIAL BALANCE		INCOME STATEMENT		BALANCE SHEET		
DEBIT	CREDIT	DEBIT	CREDIT	DEBIT	CREDIT	
2 5 6 0 00				2 5 6 0 00		1
7 4 2 8 00				7 4 2 8 00		2
6 7 9 00				6 7 9 00		3
1 9 2 00				1 9 2 00		4
4 2 7 0 00				4 2 7 0 00		5
	2 0 8 4 00				2 0 8 4 00	6
21 5 5 0 00				21 5 5 0 00		7
	8 6 2 0 00				8 6 2 0 00	8
	4 2 6 00				4 2 6 00	9
	31 3 1 4 00				31 3 1 4 00	10
60 0 0 0 00				60 0 0 0 00		11
	89 8 4 5 00		89 8 4 5 00			12
21 9 4 8 00		21 9 4 8 00				13
4 8 0 0 00		4 8 0 0 00				14
1 2 1 6 00		1 2 1 6 00				15
1 3 4 4 00		1 3 4 4 00				16
2 7 9 00		2 7 9 00				17
						18
	4 4 8 00				4 4 8 00	19
7 6 8 00		7 6 8 00				20
5 3 9 00		5 3 9 00				21
8 5 4 00		8 5 4 00				22
4 3 1 0 00		4 3 1 0 00				23
132 7 3 7 00	132 7 3 7 00	36 0 5 8 00	89 8 4 5 00	96 6 7 9 00	42 8 9 2 00	24
		53 7 8 7 00			53 7 8 7 00	25
		89 8 4 5 00	89 8 4 5 00	96 6 7 9 00	96 6 7 9 00	26

Copyright © by Houghton Mifflin Company. All rights reserved.

NAME _____ DATE _____ CLASS _____

PROBLEM 4-1A or 4-1B

_____

_____

_____

	ACCOUNT NAME	TRIAL BALANCE				ADJUSTMENTS			
		DEBIT A + Draw. + E		CREDIT Accum. Depr. + L + C + R		DEBIT		CREDIT	
1	Cash								
2	Accounts Receivable								
3	Prepaid Insurance								
4	Supplies								
5	Office Equipment								
6	Accounts Payable								
7	, Capital								
8	, Drawing								
9	Commissions Earned								
10	Rent Expense								
11	Travel Expense								
12	Utilities Expense								
13	Miscellaneous Expense								
14									
15									
16									
17									
18									
19									
20									
21									
22									
23									
24									
25									
26									
27									
28									
29									
30									
31									
32									
33									
34									
35									
36									

Copyright © by Houghton Mifflin Company. All rights reserved.

PROBLEM 4-1A or 4-1B (concluded)

_____
_____
_____

ADJUSTED TRIAL BALANCE		INCOME STATEMENT		BALANCE SHEET		
DEBIT A + Draw. + E	CREDIT Accum. Depr. + L + C + R	DEBIT E	CREDIT R	DEBIT A + Draw.	CREDIT Accum. Depr. + L + C	
						1
						2
						3
						4
						5
						6
						7
						8
						9
						10
						11
						12
						13
						14
						15
						16
						17
						18
						19
						20
						21
						22
						23
						24
						25
						26
						27
						28
						29
						30
						31
						32
						33
						34
						35
						36

Copyright © by Houghton Mifflin Company. All rights reserved.

PROBLEM 4-2A WORK SHEET

Wong Design
Work Sheet
For Month Ended March 31, 20—

ACCOUNT NAME	TRIAL BALANCE DEBIT	TRIAL BALANCE CREDIT	ADJUSTMENTS DEBIT	ADJUSTMENTS CREDIT
1 Cash	6 2 2 9 00			
2 Supplies	6 3 7 00			(a) 3 2 1 00
3 Prepaid Insurance	1 2 4 6 00			(b) 2 5 5 00
4 Equipment	6 2 8 8 00			
5 Accumulated Depreciation,				
6 Equipment		3 6 2 0 00		(c) 8 9 4 00
7 Office Furniture	3 5 8 0 00			
8 Accumulated Depreciation,				
9 Office Furniture		2 8 0 6 00		(d) 4 6 5 00
10 Truck	24 6 9 9 00			
11 Accumulated Depreciation, Truck		18 1 9 3 00		(e) 6 4 5 00
12 Accounts Payable		2 6 2 7 00		
13 H. Wong, Capital		10 6 7 2 00		
14 H. Wong, Drawing	3 2 0 0 00			
15 Professional Fees		12 1 7 6 00		
16 Salary Expense	2 0 5 5 00		(f) 4 7 7 00	
17 Rent Expense	1 0 2 5 00			
18 Travel Expense	3 4 8 00			
19 Utilities Expense	1 5 6 00			
20 Advertising Expense	4 9 6 00			
21 Miscellaneous Expense	1 3 5 00			
22	50 0 9 4 00	50 0 9 4 00		
23 Supplies Expense			(a) 3 2 1 00	
24 Insurance Expense			(b) 2 5 5 00	
25 Depreciation Expense, Equipment			(c) 8 9 4 00	
26 Depreciation Expense, Office				
27 Furniture			(d) 4 6 5 00	
28 Depreciation Expense, Truck			(e) 6 4 5 00	
29 Salaries Payable				(f) 4 7 7 00
30			3 0 5 7 00	3 0 5 7 00
31 Net Income				
32				
33				
34				
35				
36				

Copyright © by Houghton Mifflin Company. All rights reserved.

PROBLEM 4-2A (continued)

ADJUSTED TRIAL BALANCE		INCOME STATEMENT		BALANCE SHEET		
DEBIT	CREDIT	DEBIT	CREDIT	DEBIT	CREDIT	
6 2 2 9 00				6 2 2 9 00		1
3 1 6 00				3 1 6 00		2
9 9 1 00				9 9 1 00		3
6 2 8 8 00				6 2 8 8 00		4
						5
	4 5 1 4 00				4 5 1 4 00	6
3 5 8 0 00				3 5 8 0 00		7
						8
	3 2 7 1 00				3 2 7 1 00	9
24 6 9 9 00				24 6 9 9 00		10
	18 8 3 8 00				18 8 3 8 00	11
	2 6 2 7 00				2 6 2 7 00	12
	10 6 7 2 00				10 6 7 2 00	13
3 2 0 0 00				3 2 0 0 00		14
	12 1 7 6 00		12 1 7 6 00			15
2 5 3 2 00		2 5 3 2 00				16
1 0 2 5 00		1 0 2 5 00				17
3 4 8 00		3 4 8 00				18
1 5 6 00		1 5 6 00				19
4 9 6 00		4 9 6 00				20
1 3 5 00		1 3 5 00				21
						22
3 2 1 00		3 2 1 00				23
2 5 5 00		2 5 5 00				24
8 9 4 00		8 9 4 00				25
						26
4 6 5 00		4 6 5 00				27
6 4 5 00		6 4 5 00				28
	4 7 7 00				4 7 7 00	29
52 5 7 5 00	52 5 7 5 00	7 2 7 2 00	12 1 7 6 00	45 3 0 3 00	40 3 9 9 00	30
		4 9 0 4 00			4 9 0 4 00	31
		12 1 7 6 00	12 1 7 6 00	45 3 0 3 00	45 3 0 3 00	32
						33
						34
						35
						36

Copyright © by Houghton Mifflin Company. All rights reserved.

PROBLEM 4-2B WORK SHEET

Clark Design
Work Sheet
For Month Ended March 31, 20—

	ACCOUNT NAME	TRIAL BALANCE DEBIT	TRIAL BALANCE CREDIT	ADJUSTMENTS DEBIT	ADJUSTMENTS CREDIT
1	Cash	7 3 4 0 00			
2	Supplies	5 4 8 00			(a) 2 2 4 00
3	Prepaid Insurance	1 1 3 6 00			(b) 3 5 4 00
4	Equipment	7 1 7 6 00			
5	Accumulated Depreciation,				
6	Equipment		2 5 1 2 00		(c) 4 9 0 00
7	Office Furniture	4 4 7 9 00			
8	Accumulated Depreciation,				
9	Office Furniture		1 7 9 5 00		(d) 3 6 8 00
10	Truck	20 8 7 4 00			
11	Accumulated Depreciation, Truck		14 3 6 7 00		(e) 9 8 5 00
12	Accounts Payable		1 5 8 4 00		
13	J. Clark, Capital		13 6 4 8 00		
14	J. Clark, Drawing	2 8 0 0 00			
15	Professional Fees		14 8 5 2 00		
16	Salary Expense	1 8 6 4 00		(f) 3 8 7 00	
17	Rent Expense	1 2 8 5 00			
18	Travel Expense	4 4 5 00			
19	Utilities Expense	1 6 8 00			
20	Advertising Expense	4 5 8 00			
21	Miscellaneous Expense	1 8 5 00			
22		48 7 5 8 00	48 7 5 8 00		
23	Supplies Expense			(a) 2 2 4 00	
24	Insurance Expense			(b) 3 5 4 00	
25	Depreciation Expense, Equipment			(c) 4 9 0 00	
26	Depreciation Expense, Office				
27	Furniture			(d) 3 6 8 00	
28	Depreciation Expense, Truck			(e) 9 8 5 00	
29	Salaries Payable				(f) 3 8 7 00
30				2 8 0 8 00	2 8 0 8 00
31	Net Income				
32					
33					
34					
35					
36					

Copyright © by Houghton Mifflin Company. All rights reserved.

PROBLEM 4-2B (continued)

ADJUSTED TRIAL BALANCE		INCOME STATEMENT		BALANCE SHEET		
DEBIT	CREDIT	DEBIT	CREDIT	DEBIT	CREDIT	
7 3 4 0 00				7 3 4 0 00		1
3 2 4 00				3 2 4 00		2
7 8 2 00				7 8 2 00		3
7 1 7 6 00				7 1 7 6 00		4
						5
	3 0 0 2 00				3 0 0 2 00	6
4 4 7 9 00				4 4 7 9 00		7
						8
	2 1 6 3 00				2 1 6 3 00	9
20 8 7 4 00				20 8 7 4 00		10
	15 3 5 2 00				15 3 5 2 00	11
	1 5 8 4 00				1 5 8 4 00	12
	13 6 4 8 00				13 6 4 8 00	13
2 8 0 0 00				2 8 0 0 00		14
	14 8 5 2 00		14 8 5 2 00			15
2 2 5 1 00		2 2 5 1 00				16
1 2 8 5 00		1 2 8 5 00				17
4 4 5 00		4 4 5 00				18
1 6 8 00		1 6 8 00				19
4 5 8 00		4 5 8 00				20
1 8 5 00		1 8 5 00				21
						22
2 2 4 00		2 2 4 00				23
3 5 4 00		3 5 4 00				24
4 9 0 00		4 9 0 00				25
						26
3 6 8 00		3 6 8 00				27
9 8 5 00		9 8 5 00				28
	3 8 7 00				3 8 7 00	29
50 9 8 8 00	50 9 8 8 00	7 2 1 3 00	14 8 5 2 00	43 7 7 5 00	36 1 3 6 00	30
		7 6 3 9 00			7 6 3 9 00	31
		14 8 5 2 00	14 8 5 2 00	43 7 7 5 00	43 7 7 5 00	32
						33
						34
						35
						36

Copyright © by Houghton Mifflin Company. All rights reserved.

PROBLEM 4-2A or 4-2B (continued)

Copyright © by Houghton Mifflin Company. All rights reserved.

NAME _____ DATE _____ CLASS _____

PROBLEM 4-2A or 4-2B (continued)

PROBLEM 4-2A or 4-2B (continued)

Copyright © by Houghton Mifflin Company. All rights reserved.

PROBLEM 4-2A or 4-2B (concluded)

GENERAL JOURNAL   PAGE _____

	DATE		DESCRIPTION	POST. REF.	DEBIT	CREDIT	
1							1
2							2
3							3
4							4
5							5
6							6
7							7
8							8
9							9
10							10
11							11
12							12
13							13
14							14
15							15
16							16
17							17
18							18
19							19
20							20
21							21
22							22
23							23
24							24
25							25
26							26
27							27
28							28
29							29
30							30
31							31
32							32
33							33
34							34
35							35
36							36
37							37

Copyright © by Houghton Mifflin Company. All rights reserved.

PROBLEM 4-3A or 4-3B

_____

_____

_____

	ACCOUNT NAME	TRIAL BALANCE		ADJUSTMENTS	
		DEBIT	CREDIT	DEBIT	CREDIT
1	Cash				
2	Supplies				
3	Prepaid Insurance				
4	Equipment				
5	Accumulated Depreciation,				
6	Equipment				
7	Accounts Payable				
8	, Capital				
9	, Drawing				
10	Income from Services				
11	Wages Expense				
12	Rent Expense				
13	Utilities Expense				
14	Telephone Expense				
15	Miscellaneous Expense				
16					
17					
18					
19					
20					
21					
22					
23					
24					
25					
26					
27					
28					
29					
30					
31					
32					
33					
34					
35					
36					

Copyright © by Houghton Mifflin Company. All rights reserved.

PROBLEM 4-3A or 4-3B (continued)

ADJUSTED TRIAL BALANCE		INCOME STATEMENT		BALANCE SHEET		
DEBIT	CREDIT	DEBIT	CREDIT	DEBIT	CREDIT	
						1
						2
						3
						4
						5
						6
						7
						8
						9
						10
						11
						12
						13
						14
						15
						16
						17
						18
						19
						20
						21
						22
						23
						24
						25
						26
						27
						28
						29
						30
						31
						32
						33
						34
						35
						36

Copyright © by Houghton Mifflin Company. All rights reserved.

PROBLEM 4-3A or 4-3B (concluded)

GENERAL JOURNAL

PAGE _____

	DATE		DESCRIPTION	POST. REF.	DEBIT	CREDIT	
1							1
2							2
3							3
4							4
5							5
6							6
7							7
8							8
9							9
10							10
11							11
12							12
13							13
14							14
15							15
16							16
17							17
18							18
19							19
20							20
21							21
22							22
23							23
24							24
25							25
26							26
27							27
28							28
29							29
30							30
31							31
32							32
33							33
34							34
35							35
36							36
37							37

Copyright © by Houghton Mifflin Company. All rights reserved.

EXTRA FORM

GENERAL JOURNAL

	DATE		DESCRIPTION	POST. REF.	DEBIT	CREDIT	
1							1
2							2
3							3
4							4
5							5
6							6
7							7
8							8
9							9
10							10
11							11
12							12
13							13
14							14
15							15
16							16
17							17
18							18
19							19
20							20
21							21
22							22
23							23
24							24
25							25
26							26
27							27
28							28
29							29
30							30
31							31
32							32
33							33
34							34
35							35
36							36
37							37

Copyright © by Houghton Mifflin Company. All rights reserved.

PROBLEM 4-4A or 4-4B

_____

_____

_____

	ACCOUNT NAME	TRIAL BALANCE		ADJUSTMENTS	
		DEBIT	CREDIT	DEBIT	CREDIT
1	Cash				
2	Supplies				
3	Prepaid Insurance				
4	Equipment				
5	Accumulated Depreciation,				
6	Equipment				
7	Repair Equipment				
8	Accumulated Depreciation,				
9	Repair Equipment				
10	Accounts Payable				
11	, Capital				
12	, Drawing				
13	Golf Fees Income				
14	Concessions Income				
15	Wages Expense				
16	Rent Expense				
17	Utilities Expense				
18	Repair Expense				
19	Miscellaneous Expense				
20					
21					
22					
23					
24					
25					
26					
27					
28					
29					
30					
31					
32					
33					
34					
35					
36					

Copyright © by Houghton Mifflin Company. All rights reserved.

PROBLEM 4-4A or 4-4B (continued)

	ADJUSTED TRIAL BALANCE		INCOME STATEMENT		BALANCE SHEET		
	DEBIT	CREDIT	DEBIT	CREDIT	DEBIT	CREDIT	
							1
							2
							3
							4
							5
							6
							7
							8
							9
							10
							11
							12
							13
							14
							15
							16
							17
							18
							19
							20
							21
							22
							23
							24
							25
							26
							27
							28
							29
							30
							31
							32
							33
							34
							35
							36

Copyright © by Houghton Mifflin Company. All rights reserved.

PROBLEM 4-4A or 4-4B (continued)

Copyright © by Houghton Mifflin Company. All rights reserved.

PROBLEM 4-4A or 4-4B (continued)

Copyright © by Houghton Mifflin Company. All rights reserved.

PROBLEM 4-4A or 4-4B (continued)

Copyright © by Houghton Mifflin Company. All rights reserved.

NAME _____ DATE _____ CLASS _____

PROBLEM 4-4A or 4-4B (concluded)

GENERAL JOURNAL   PAGE _____

	DATE	DESCRIPTION	POST. REF.	DEBIT	CREDIT	
1						1
2						2
3						3
4						4
5						5
6						6
7						7
8						8
9						9
10						10
11						11
12						12
13						13
14						14
15						15
16						16
17						17
18						18
19						19
20						20
21						21
22						22
23						23
24						24
25						25
26						26
27						27
28						28
29						29
30						30
31						31
32						32
33						33
34						34
35						35
36						36
37						37

Copyright © by Houghton Mifflin Company. All rights reserved.

PROBLEM A-I

Year	Depreciation for the Year	Accumulated Depreciation	Book Value

PROBLEM A-2

Year	Depreciation for the Year	Accumulated Depreciation	Book Value

PROBLEM A-3

Year	Depreciation for the Year	Accumulated Depreciation	Book Value

Copyright © by Houghton Mifflin Company. All rights reserved.

5 | Closing Entries and the Post-Closing Trial Balance

PERFORMANCE OBJECTIVES

1. List the steps in the accounting cycle.
2. Journalize and post closing entries for a service enterprise.
3. Prepare a post-closing trial balance.
4. Define the following methods of accounting: accrual basis, cash-receipts-and-disbursements basis, modified cash basis.
5. Prepare interim statements.

KEY TERMS

Accrual basis
Cash-receipts-and-disbursements basis
Closing entries
Income Summary
Interim statements

Modified cash basis
Nominal or temporary-equity accounts
Post-closing trial balance
Real or permanent accounts

STUDY GUIDE QUESTIONS

PART 1   True/False

For each of the following statements, circle T if the statement is true and F if the statement is false:

T   F   1. The first step in the closing procedure is to close the expense accounts into the Income Summary account.

T   F   2. The post-closing trial balance is final proof that the total of the debit balances equals the total of the credit balances.

T   F   3. After the closing entries have been posted, the final balance of the Capital account is the same as the amount recorded on the last line of the statement of owner's equity.

T   F   4. Generally, the closing procedure is completed by making three entries.

T   F   5. The purpose of the closing entries is to close off the asset and liability accounts because their balances apply to only one fiscal period.

T   F   6. The total of the expense accounts is recorded in Income Summary as a credit.

T   F   7. The last step in the closing procedure is to close the Drawing account into the Capital account.

T   F   8. If you have to debit Income Summary to close it, this indicates a net loss.

T   F   9. Income Summary is an example of a nominal or temporary-equity account.

T   F   10. The post-closing trial balance includes only the balances of real or permanent accounts.

Copyright © by Houghton Mifflin Company. All rights reserved.

PART 2 Completion—Language of Business

Complete each of the following statements by writing the appropriate words in the spaces provided.

1. After the closing entries have been journalized and posted, the _____ _____ is prepared as final proof that the accounts are in balance.

2. The accounts that have balances that are carried over to the next fiscal period are called _____ accounts.

3. Financial statements that are prepared during the fiscal period and cover a period of time less than the fiscal period are called _____ statements.

4. The _____ account is brought into existence to have a debit and credit for each closing entry.

5. A journal entry that is made to clear an account or make the balance of that account equal to zero is called a(n) _____ entry.

6. The _____ accounts apply to only one fiscal period and are closed at the end of the fiscal period.

7. An accounting basis under which revenue is recorded only when it is earned and expenses are recorded only when they are incurred is called the _____ .

8. The _____ is an accounting basis under which revenue is recorded only when it is received in cash and most expenses are recorded only when they are paid in cash. Expenses to be counted that are not paid in cash include Depreciation Expense, Supplies Expense, and Insurance Expense.

PART 3 Closing Entries

Using the following list of account titles, determine the account titles to be debited and credited for the closing entries below.

a. Rent Expense   **c.** L. Drew, Drawing   **e.** L. Drew, Capital
b. Service Income   **d.** Income Summary   **f.** Wages Expense

	Debit	Credit
1. Close out the balance of the revenue account.	____	____
2. Close out the balances of the expense accounts.	____	____
3. Close out the amount of the net income for the period.	____	____
4. Close out the balance of the Drawing account.	____	____

PART 4 Posting Closing Entries

After the first closing entries have been journalized and posted, the remaining accounts are shown below in T account form. Based on the T accounts, answer the following questions.

Income Summary		J. See, Capital		J. See, Drawing	
Debit	Credit	Debit	Credit	Debit	Credit
46,000	41,000		Bal. 150,000	Bal. 22,000	

1. The amount of the total revenue is $_____ .
2. The amount of the total expenses is $_____ .
3. The amount of the net income or net loss is $_____ .
4. The amount of the total withdrawals is $_____ .
5. The entry to close Income Summary is a debit to _____ and a credit to _____ .
6. The entry to close J. See, Drawing, is a debit to _____ and a credit to _____ .
7. The amount of the increase or decrease in capital for the period is $_____ .
8. The ending balance of J. See, Capital, is $_____ .

Copyright © by Houghton Mifflin Company. All rights reserved.

DEMONSTRATION PROBLEM

After the adjusting entries have been posted, the ledger of W. T. Wicker, a financial planner, contains the following account balances as of December 31:

Cash	$ 3,064
Accounts Receivable	8,450
Supplies	420
Equipment	10,500
Accumulated Depreciation, Equipment	4,200
Accounts Payable	756
W. T. Wicker, Capital	18,378
W. T. Wicker, Drawing	80,000
Income Summary	—
Commissions Earned	92,824
Income from Services	23,050
Salary Expense	21,600
Rent Expense	11,200
Supplies Expense	1,215
Depreciation Expense, Equipment	2,100
Miscellaneous Expense	659

Instructions

Record the closing entries in general journal form.

SOLUTION

GENERAL JOURNAL

PAGE _____

DATE		DESCRIPTION	POST. REF.	DEBIT	CREDIT
20—		*Closing Entries*			
Dec.	31	*Commissions Earned*		92 8 2 4 00	
		Income from Services		23 0 5 0 00	
		Income Summary			115 8 7 4 00
	31	*Income Summary*		36 7 7 4 00	
		Salary Expense			21 6 0 0 00
		Rent Expense			11 2 0 0 00
		Supplies Expense			1 2 1 5 00
		Depreciation Expense, Equipment			2 1 0 0 00
		Miscellaneous Expense			6 5 9 00
	31	*Income Summary*		79 1 0 0 00	
		W. T. Wicker, Capital			79 1 0 0 00
	31	*W. T. Wicker, Capital*		80 0 0 0 00	
		W. T. Wicker, Drawing			80 0 0 0 00

Copyright © by Houghton Mifflin Company. All rights reserved.

NAME _____ DATE _____ CLASS _____

PROBLEM 5-1A or 5-1B

Assets		=	Liabilities		+	Owner's Equity		+	Revenue		−	Expenses	
Dr.	Cr.		Dr.	Cr.		Dr.	Cr.		Dr.	Cr.		Dr.	Cr.
+	−		−	+		−	+		−	+		+	−

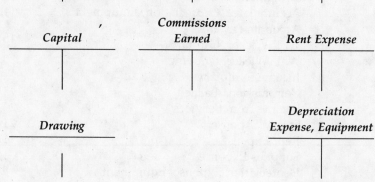

Capital

Commissions
Earned

Rent Expense

Drawing

Depreciation
Expense, Equipment

Income Summary

Utilities Expense

Miscellaneous
Expense

Copyright © by Houghton Mifflin Company. All rights reserved.

PROBLEM 5-1A or 5-1B (concluded)

GENERAL JOURNAL

PAGE _____

	DATE		DESCRIPTION	POST. REF.	DEBIT	CREDIT	
1							1
2							2
3							3
4							4
5							5
6							6
7							7
8							8
9							9
10							10
11							11
12							12
13							13
14							14
15							15
16							16
17							17
18							18
19							19
20							20
21							21
22							22
23							23
24							24
25							25
26							26
27							27
28							28
29							29
30							30
31							31
32							32
33							33
34							34
35							35
36							36
37							37

Copyright © by Houghton Mifflin Company. All rights reserved.

PROBLEM 5-2A or 5-2B

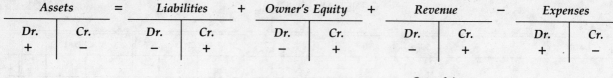

Assets		=	Liabilities		+	Owner's Equity		+	Revenue		−	Expenses	
Dr.	Cr.		Dr.	Cr.		Dr.	Cr.		Dr.	Cr.		Dr.	Cr.
+	−		−	+		−	+		−	+		+	−

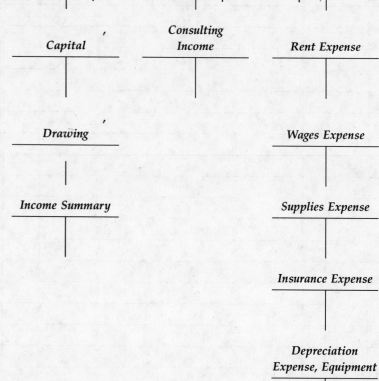

Capital ,

Consulting Income

Rent Expense

Drawing ,

Wages Expense

Income Summary

Supplies Expense

Insurance Expense

Depreciation Expense, Equipment

Miscellaneous Expense

Copyright © by Houghton Mifflin Company. All rights reserved.

NAME _____ DATE _____ CLASS _____

PROBLEM 5-2A or 5-2B (concluded)

GENERAL JOURNAL   PAGE _____

	DATE	DESCRIPTION	POST. REF.	DEBIT	CREDIT	
1						1
2						2
3						3
4						4
5						5
6						6
7						7
8						8
9						9
10						10
11						11
12						12
13						13
14						14
15						15
16						16
17						17
18						18
19						19
20						20
21						21
22						22
23						23
24						24
25						25
26						26
27						27
28						28
29						29
30						30
31						31
32						32
33						33
34						34
35						35
36						36
37						37

Copyright © by Houghton Mifflin Company. All rights reserved.

PROBLEM 5-3A WORK SHEET

Kathy's Tour Company
Work Sheet
For Year Ended December 31, 20—

	ACCOUNT NAME	TRIAL BALANCE DEBIT	TRIAL BALANCE CREDIT	ADJUSTMENTS DEBIT	ADJUSTMENTS CREDIT
1	Cash	3 9 4 8 00			
2	Office Supplies	3 2 8 00			(a) 2 1 6 00
3	Office Equipment	3 4 6 0 00			
4	Accumulated Depreciation, Office				
5	Equipment		3 8 0 00		(b) 3 2 0 00
6	K. Dunn, Capital		5 7 3 9 00		
7	K. Dunn, Drawing	19 0 0 0 00			
8	Fees Earned		43 4 0 0 00		
9	Wages Expense	18 5 0 0 00		(c) 4 2 5 00	
10	Rent Expense	2 4 0 0 00			
11	Telephone Expense	7 3 6 00			
12	Advertising Expense	9 2 6 00			
13	Miscellaneous Expense	2 2 1 00			
14		49 5 1 9 00	49 5 1 9 00		
15	Office Supplies Expense			(a) 2 1 6 00	
16	Depreciation Expense, Office				
17	Equipment			(b) 3 2 0 00	
18	Wages Payable				(c) 4 2 5 00
19				9 6 1 00	9 6 1 00
20	Net Income				

Copyright © by Houghton Mifflin Company. All rights reserved.

PROBLEM 5-3A (continued)

ADJUSTED TRIAL BALANCE		INCOME STATEMENT		BALANCE SHEET		
DEBIT	CREDIT	DEBIT	CREDIT	DEBIT	CREDIT	
3 9 4 8 00				3 9 4 8 00		1
1 1 2 00				1 1 2 00		2
3 4 6 0 00				3 4 6 0 00		3
						4
	7 0 0 00				7 0 0 00	5
	5 7 3 9 00				5 7 3 9 00	6
19 0 0 0 00				19 0 0 0 00		7
	43 4 0 0 00		43 4 0 0 00			8
18 9 2 5 00		18 9 2 5 00				9
2 4 0 0 00		2 4 0 0 00				10
7 3 6 00		7 3 6 00				11
9 2 6 00		9 2 6 00				12
2 2 1 00		2 2 1 00				13
						14
2 1 6 00		2 1 6 00				15
						16
3 2 0 00		3 2 0 00				17
	4 2 5 00				4 2 5 00	18
50 2 6 4 00	50 2 6 4 00	23 7 4 4 00	43 4 0 0 00	26 5 2 0 00	6 8 6 4 00	19
		19 6 5 6 00			19 6 5 6 00	20
		43 4 0 0 00	43 4 0 0 00	26 5 2 0 00	26 5 2 0 00	21
						22
						23
						24
						25
						26
						27
						28
						29
						30
						31
						32
						33
						34
						35
						36

Copyright © by Houghton Mifflin Company. All rights reserved.

PROBLEM 5-3B WORK SHEET

Dunn Insurance Agency
Work Sheet
For Year Ended December 31, 20—

	ACCOUNT NAME	TRIAL BALANCE DEBIT	TRIAL BALANCE CREDIT	ADJUSTMENTS DEBIT	ADJUSTMENTS CREDIT
1	Cash	4 7 3 7 60			
2	Office Supplies	3 9 3 60			(a) 2 5 9 20
3	Office Equipment	4 1 5 2 00			
4	Accumulated Depreciation, Office				
5	Equipment		4 5 6 00		(b) 3 8 4 00
6	M. Dunn, Capital		6 8 8 6 80		
7	M. Dunn, Drawing	22 8 0 0 00			
8	Fees Earned		52 0 8 0 00		
9	Wages Expense	22 2 0 0 00		(c) 5 1 0 00	
10	Rent Expense	2 8 8 0 00			
11	Telephone Expense	8 8 3 20			
12	Advertising Expense	1 1 1 1 20			
13	Miscellaneous Expense	2 6 5 20			
14		59 4 2 2 80	59 4 2 2 80		
15	Office Supplies Expense			(a) 2 5 9 20	
16	Depreciation Expense, Office				
17	Equipment			(b) 3 8 4 00	
18	Wages Payable				(c) 5 1 0 00
19				1 1 5 3 20	1 1 5 3 20
20	Net Income				
21					
22					
23					
24					
25					
26					
27					
28					
29					
30					
31					
32					
33					
34					
35					
36					

Copyright © by Houghton Mifflin Company. All rights reserved.

PROBLEM 5-3B (continued)

ADJUSTED TRIAL BALANCE		INCOME STATEMENT		BALANCE SHEET		
DEBIT	CREDIT	DEBIT	CREDIT	DEBIT	CREDIT	
4 7 3 7 60				4 7 3 7 60		1
1 3 4 40				1 3 4 40		2
4 1 5 2 00				4 1 5 2 00		3
						4
	8 4 0 00				8 4 0 00	5
	6 8 8 6 80				6 8 8 6 80	6
22 8 0 0 00				22 8 0 0 00		7
	52 0 8 0 00		52 0 8 0 00			8
22 7 1 0 00		22 7 1 0 00				9
2 8 8 0 00		2 8 8 0 00				10
8 8 3 20		8 8 3 20				11
1 1 1 1 20		1 1 1 1 20				12
2 6 5 20		2 6 5 20				13
						14
2 5 9 20		2 5 9 20				15
						16
3 8 4 00		3 8 4 00				17
	5 1 0 00				5 1 0 00	18
60 3 1 6 80	60 3 1 6 80	28 4 9 2 80	52 0 8 0 00	31 8 2 4 00	8 2 3 6 80	19
		23 5 8 7 20			23 5 8 7 20	20
		52 0 8 0 00	52 0 8 0 00	31 8 2 4 00	31 8 2 4 00	21

Copyright © by Houghton Mifflin Company. All rights reserved.

PROBLEM 5-3A or 5-3B (continued)

GENERAL LEDGER

ACCOUNT _Cash_ _____ ACCOUNT NO. _111_

DATE	ITEM	POST. REF.	DEBIT	CREDIT	BALANCE	
					DEBIT	CREDIT

ACCOUNT _Office Supplies_ _____ ACCOUNT NO. _115_

DATE	ITEM	POST. REF.	DEBIT	CREDIT	BALANCE	
					DEBIT	CREDIT

ACCOUNT _Office Equipment_ _____ ACCOUNT NO. _124_

DATE	ITEM	POST. REF.	DEBIT	CREDIT	BALANCE	
					DEBIT	CREDIT

ACCOUNT _Accumulated Depreciation, Office Equipment_ _____ ACCOUNT NO. _125_

DATE	ITEM	POST. REF.	DEBIT	CREDIT	BALANCE	
					DEBIT	CREDIT

ACCOUNT _Wages Payable_ _____ ACCOUNT NO. _222_

DATE	ITEM	POST. REF.	DEBIT	CREDIT	BALANCE	
					DEBIT	CREDIT

Copyright © by Houghton Mifflin Company. All rights reserved.

PROBLEM 5-3A or 5-3B (continued)

ACCOUNT _____ , *Capital* _____ ACCOUNT NO. _*311*_

DATE	ITEM	POST. REF.	DEBIT	CREDIT	BALANCE	
					DEBIT	CREDIT

ACCOUNT _____ , *Drawing* _____ ACCOUNT NO. _*312*_

DATE	ITEM	POST. REF.	DEBIT	CREDIT	BALANCE	
					DEBIT	CREDIT

ACCOUNT _*Income Summary*_ _____ ACCOUNT NO. _*313*_

DATE	ITEM	POST. REF.	DEBIT	CREDIT	BALANCE	
					DEBIT	CREDIT

ACCOUNT _*Fees Earned*_ _____ ACCOUNT NO. _*411*_

DATE	ITEM	POST. REF.	DEBIT	CREDIT	BALANCE	
					DEBIT	CREDIT

Copyright © by Houghton Mifflin Company. All rights reserved.

PROBLEM 5-3A or 5-3B (continued)

ACCOUNT _*Wages Expense*_____ ACCOUNT NO. _*511*_

DATE	ITEM	POST. REF.	DEBIT	CREDIT	BALANCE	
					DEBIT	CREDIT

ACCOUNT _*Rent Expense*_____ ACCOUNT NO. _*512*_

DATE	ITEM	POST. REF.	DEBIT	CREDIT	BALANCE	
					DEBIT	CREDIT

ACCOUNT _*Office Supplies Expense*_____ ACCOUNT NO. _*513*_

DATE	ITEM	POST. REF.	DEBIT	CREDIT	BALANCE	
					DEBIT	CREDIT

ACCOUNT _*Depreciation Expense, Office Equipment*_____ ACCOUNT NO. _*514*_

DATE	ITEM	POST. REF.	DEBIT	CREDIT	BALANCE	
					DEBIT	CREDIT

Copyright © by Houghton Mifflin Company. All rights reserved.

PROBLEM 5-3A or 5-3B (continued)

ACCOUNT *Telephone Expense* _____ ACCOUNT NO. *515*

DATE	ITEM	POST. REF.	DEBIT	CREDIT	BALANCE	
					DEBIT	CREDIT

ACCOUNT *Advertising Expense* _____ ACCOUNT NO. *516*

DATE	ITEM	POST. REF.	DEBIT	CREDIT	BALANCE	
					DEBIT	CREDIT

ACCOUNT *Miscellaneous Expense* _____ ACCOUNT NO. *519*

DATE	ITEM	POST. REF.	DEBIT	CREDIT	BALANCE	
					DEBIT	CREDIT

Copyright © by Houghton Mifflin Company. All rights reserved.

PROBLEM 5-3A or 5-3B (continued)

GENERAL JOURNAL

	DATE	DESCRIPTION	POST. REF.	DEBIT	CREDIT	
1						1
2						2
3						3
4						4
5						5
6						6
7						7
8						8
9						9
10						10
11						11
12						12
13						13
14						14
15						15
16						16
17						17
18						18
19						19
20						20
21						21
22						22
23						23
24						24
25						25
26						26
27						27
28						28
29						29
30						30
31						31
32						32
33						33
34						34
35						35
36						36

Copyright © by Houghton Mifflin Company. All rights reserved.

NAME _____ DATE _____ CLASS _____

PROBLEM 5-3A or 5-3B (concluded)

ACCOUNT NAME	DEBIT	CREDIT

Copyright © by Houghton Mifflin Company. All rights reserved.

PROBLEM 5-4A or 5-4B

_____

_____

_____

	ACCOUNT NAME	TRIAL BALANCE		ADJUSTMENTS	
		DEBIT	CREDIT	DEBIT	CREDIT
1					
2					
3					
4					
5					
6					
7					
8					
9					
10					
11					
12					
13					
14					
15					
16					
17					
18					
19					
20					
21					
22					
23					
24					
25					
26					
27					
28					
29					
30					
31					
32					
33					
34					
35					
36					

Copyright © by Houghton Mifflin Company. All rights reserved.

PROBLEM 5-4A or 5-4B (continued)

	ADJUSTED TRIAL BALANCE		INCOME STATEMENT		BALANCE SHEET		
	DEBIT	CREDIT	DEBIT	CREDIT	DEBIT	CREDIT	
							1
							2
							3
							4
							5
							6
							7
							8
							9
							10
							11
							12
							13
							14
							15
							16
							17
							18
							19
							20
							21
							22
							23
							24
							25
							26
							27
							28
							29
							30
							31
							32
							33
							34
							35
							36

Copyright © by Houghton Mifflin Company. All rights reserved.

PROBLEM 5-4A or 5-4B (continued)

Copyright © by Houghton Mifflin Company. All rights reserved.

PROBLEM 5-4A or 5-4B (continued)

PROBLEM 5-4A or 5-4B (concluded)

GENERAL JOURNAL

PAGE _____

	DATE		DESCRIPTION	POST. REF.	DEBIT	CREDIT	
1							1
2							2
3							3
4							4
5							5
6							6
7							7
8							8
9							9
10							10
11							11
12							12
13							13
14							14
15							15
16							16
17							17
18							18
19							19
20							20
21							21
22							22
23							23
24							24
25							25
26							26
27							27
28							28
29							29
30							30
31							31
32							32
33							33
34							34
35							35
36							36
37							37

Copyright © by Houghton Mifflin Company. All rights reserved.

NAME _____ DATE _____ CLASS _____

CUMULATIVE SELF-CHECK: Chapters 4–5

Part II:

GENERAL JOURNAL   PAGE _____

	DATE	DESCRIPTION	POST. REF.	DEBIT	CREDIT	
1						1
2						2
3						3
4						4
5						5
6						6
7						7
8						8
9						9
10						10
11						11
12						12
13						13
14						14
15						15
16						16
17						17
18						18
19						19

Copyright © by Houghton Mifflin Company. All rights reserved.

ACCOUNTING CYCLE REVIEW PROBLEM A

GENERAL JOURNAL   PAGE _____

	DATE	DESCRIPTION	POST. REF.	DEBIT	CREDIT	
1						1
2						2
3						3
4						4
5						5
6						6
7						7
8						8
9						9
10						10
11						11
12						12
13						13
14						14
15						15
16						16
17						17
18						18
19						19
20						20
21						21
22						22
23						23
24						24
25						25
26						26
27						27
28						28
29						29
30						30
31						31
32						32
33						33
34						34
35						35
36						36

Copyright © by Houghton Mifflin Company. All rights reserved.

ACCOUNTING CYCLE REVIEW PROBLEM A (continued)

GENERAL JOURNAL   PAGE _____

	DATE		DESCRIPTION	POST. REF.	DEBIT	CREDIT	
1							1
2							2
3							3
4							4
5							5
6							6
7							7
8							8
9							9
10							10
11							11
12							12
13							13
14							14
15							15
16							16
17							17
18							18
19							19
20							20
21							21
22							22
23							23
24							24
25							25
26							26
27							27
28							28
29							29
30							30
31							31
32							32
33							33
34							34
35							35
36							36
37							37

Copyright © by Houghton Mifflin Company. All rights reserved.

ACCOUNTING CYCLE REVIEW PROBLEM A (continued)

GENERAL JOURNAL

PAGE _____

	DATE	DESCRIPTION	POST. REF.	DEBIT	CREDIT	
1						1
2						2
3						3
4						4
5						5
6						6
7						7
8						8
9						9
10						10
11						11
12						12
13						13
14						14
15						15
16						16
17						17
18						18
19						19
20						20
21						21
22						22
23						23
24						24
25						25
26						26
27						27
28						28
29						29
30						30
31						31
32						32
33						33
34						34
35						35
36						36
37						37

Copyright © by Houghton Mifflin Company. All rights reserved.

ACCOUNTING CYCLE REVIEW PROBLEM A (continued)

GENERAL JOURNAL   PAGE _____

	DATE	DESCRIPTION	POST. REF.	DEBIT	CREDIT	
1						1
2						2
3						3
4						4
5						5
6						6
7						7
8						8
9						9
10						10
11						11
12						12
13						13
14						14
15						15
16						16
17						17
18						18
19						19
20						20
21						21
22						22
23						23
24						24
25						25
26						26
27						27
28						28
29						29
30						30
31						31
32						32
33						33
34						34
35						35
36						36
37						37

Copyright © by Houghton Mifflin Company. All rights reserved.

ACCOUNTING CYCLE REVIEW PROBLEM A (continued)

GENERAL JOURNAL

PAGE _____

	DATE	DESCRIPTION	POST. REF.	DEBIT	CREDIT	
1						1
2						2
3						3
4						4
5						5
6						6
7						7
8						8
9						9
10						10
11						11
12						12
13						13
14						14
15						15
16						16
17						17
18						18
19						19
20						20
21						21
22						22
23						23
24						24
25						25
26						26
27						27
28						28
29						29
30						30
31						31
32						32
33						33
34						34
35						35
36						36
37						37

Copyright © by Houghton Mifflin Company. All rights reserved.

NAME _____ DATE _____ CLASS _____

ACCOUNTING CYCLE REVIEW PROBLEM A (continued)

GENERAL JOURNAL   PAGE _____

	DATE	DESCRIPTION	POST. REF.	DEBIT	CREDIT	
1						1
2						2
3						3
4						4
5						5
6						6
7						7
8						8
9						9
10						10
11						11
12						12
13						13
14						14
15						15
16						16
17						17
18						18
19						19
20						20
21						21
22						22
23						23
24						24
25						25
26						26
27						27
28						28
29						29
30						30
31						31
32						32
33						33
34						34
35						35
36						36
37						37

Copyright © by Houghton Mifflin Company. All rights reserved.

ACCOUNTING CYCLE REVIEW PROBLEM A (continued)

GENERAL LEDGER

ACCOUNT *Cash* ACCOUNT NO. *111*

DATE	ITEM	POST. REF.	DEBIT	CREDIT	BALANCE	
					DEBIT	CREDIT

ACCOUNT *Accounts Receivable* ACCOUNT NO. *112*

DATE	ITEM	POST. REF.	DEBIT	CREDIT	BALANCE	
					DEBIT	CREDIT

Copyright © by Houghton Mifflin Company. All rights reserved.

ACCOUNTING CYCLE REVIEW PROBLEM A (continued)

ACCOUNT *Supplies* _____ ACCOUNT NO. __113__

DATE	ITEM	POST. REF.	DEBIT	CREDIT	BALANCE	
					DEBIT	CREDIT

ACCOUNT *Prepaid Insurance* _____ ACCOUNT NO. __114__

DATE	ITEM	POST. REF.	DEBIT	CREDIT	BALANCE	
					DEBIT	CREDIT

ACCOUNT *Land* _____ ACCOUNT NO. __121__

DATE	ITEM	POST. REF.	DEBIT	CREDIT	BALANCE	
					DEBIT	CREDIT

ACCOUNT *Building* _____ ACCOUNT NO. __122__

DATE	ITEM	POST. REF.	DEBIT	CREDIT	BALANCE	
					DEBIT	CREDIT

Copyright © by Houghton Mifflin Company. All rights reserved.

ACCOUNTING CYCLE REVIEW PROBLEM A (continued)

ACCOUNT *Accumulated Depreciation, Building*   ACCOUNT NO. *123*

DATE	ITEM	POST. REF.	DEBIT	CREDIT	BALANCE	
					DEBIT	CREDIT

ACCOUNT *Pool/Slide Facility*   ACCOUNT NO. *124*

DATE	ITEM	POST. REF.	DEBIT	CREDIT	BALANCE	
					DEBIT	CREDIT

ACCOUNT *Accumulated Depreciation, Pool/Slide Facility*   ACCOUNT NO. *125*

DATE	ITEM	POST. REF.	DEBIT	CREDIT	BALANCE	
					DEBIT	CREDIT

ACCOUNT *Pool Furniture*   ACCOUNT NO. *126*

DATE	ITEM	POST. REF.	DEBIT	CREDIT	BALANCE	
					DEBIT	CREDIT

Copyright © by Houghton Mifflin Company. All rights reserved.

ACCOUNTING CYCLE REVIEW PROBLEM A (continued)

ACCOUNT *Accumulated Depreciation, Pool Furniture*   ACCOUNT NO. *127*

DATE	ITEM	POST. REF.	DEBIT	CREDIT	BALANCE	
					DEBIT	CREDIT

ACCOUNT *Accounts Payable*   ACCOUNT NO. *221*

DATE	ITEM	POST. REF.	DEBIT	CREDIT	BALANCE	
					DEBIT	CREDIT

ACCOUNT *Wages Payable*   ACCOUNT NO. *222*

DATE	ITEM	POST. REF.	DEBIT	CREDIT	BALANCE	
					DEBIT	CREDIT

Copyright © by Houghton Mifflin Company. All rights reserved.

ACCOUNTING CYCLE REVIEW PROBLEM A (continued)

ACCOUNT *Mortgage Payable*   ACCOUNT NO. 223

DATE	ITEM	POST. REF.	DEBIT	CREDIT	BALANCE	
					DEBIT	CREDIT

ACCOUNT *K. Taylor, Capital*   ACCOUNT NO. 311

DATE	ITEM	POST. REF.	DEBIT	CREDIT	BALANCE	
					DEBIT	CREDIT

ACCOUNT *K. Taylor, Drawing*   ACCOUNT NO. 312

DATE	ITEM	POST. REF.	DEBIT	CREDIT	BALANCE	
					DEBIT	CREDIT

ACCOUNT *Income Summary*   ACCOUNT NO. 313

DATE	ITEM	POST. REF.	DEBIT	CREDIT	BALANCE	
					DEBIT	CREDIT

Copyright © by Houghton Mifflin Company. All rights reserved.

ACCOUNTING CYCLE REVIEW PROBLEM A (continued)

ACCOUNT _Income from Services_   ACCOUNT NO. **411**

DATE	ITEM	POST. REF.	DEBIT	CREDIT	BALANCE DEBIT	BALANCE CREDIT

ACCOUNT _Concessions Income_   ACCOUNT NO. **412**

DATE	ITEM	POST. REF.	DEBIT	CREDIT	BALANCE DEBIT	BALANCE CREDIT

ACCOUNT _Pool Maintenance Expense_   ACCOUNT NO. **511**

DATE	ITEM	POST. REF.	DEBIT	CREDIT	BALANCE DEBIT	BALANCE CREDIT

ACCOUNT _Wages Expense_   ACCOUNT NO. **512**

DATE	ITEM	POST. REF.	DEBIT	CREDIT	BALANCE DEBIT	BALANCE CREDIT

Copyright © by Houghton Mifflin Company. All rights reserved.

ACCOUNTING CYCLE REVIEW PROBLEM A (continued)

ACCOUNT _Advertising Expense_   ACCOUNT NO. _513_

DATE	ITEM	POST. REF.	DEBIT	CREDIT	BALANCE	
					DEBIT	CREDIT

ACCOUNT _Utilities Expense_   ACCOUNT NO. _514_

DATE	ITEM	POST. REF.	DEBIT	CREDIT	BALANCE	
					DEBIT	CREDIT

ACCOUNT _Interest Expense_   ACCOUNT NO. _515_

DATE	ITEM	POST. REF.	DEBIT	CREDIT	BALANCE	
					DEBIT	CREDIT

ACCOUNT _Supplies Expense_   ACCOUNT NO. _516_

DATE	ITEM	POST. REF.	DEBIT	CREDIT	BALANCE	
					DEBIT	CREDIT

Copyright © by Houghton Mifflin Company. All rights reserved.

ACCOUNTING CYCLE REVIEW PROBLEM A (continued)

ACCOUNT *Insurance Expense* _____ ACCOUNT NO. **517**

DATE	ITEM	POST. REF.	DEBIT	CREDIT	BALANCE DEBIT	BALANCE CREDIT

ACCOUNT *Depreciation Expense, Building* _____ ACCOUNT NO. **518**

DATE	ITEM	POST. REF.	DEBIT	CREDIT	BALANCE DEBIT	BALANCE CREDIT

ACCOUNT *Depreciation Expense, Pool/Slide Facility* _____ ACCOUNT NO. **519**

DATE	ITEM	POST. REF.	DEBIT	CREDIT	BALANCE DEBIT	BALANCE CREDIT

ACCOUNT *Depreciation Expense, Pool Furniture* _____ ACCOUNT NO. **520**

DATE	ITEM	POST. REF.	DEBIT	CREDIT	BALANCE DEBIT	BALANCE CREDIT

Copyright © by Houghton Mifflin Company. All rights reserved.

ACCOUNTING CYCLE REVIEW PROBLEM A (continued)

ACCOUNT *Miscellaneous Expense*   ACCOUNT NO. 522

DATE	ITEM	POST. REF.	DEBIT	CREDIT	BALANCE	
					DEBIT	CREDIT

ACCOUNT _____ ACCOUNT NO. _____

DATE	ITEM	POST. REF.	DEBIT	CREDIT	BALANCE	
					DEBIT	CREDIT

ACCOUNT _____ ACCOUNT NO. _____

DATE	ITEM	POST. REF.	DEBIT	CREDIT	BALANCE	
					DEBIT	CREDIT

ACCOUNT _____ ACCOUNT NO. _____

DATE	ITEM	POST. REF.	DEBIT	CREDIT	BALANCE	
					DEBIT	CREDIT

Copyright © by Houghton Mifflin Company. All rights reserved.

EXTRA FORMS

ACCOUNT _____ ACCOUNT NO. _____

DATE	ITEM	POST. REF.	DEBIT	CREDIT	BALANCE	
					DEBIT	CREDIT

ACCOUNT _____ ACCOUNT NO. _____

DATE	ITEM	POST. REF.	DEBIT	CREDIT	BALANCE	
					DEBIT	CREDIT

ACCOUNT _____ ACCOUNT NO. _____

DATE	ITEM	POST. REF.	DEBIT	CREDIT	BALANCE	
					DEBIT	CREDIT

ACCOUNT _____ ACCOUNT NO. _____

DATE	ITEM	POST. REF.	DEBIT	CREDIT	BALANCE	
					DEBIT	CREDIT

Copyright © by Houghton Mifflin Company. All rights reserved.

ACCOUNTING CYCLE REVIEW PROBLEM A (continued)

	ACCOUNT NAME	TRIAL BALANCE		ADJUSTMENTS	
		DEBIT	CREDIT	DEBIT	CREDIT
1					
2					
3					
4					
5					
6					
7					
8					
9					
10					
11					
12					
13					
14					
15					
16					
17					
18					
19					
20					
21					
22					
23					
24					
25					
26					
27					
28					
29					
30					
31					
32					
33					
34					
35					
36					

Copyright © by Houghton Mifflin Company. All rights reserved.

ACCOUNTING CYCLE REVIEW PROBLEM A (continued)

ADJUSTED TRIAL BALANCE		INCOME STATEMENT		BALANCE SHEET		
DEBIT	CREDIT	DEBIT	CREDIT	DEBIT	CREDIT	
						1
						2
						3
						4
						5
						6
						7
						8
						9
						10
						11
						12
						13
						14
						15
						16
						17
						18
						19
						20
						21
						22
						23
						24
						25
						26
						27
						28
						29
						30
						31
						32
						33
						34
						35
						36

Copyright © by Houghton Mifflin Company. All rights reserved.

ACCOUNTING CYCLE REVIEW PROBLEM A (continued)

Copyright © by Houghton Mifflin Company. All rights reserved.

ACCOUNTING CYCLE REVIEW PROBLEM A (continued)

Copyright © by Houghton Mifflin Company. All rights reserved.

NAME _____ DATE _____ CLASS _____

ACCOUNTING CYCLE REVIEW PROBLEM A (concluded)

ACCOUNT NAME	DEBIT	CREDIT

Copyright © by Houghton Mifflin Company. All rights reserved.

NAME _____ DATE _____ CLASS _____

ACCOUNTING CYCLE REVIEW PROBLEM B

GENERAL JOURNAL   PAGE _____

	DATE		DESCRIPTION	POST. REF.	DEBIT	CREDIT	
1							1
2							2
3							3
4							4
5							5
6							6
7							7
8							8
9							9
10							10
11							11
12							12
13							13
14							14
15							15
16							16
17							17
18							18
19							19
20							20
21							21
22							22
23							23
24							24
25							25
26							26
27							27
28							28
29							29
30							30
31							31
32							32
33							33
34							34
35							35
36							36

Copyright © by Houghton Mifflin Company. All rights reserved.

ACCOUNTING CYCLE REVIEW PROBLEM B (continued)

GENERAL JOURNAL

	DATE		DESCRIPTION	POST. REF.	DEBIT	CREDIT	
1							1
2							2
3							3
4							4
5							5
6							6
7							7
8							8
9							9
10							10
11							11
12							12
13							13
14							14
15							15
16							16
17							17
18							18
19							19
20							20
21							21
22							22
23							23
24							24
25							25
26							26
27							27
28							28
29							29
30							30
31							31
32							32
33							33
34							34
35							35
36							36
37							37

Copyright © by Houghton Mifflin Company. All rights reserved.

NAME _____ DATE _____ CLASS _____

ACCOUNTING CYCLE REVIEW PROBLEM B (continued)

GENERAL JOURNAL

PAGE _____

	DATE	DESCRIPTION	POST. REF.	DEBIT	CREDIT	
1						1
2						2
3						3
4						4
5						5
6						6
7						7
8						8
9						9
10						10
11						11
12						12
13						13
14						14
15						15
16						16
17						17
18						18
19						19
20						20
21						21
22						22
23						23
24						24
25						25
26						26
27						27
28						28
29						29
30						30
31						31
32						32
33						33
34						34
35						35
36						36
37						37

Copyright © by Houghton Mifflin Company. All rights reserved.

ACCOUNTING CYCLE REVIEW PROBLEM B (continued)

GENERAL JOURNAL

PAGE _____

	DATE		DESCRIPTION	POST. REF.	DEBIT	CREDIT	
1							1
2							2
3							3
4							4
5							5
6							6
7							7
8							8
9							9
10							10
11							11
12							12
13							13
14							14
15							15
16							16
17							17
18							18
19							19
20							20
21							21
22							22
23							23
24							24
25							25
26							26
27							27
28							28
29							29
30							30
31							31
32							32
33							33
34							34
35							35
36							36
37							37

Copyright © by Houghton Mifflin Company. All rights reserved.

NAME _____ DATE _____ CLASS _____

ACCOUNTING CYCLE REVIEW PROBLEM B (continued)

GENERAL JOURNAL   PAGE _____

	DATE	DESCRIPTION	POST. REF.	DEBIT	CREDIT	
1						1
2						2
3						3
4						4
5						5
6						6
7						7
8						8
9						9
10						10
11						11
12						12
13						13
14						14
15						15
16						16
17						17
18						18
19						19
20						20
21						21
22						22
23						23
24						24
25						25
26						26
27						27
28						28
29						29
30						30
31						31
32						32
33						33
34						34
35						35
36						36
37						37

Copyright © by Houghton Mifflin Company. All rights reserved.

ACCOUNTING CYCLE REVIEW PROBLEM B (continued)

GENERAL JOURNAL

PAGE _____

	DATE		DESCRIPTION	POST. REF.	DEBIT	CREDIT	
1							1
2							2
3							3
4							4
5							5
6							6
7							7
8							8
9							9
10							10
11							11
12							12
13							13
14							14
15							15
16							16
17							17
18							18
19							19
20							20
21							21
22							22
23							23
24							24
25							25
26							26
27							27
28							28
29							29
30							30
31							31
32							32
33							33
34							34
35							35
36							36
37							37

Copyright © by Houghton Mifflin Company. All rights reserved.

ACCOUNTING CYCLE REVIEW PROBLEM B (continued)

GENERAL LEDGER

ACCOUNT _Cash_ _____ ACCOUNT NO. _111_

DATE	ITEM	POST. REF.	DEBIT	CREDIT	BALANCE	
					DEBIT	CREDIT

ACCOUNT _Accounts Receivable_ _____ ACCOUNT NO. _112_

DATE	ITEM	POST. REF.	DEBIT	CREDIT	BALANCE	
					DEBIT	CREDIT

Copyright © by Houghton Mifflin Company. All rights reserved.

ACCOUNTING CYCLE REVIEW PROBLEM B (continued)

ACCOUNT *Prepaid Insurance* ACCOUNT NO. *114*

DATE	ITEM	POST. REF.	DEBIT	CREDIT	BALANCE	
					DEBIT	CREDIT

ACCOUNT *Land* ACCOUNT NO. *121*

DATE	ITEM	POST. REF.	DEBIT	CREDIT	BALANCE	
					DEBIT	CREDIT

ACCOUNT *Pool Structure* ACCOUNT NO. *125*

DATE	ITEM	POST. REF.	DEBIT	CREDIT	BALANCE	
					DEBIT	CREDIT

ACCOUNT *Accumulated Depreciation, Pool Structure* ACCOUNT NO. *126*

DATE	ITEM	POST. REF.	DEBIT	CREDIT	BALANCE	
					DEBIT	CREDIT

Copyright © by Houghton Mifflin Company. All rights reserved.

ACCOUNTING CYCLE REVIEW PROBLEM B (continued)

ACCOUNT *Fan System*   ACCOUNT NO. __127__

DATE	ITEM	POST. REF.	DEBIT	CREDIT	BALANCE	
					DEBIT	CREDIT

ACCOUNT *Accumulated Depreciation, Fan System*   ACCOUNT NO. __128__

DATE	ITEM	POST. REF.	DEBIT	CREDIT	BALANCE	
					DEBIT	CREDIT

ACCOUNT *Sailboats*   ACCOUNT NO. __129__

DATE	ITEM	POST. REF.	DEBIT	CREDIT	BALANCE	
					DEBIT	CREDIT

ACCOUNT *Accumulated Depreciation, Sailboats*   ACCOUNT NO. __130__

DATE	ITEM	POST. REF.	DEBIT	CREDIT	BALANCE	
					DEBIT	CREDIT

Copyright © by Houghton Mifflin Company. All rights reserved.

ACCOUNTING CYCLE REVIEW PROBLEM B (continued)

ACCOUNT *Accounts Payable*   ACCOUNT NO. *221*

DATE	ITEM	POST. REF.	DEBIT	CREDIT	BALANCE	
					DEBIT	CREDIT

ACCOUNT *Wages Payable*   ACCOUNT NO. *222*

DATE	ITEM	POST. REF.	DEBIT	CREDIT	BALANCE	
					DEBIT	CREDIT

ACCOUNT *Mortgage Payable*   ACCOUNT NO. *223*

DATE	ITEM	POST. REF.	DEBIT	CREDIT	BALANCE	
					DEBIT	CREDIT

Copyright © by Houghton Mifflin Company. All rights reserved.

ACCOUNTING CYCLE REVIEW PROBLEM B (continued)

ACCOUNT _J. Moore, Capital_   ACCOUNT NO. _311_

DATE	ITEM	POST. REF.	DEBIT	CREDIT	BALANCE DEBIT	BALANCE CREDIT

ACCOUNT _J. Moore, Drawing_   ACCOUNT NO. _312_

DATE	ITEM	POST. REF.	DEBIT	CREDIT	BALANCE DEBIT	BALANCE CREDIT

ACCOUNT _Income Summary_   ACCOUNT NO. _313_

DATE	ITEM	POST. REF.	DEBIT	CREDIT	BALANCE DEBIT	BALANCE CREDIT

ACCOUNT _Income from Services_   ACCOUNT NO. _411_

DATE	ITEM	POST. REF.	DEBIT	CREDIT	BALANCE DEBIT	BALANCE CREDIT

Copyright © by Houghton Mifflin Company. All rights reserved.

ACCOUNTING CYCLE REVIEW PROBLEM B (continued)

ACCOUNT *Concessions Income*   ACCOUNT NO. *412*

DATE	ITEM	POST. REF.	DEBIT	CREDIT	BALANCE	
					DEBIT	CREDIT

ACCOUNT *Sailboat Rental Expense*   ACCOUNT NO. *511*

DATE	ITEM	POST. REF.	DEBIT	CREDIT	BALANCE	
					DEBIT	CREDIT

ACCOUNT *Wages Expense*   ACCOUNT NO. *512*

DATE	ITEM	POST. REF.	DEBIT	CREDIT	BALANCE	
					DEBIT	CREDIT

ACCOUNT *Advertising Expense*   ACCOUNT NO. *513*

DATE	ITEM	POST. REF.	DEBIT	CREDIT	BALANCE	
					DEBIT	CREDIT

Copyright © by Houghton Mifflin Company. All rights reserved.

ACCOUNTING CYCLE REVIEW PROBLEM B (continued)

ACCOUNT _Utilities Expense_   ACCOUNT NO. _514_

DATE	ITEM	POST. REF.	DEBIT	CREDIT	BALANCE	
					DEBIT	CREDIT

ACCOUNT _Interest Expense_   ACCOUNT NO. _515_

DATE	ITEM	POST. REF.	DEBIT	CREDIT	BALANCE	
					DEBIT	CREDIT

ACCOUNT _Insurance Expense_   ACCOUNT NO. _516_

DATE	ITEM	POST. REF.	DEBIT	CREDIT	BALANCE	
					DEBIT	CREDIT

Copyright © by Houghton Mifflin Company. All rights reserved.

ACCOUNTING CYCLE REVIEW PROBLEM B (continued)

ACCOUNT *Depreciation Expense, Pool Structure*   ACCOUNT NO. *517*

DATE	ITEM	POST. REF.	DEBIT	CREDIT	BALANCE	
					DEBIT	CREDIT

ACCOUNT *Depreciation Expense, Fan System*   ACCOUNT NO. *518*

DATE	ITEM	POST. REF.	DEBIT	CREDIT	BALANCE	
					DEBIT	CREDIT

ACCOUNT *Depreciation Expense, Sailboats*   ACCOUNT NO. *519*

DATE	ITEM	POST. REF.	DEBIT	CREDIT	BALANCE	
					DEBIT	CREDIT

ACCOUNT *Miscellaneous Expense*   ACCOUNT NO. *522*

DATE	ITEM	POST. REF.	DEBIT	CREDIT	BALANCE	
					DEBIT	CREDIT

Copyright © by Houghton Mifflin Company. All rights reserved.

NAME _____ DATE _____ CLASS _____

EXTRA FORMS

ACCOUNT _____ ACCOUNT NO. _____

DATE	ITEM	POST. REF.	DEBIT	CREDIT	BALANCE	
					DEBIT	CREDIT

ACCOUNT _____ ACCOUNT NO. _____

DATE	ITEM	POST. REF.	DEBIT	CREDIT	BALANCE	
					DEBIT	CREDIT

ACCOUNT _____ ACCOUNT NO. _____

DATE	ITEM	POST. REF.	DEBIT	CREDIT	BALANCE	
					DEBIT	CREDIT

ACCOUNT _____ ACCOUNT NO. _____

DATE	ITEM	POST. REF.	DEBIT	CREDIT	BALANCE	
					DEBIT	CREDIT

Copyright © by Houghton Mifflin Company. All rights reserved.

ACCOUNTING CYCLE REVIEW PROBLEM B (continued)

	ACCOUNT NAME	TRIAL BALANCE		ADJUSTMENTS	
		DEBIT	CREDIT	DEBIT	CREDIT
1					
2					
3					
4					
5					
6					
7					
8					
9					
10					
11					
12					
13					
14					
15					
16					
17					
18					
19					
20					
21					
22					
23					
24					
25					
26					
27					
28					
29					
30					
31					
32					
33					
34					
35					
36					

Copyright © by Houghton Mifflin Company. All rights reserved.

ACCOUNTING CYCLE REVIEW PROBLEM B (continued)

_____

_____

_____

ADJUSTED TRIAL BALANCE		INCOME STATEMENT		BALANCE SHEET		
DEBIT	CREDIT	DEBIT	CREDIT	DEBIT	CREDIT	
						1
						2
						3
						4
						5
						6
						7
						8
						9
						10
						11
						12
						13
						14
						15
						16
						17
						18
						19
						20
						21
						22
						23
						24
						25
						26
						27
						28
						29
						30
						31
						32
						33
						34
						35
						36

Copyright © by Houghton Mifflin Company. All rights reserved.

ACCOUNTING CYCLE REVIEW PROBLEM B (continued)

Copyright © by Houghton Mifflin Company. All rights reserved.

ACCOUNTING CYCLE REVIEW PROBLEM B (continued)

ACCOUNTING CYCLE REVIEW PROBLEM B (continued)

Copyright © by Houghton Mifflin Company. All rights reserved.

ACCOUNTING CYCLE REVIEW PROBLEM B (concluded)

ACCOUNT NAME	DEBIT	CREDIT

Copyright © by Houghton Mifflin Company. All rights reserved.

<table>
<tr><td>

6

</td><td>

Accounting for Professional Enterprises: The Combined Journal *(Optional)*

</td></tr>
</table>

PERFORMANCE OBJECTIVES

1. Describe the accounting records for a professional enterprise.
2. Record transactions for both a professional and a service enterprise in a combined journal.
3. Post from the combined journal and determine the cash balance.
4. Prepare a work sheet for a professional enterprise.
5. Prepare financial statements for a professional enterprise.
6. Record adjusting and closing entries in a combined journal.

KEY TERMS

Combined journal
Patient's ledger record

Professional enterprise
Special columns

STUDY GUIDE QUESTIONS

PART 1   True/False

For each of the following statements, circle T if the statement is true and F if the statement is false:

T   F   1. When one is using the modified cash basis, there is no adjustment for accrued salaries.

T   F   2. Individuals filing their personal income tax returns use the accrual basis.

T   F   3. Accountants feel strongly that the modified cash basis gives the most realistic picture of net income.

T   F   4. The modified cash basis could be used to keep books for a shoe repair shop.

T   F   5. The combined journal is used widely by professional and service-type enterprises.

T   F   6. The cash-receipts-and-disbursements basis of accounting is ideal for firms having large amounts of equipment.

T   F   7. Each amount in the Sundry Debit column of a combined journal is posted as a part of the column total.

T   F   8. A dash in the Post. Ref. column of a combined journal indicates that individual amounts in the special columns are being posted as totals.

T   F   9. There are no adjusting entries when using the cash-receipts-and-disbursements basis.

T   F   10. When a combined journal is being used, the cash balance may be determined at any time during the month by taking the beginning balance of cash, adding the total cash credits so far during the month, and subtracting the total cash debits so far during the month.

Copyright © by Houghton Mifflin Company. All rights reserved.

PART 2   Chart of Accounts

L. Barnes, the owner of a television repair shop, has asked you to set up a tentative chart of accounts for his business. He rents space in a shopping center and has one employee. He operates a service truck. Revenue is only in the form of cash. The firm does a considerable amount of advertising for the business.

Chart of Accounts

Assets

_____

_____

_____

_____

_____

_____

Liabilities

_____

_____

Owner's Equity

_____

_____

_____

Revenue

_____

_____

Expenses

_____

_____

_____

_____

_____

_____

_____

_____

Copyright © by Houghton Mifflin Company. All rights reserved.

PART 3

L. Barnes decides to use a combined journal. Make a tentative list of the headings for the money columns for a combined journal.

_____

_____

_____

_____

_____

_____

Copyright © by Houghton Mifflin Company. All rights reserved.

DEMONSTRATION PROBLEM

Transactions for Heins' Cleaners are presented below. Assume the posting has been completed.

June

1 N. L. Heins invests $40,000 cash in his new business.

2 Buys equipment costing $22,000, paying cash from Craig Co. (Ck. No. 1).

2 Buys equipment costing $4,000 on credit from Drake Equipment Company.

5 Pays $1,000 to Drake Equipment Company to be applied against the firm's liability of $4,000 (Ck. No. 2).

5 Buys cleaning fluid and garment bags on account from Blair Supply Company for $400.

7 Cash revenue received for the first week, $960.

8 Pays rent for the month, $500 (Ck. No. 3).

10 Pays wages to a part-time employee, for the period June 1 through June 10, $440 (Ck. No. 4).

11 Pays $360 for a two-year liability insurance policy (Ck. No. 5).

14 Cash revenue received for the second week, $980.

14 Receives bill from the *City News* for newspaper advertising, $180.

15 Pays $1,800 to Drake Equipment Company as part payment on account (Ck. No. 6).

15 Receives and pays bills for utilities, $220 (Ck. No. 7).

15 Pays $180 to *City News* for advertising (Ck. No. 8). (This bill has been previously recorded.)

21 Cash revenue received for the third week, $830.

23 Heins' Cleaners enters into a contract with Formal Rentals to clean formal garments on a credit basis. Heins' Cleaners bills Formal Rentals for services performed, $140.

24 Pays wages to part-time employee, $490, for June 11 through June 24 (Ck. No. 9).

26 Buys additional equipment for $940 from Drake Equipment Company, paying $140 down, with the remaining $800 on account (Ck. No. 10).

30 Cash received for the remainder of the month, $960.

30 Receives $90 from Formal Rentals to apply on amount previously billed.

30 Heins withdraws $1,200 in cash for personal use (Ck. No. 11).

Instructions

Record the June transactions in a combined journal.

SOLUTION

Notice the first transaction of June 5, involving payment to a creditor on account. The name of the creditor is recorded in the Account Name column. Likewise, in receiving cash from a customer on account (second entry of June 30), the name of the charge customer is recorded in the Account Name column.

COMBINED

	CASH DEBIT	CASH CREDIT	CK. NO.	DATE	ACCOUNT NAME	POST. REF.	OTHER ACCOUNTS DEBIT	OTHER ACCOUNTS CREDIT
1				20—				
2	40 000 00			June 1	N. L. Heins, Capital			40 000 00
3		22 000 00	1	2	Equipment, Craig Co.		22 000 00	
4				2	Equipment, Drake			
5					Equip. Co.		4 000 00	
6		1 000 00	2	5	Drake Equipment Co.	—		
7				5	Supplies, Blair			
8					Supply Co.		4 00 00	
9	9 60 00			7	————	—		
10		5 00 00	3	8	Rent Expense		5 00 00	
11		4 40 00	4	10		—		
12		3 60 00	5	11	Prepaid Insurance		3 60 00	
13	9 80 00			14				
14				14	Advertising Expense,			
15					City News		1 80 00	
16		1 800 00	6	15	Drake Equipment Co.	—		
17		2 20 00	7	15	Utilities Expense		2 20 00	
18		1 80 00	8	15	City News	—		
19	8 30 00			21		—		
20				23	Formal Rentals	—		
21		4 90 00	9	24		—		
22		1 40 00	10	26	Equipment, Drake			
23					Equip. Co.		9 40 00	
24	9 60 00			30	————	—		
25	90 00			30	Formal Rentals	—		
26		1 200 00	11	30	N. L. Heins, Drawing		1 2 00 00	
27	43 820 00	28 330 00		30			29 800 00	40 000 00
28								
29								

Debits	$43,820		Credits	$28,330
	29,800			40,000
	140			90
	2,980			5,380
	930			3,870
	$77,670			$77,670

Copyright © by Houghton Mifflin Company. All rights reserved.

ACCOUNTS RECEIVABLE		ACCOUNTS PAYABLE		INCOME FROM SERVICES	WAGES EXPENSE	
DEBIT	CREDIT	DEBIT	CREDIT	CREDIT	DEBIT	
						1
						2
						3
						4
			400 00			5
		1000 00				6
						7
			40 00			8
				960 00		9
						10
					440 00	11
						12
				980 00		13
						14
			180 00			15
		1800 00				16
						17
		180 00				18
				830 00		19
140 00				140 00		20
					490 00	21
						22
			800 00			23
				960 00		24
	90 00					25
						26
140 00	90 00	2980 00	5380 00	3870 00	930 00	27
						28
						29

Copyright © by Houghton Mifflin Company. All rights reserved.

PROBLEM 6-1A or 6-1B

COMBINED

	CASH							OTHER ACCOUNTS	
	DEBIT	CREDIT	CK. NO.	DATE	ACCOUNT NAME	POST. REF.		DEBIT	CREDIT
1									
2									
3									
4									
5									
6									
7									
8									
9									
10									
11									
12									
13									
14									
15									
16									
17									
18									
19									
20									
21									
22									
23									
24									
25									
26									
27									
28									
29									
30									
31									
32									
33									
34									
35									
36									
37									

178

Copyright © by Houghton Mifflin Company. All rights reserved.

PROBLEM 6-1A or 6-1B (concluded)
JOURNAL

MEDICAL SUPPLIES	DRAWING	PROFESSIONAL FEES	LABORATORY EXPENSE	CLEANING EXPENSE	MISCELLANEOUS EXPENSE	
DEBIT	DEBIT	CREDIT	DEBIT	DEBIT	DEBIT	
						1
						2
						3
						4
						5
						6
						7
						8
						9
						10
						11
						12
						13
						14
						15
						16
						17
						18
						19
						20
						21
						22
						23
						24
						25
						26
						27
						28
						29
						30
						31
						32
						33
						34
						35
						36
						37

Copyright © by Houghton Mifflin Company. All rights reserved.

PROBLEM 6-2A or 6-2B

COMBINED

	CASH		CK. NO.	DATE	ACCOUNT NAME	POST. REF.	OTHER ACCOUNTS	
	DEBIT	CREDIT					DEBIT	CREDIT
1								
2								
3								
4								
5								
6								
7								
8								
9								
10								
11								
12								
13								
14								
15								
16								
17								
18								
19								
20								
21								
22								
23								
24								
25								
26								
27								
28								
29								
30								
31								
32								
33								
34								
35								

Copyright © by Houghton Mifflin Company. All rights reserved.

NAME _____ DATE _____ CLASS _____

PROBLEM 6-2A or 6-2B (concluded)

JOURNAL   PAGE _____

SUPPLIES	DRAWING	ADVERTISING EXPENSE	PROFESSIONAL FEES	TRAVEL EXPENSE	MISCELLANEOUS EXPENSE	
DEBIT	DEBIT	DEBIT	DEBIT	DEBIT	DEBIT	
						1
						2
						3
						4
						5
						6
						7
						8
						9
						10
						11
						12
						13
						14
						15
						16
						17
						18
						19
						20
						21
						22
						23
						24
						25
						26
						27
						28
						29
						30
						31
						32
						33
						34
						35

Copyright © by Houghton Mifflin Company. All rights reserved.

PROBLEM 6-3A or 6-3B

COMBINED

CASH		CK. NO.	DATE	ACCOUNT NAME	POST. REF.	OTHER ACCOUNTS	
DEBIT	CREDIT					DEBIT	CREDIT
1							
2							
3							
4							
5							
6							
7							
8							
9							
10							
11							
12							
13							
14							
15							
16							
17							
18							
19							
20							
21							
22							
23							
24							
25							
26							
27							
28							
29							
30							
31							
32							
33							
34							
35							
36							
37							

Copyright © by Houghton Mifflin Company. All rights reserved.

PROBLEM 6-3A or 6-3B (continued)
JOURNAL

PAGE _____

ACCOUNTS RECEIVABLE		PROFESSIONAL FEES	SALARY EXPENSE	UTILITIES EXPENSE	
DEBIT	CREDIT	CREDIT	DEBIT	DEBIT	
					1
					2
					3
					4
					5
					6
					7
					8
					9
					10
					11
					12
					13
					14
					15
					16
					17
					18
					19
					20
					21
					22
					23
					24
					25
					26
					27
					28
					29
					30
					31
					32
					33
					34
					35
					36
					37

Copyright © by Houghton Mifflin Company. All rights reserved.

PROBLEM 6-3A or 6-3B (continued)

GENERAL LEDGER

ACCOUNT *Cash* — ACCOUNT NO. *111*

DATE		ITEM	POST. REF.	DEBIT	CREDIT	BALANCE	
						DEBIT	CREDIT
20—							
Aug.	31	Balance	✓			6 2 8 8 00	

ACCOUNT *Accounts Receivable* — ACCOUNT NO. *112*

DATE		ITEM	POST. REF.	DEBIT	CREDIT	BALANCE	
						DEBIT	CREDIT
20—							
Aug.	31	Balance	✓			4 4 9 6 00	✓

ACCOUNT *Supplies* — ACCOUNT NO. *113*

DATE		ITEM	POST. REF.	DEBIT	CREDIT	BALANCE	
						DEBIT	CREDIT
20—							
Aug.	31	Balance	✓			2 2 8 0 00	

ACCOUNT *Prepaid Insurance* — ACCOUNT NO. *114*

DATE		ITEM	POST. REF.	DEBIT	CREDIT	BALANCE	
						DEBIT	CREDIT
20—							
Aug.	31	Balance	✓			3 6 0 0 00	

ACCOUNT *Equipment* — ACCOUNT NO. *121*

DATE		ITEM	POST. REF.	DEBIT	CREDIT	BALANCE	
						DEBIT	CREDIT
20—							
Aug.	31	Balance	✓			18 9 2 0 00	

184

Copyright © by Houghton Mifflin Company. All rights reserved.

PROBLEM 6-3A or 6-3B (continued)

ACCOUNT *Accumulated Depreciation, Equipment* ACCOUNT NO. **122**

DATE		ITEM	POST. REF.	DEBIT	CREDIT	BALANCE	
						DEBIT	CREDIT
20—							
Aug.	31	Balance	√				10 3 6 2 00

ACCOUNT *Accounts Payable* ACCOUNT NO. **221**

DATE		ITEM	POST. REF.	DEBIT	CREDIT	BALANCE	
						DEBIT	CREDIT
20—							
Aug.	31	Balance	√				3 2 0 50

ACCOUNT _____ *, Capital* ACCOUNT NO. **311**

DATE		ITEM	POST. REF.	DEBIT	CREDIT	BALANCE	
						DEBIT	CREDIT
20—							
Aug.	31	Balance	√				40 1 1 5 00

ACCOUNT _____ *, Drawing* ACCOUNT NO. **312**

DATE		ITEM	POST. REF.	DEBIT	CREDIT	BALANCE	
						DEBIT	CREDIT
20—							
Aug.	31	Balance	√			16 7 5 0 00	

ACCOUNT *Income Summary* ACCOUNT NO. **313**

DATE		ITEM	POST. REF.	DEBIT	CREDIT	BALANCE	
						DEBIT	CREDIT

Copyright © by Houghton Mifflin Company. All rights reserved.

PROBLEM 6-3A or 6-3B (continued)

ACCOUNT _Professional Fees_   ACCOUNT NO. _411_

DATE		ITEM	POST. REF.	DEBIT	CREDIT	BALANCE	
						DEBIT	CREDIT
20—							
Aug.	31	Balance	√				33 1 0 0 00

ACCOUNT _Salary Expense_   ACCOUNT NO. _511_

DATE		ITEM	POST. REF.	DEBIT	CREDIT	BALANCE	
						DEBIT	CREDIT
20—							
Aug.	31	Balance	√			17 3 5 0 00	

ACCOUNT _Rent Expense_   ACCOUNT NO. _512_

DATE		ITEM	POST. REF.	DEBIT	CREDIT	BALANCE	
						DEBIT	CREDIT
20—							
Aug.	31	Balance	√			7 2 0 0 00	

ACCOUNT _Laboratory Expense_   ACCOUNT NO. _513_

DATE		ITEM	POST. REF.	DEBIT	CREDIT	BALANCE	
						DEBIT	CREDIT
20—							
Aug.	31	Balance	√			4 2 5 0 00	

Copyright © by Houghton Mifflin Company. All rights reserved.

PROBLEM 6-3A or 6-3B (continued)

ACCOUNT *Utilities Expense*   ACCOUNT NO. **514**

DATE		ITEM	POST. REF.	DEBIT	CREDIT	BALANCE	
						DEBIT	CREDIT
20—							
Aug.	31	Balance	√			1 7 6 5 50	

ACCOUNT *Depreciation Expense, Equipment*   ACCOUNT NO. **515**

DATE	ITEM	POST. REF.	DEBIT	CREDIT	BALANCE	
					DEBIT	CREDIT

ACCOUNT *Miscellaneous Expense*   ACCOUNT NO. **516**

DATE		ITEM	POST. REF.	DEBIT	CREDIT	BALANCE	
						DEBIT	CREDIT
20—							
Aug.	31	Balance	√			9 9 8 00	

Copyright © by Houghton Mifflin Company. All rights reserved.

PROBLEM 6-3A or 6-3B (concluded)

ACCOUNT NAME	DEBIT	CREDIT

Copyright © by Houghton Mifflin Company. All rights reserved.

PROBLEM 6-4A or 6-4B

Chart of Accounts

Assets

Revenue

Expenses

Liabilities

Owner's Equity

Copyright © by Houghton Mifflin Company. All rights reserved.

PROBLEM 6-4A or 6-4B (continued)

COMBINED

	CASH		CK. NO.	DATE	ACCOUNT NAME	POST. REF.	OTHER ACCOUNTS	
	DEBIT	CREDIT					DEBIT	CREDIT
1								
2								
3								
4								
5								
6								
7								
8								
9								
10								
11								
12								
13								
14								
15								
16								
17								
18								
19								
20								
21								
22								
23								
24								
25								
26								
27								
28								
29								
30								
31								
32								
33								
34								
35								
36								
37								

Copyright © by Houghton Mifflin Company. All rights reserved.

PROBLEM 6-4A or 6-4B (concluded)

JOURNAL   PAGE _____

ACCOUNTS PAYABLE		INCOME FROM SERVICES	WAGES EXPENSE	
DEBIT	CREDIT	CREDIT	DEBIT	
				1
				2
				3
				4
				5
				6
				7
				8
				9
				10
				11
				12
				13
				14
				15
				16
				17
				18
				19
				20
				21
				22
				23
				24
				25
				26
				27
				28
				29
				30
				31
				32
				33
				34
				35
				36
				37

Copyright © by Houghton Mifflin Company. All rights reserved.

Bank Accounts and Cash Funds

PERFORMANCE OBJECTIVES

1. Describe the procedure for depositing checks.
2. Reconcile a bank statement.
3. Record the required journal entries directly from the bank reconciliation.
4. Record journal entries to establish and reimburse Petty Cash Fund.
5. Complete petty cash vouchers and petty cash payments records.
6. Record the journal entries to establish a Change Fund.
7. Record journal entries for transactions involving Cash Short and Over.

KEY TERMS

ABA number	Endorsement
ATM (automated teller machine)	Ledger balance of cash
Bank reconciliation	MICR
Bank statement	NSF (not sufficient funds) checks
Blank endorsement	Outstanding checks
Canceled checks	Payee
Cash funds	Petty Cash Fund
Change Fund	Petty cash payments record
Check writer	Petty cash voucher
Collections	Promissory note
Denominations	Qualified endorsement
Deposit in transit	Restrictive endorsement
Deposit slips	Service charge
Drawer	Signature card

STUDY GUIDE QUESTIONS

PART 1   True/False

For each of the following statements, circle T if the statement is true and F if the statement is false:

T   F   1. Cash receipts, deposits, and bank reconciliation should always be handled by the same person.

T   F   2. Each petty cash payment is entered separately in the general journal.

T   F   3. If the final balance of Cash Short and Over is a debit balance, it is treated as a deduction from Sales.

T   F   4. A qualified endorsement prevents any further transferring of a check by signing over the check from one person to another.

T   F   5. On a bank reconciliation, outstanding checks are deducted from the bank statement balance.

T   F   6. Payments made from the petty cash fund are journalized when the petty cash fund is reimbursed.

Copyright © by Houghton Mifflin Company. All rights reserved.

T F   7. A credit memo increases the depositor's bank balance.

T F   8. The entry to reimburse the Petty Cash Fund involves a debit to Petty Cash Fund and a credit to Cash.

T F   9. The entry for an NSF check involves a debit to Accounts Payable and a credit to Cash.

T F   10. A credit balance in the Cash Short and Over account is listed on the income statement under Miscellaneous Expense.

PART 2   Completion—Language of Business

Complete each of the following statements by writing the appropriate word(s) in the spaces provided:

1. The party to whom a check is made out is called the _____ .
2. The amount that the bank charges a depositor for handling checks and collections is called a(n) _____ .
3. The method used to transfer title of a check is known as a(n) _____ .
4. Varieties of coins and currency are called _____ .
5. Checks issued by the depositor that have been paid by the bank and included with the bank statement are called _____ .
6. An endorsement that prevents further circulation of a check is called a(n) _____
   _____ .
7. The party who writes the check is called the _____ .
8. On a bank reconciliation, the balance of the Cash account in the general ledger is called the _____ .
9. A deposit not recorded on the bank statement because the deposit was made between the bank's cut-off date and the time the statement is received is called a(n) _____
   _____ .
10. The _____ is a cash fund used to handle transactions where customers pay cash for goods and services.
11. An endorsement of a check that contains the words "without recourse" is called a(n)
    _____ .
12. The procedure used to determine why there is a difference between the balance of Cash in the company's general ledger and in the company's bank records is called a(n) _____
    _____ .
13. _____ are checks that have been written by the depositor and deducted on the depositor's records but have not yet reached the bank for payment.
14. In a(n) _____ , the holder (payee) of a check simply signs her or his name on the back of the check.

Copyright © by Houghton Mifflin Company. All rights reserved.

PART 3 Reimbursing the Petty Cash Fund

Quality Bakery has the petty cash payments record shown on the next page. The amount of the debit balance of the Petty Cash Fund account is $ _____ . Record the entry in general journal form to reimburse the Petty Cash Fund.

GENERAL JOURNAL   PAGE _____

	DATE	DESCRIPTION	POST. REF.	DEBIT	CREDIT	
1						1
2						2
3						3
4						4
5						5
6						6
7						7
8						8
9						9
10						10
11						11
12						12
13						13

194

Copyright © by Houghton Mifflin Company. All rights reserved.

PERIOD OF TIME _____ June 20 — _____

PETTY CASH PAYMENTS RECORD

DATE	VOU. NO.	EXPLANATION	PAYMENTS	DISTRIBUTION OF PAYMENTS			OTHER ACCOUNTS	
				REPAIR EXPENSE	DELIVERY EXPENSE	MISCELLANEOUS EXPENSE	ACCOUNT	AMOUNT
20—								
June 3	1	H. Ball	7 00				H. Ball, Drawing	7 00
7	2	Marking pens	5 16			5 16		
9	3	Ben's Delivery	4 20		4 20			
12	4	Lightbulbs	6 32			6 32		
17	5	Postage stamps	5 00			5 00		
21	6	Repair fuses	7 10	7 10				
29	7	H. Ball	4 50				H. Ball, Drawing	4 50
30		Totals	39 28	7 10	4 20	16 48		11 50
		Balance in fund $20.72						
		Reimbursed Ck. No. 711 $39.28						
		Total $60.00						

Copyright © by Houghton Mifflin Company. All rights reserved.

DEMONSTRATION PROBLEM

The Reading Company made the following transactions during June of this year involving its Petty Cash Fund, its Change Fund, its Cash Short and Over, and its Income from Services accounts:

June   1 Established a Change Fund, $200.

       3 Established a Petty Cash Fund, $100.

    14 Recorded cash revenue for period June 1 through 14: cash register tape, $4,980.21; cash count, $5,175.39.

    30 Reimbursed the Petty Cash Fund, $94. The petty cash payments record indicated the following expenditures: Supplies, $32; Delivery Expense, $16; Advertising Expense, $35; Miscellaneous Expense, $11.

    30 Recorded cash revenue for period June 15 through 30: cash register tape, $5,239.16; cash count, $5,441.09.

    30 Recorded an NSF check received from J. Blakely listed on the bank reconciliation, $157.

Instructions

Record the transactions in general journal form.

Copyright © by Houghton Mifflin Company. All rights reserved.

SOLUTION

GENERAL JOURNAL

PAGE _____

DATE		DESCRIPTION	POST. REF.	DEBIT	CREDIT
20—					
June	1	Change Fund		2 0 0 00	
		Cash			2 0 0 00
		Established a Change Fund.			
	3	Petty Cash Fund		1 0 0 00	
		Cash			1 0 0 00
		Established a Petty Cash Fund.			
	14	Cash		4 9 7 5 39	
		Cash Short and Over		4 82	
		Income from Services			4 9 8 0 21
		To record cash revenue for period			
		June 1 through 14 involving a			
		cash shortage of $4.82.			
	30	Supplies		3 2 00	
		Delivery Expense		1 6 00	
		Advertising Expense		3 5 00	
		Miscellaneous Expense		1 1 00	
		Cash			9 4 00
		Reimbursed the Petty Cash			
		Fund.			
	30	Cash		5 2 4 1 09	
		Income from Services			5 2 3 9 16
		Cash Short and Over			1 93
		To record cash revenue for period			
		June 15 through 30 involving			
		a cash overage of $1.93.			
	30	Accounts Receivable		1 5 7 00	
		Cash			1 5 7 00
		To record an NSF check			
		received from J. Blakely.			

Copyright © by Houghton Mifflin Company. All rights reserved.

PROBLEM 7-1A or 7-1B

Bank Reconciliation

Bank Statement Balance $ _____

Add: _____

                                                             $ _____

Deduct: _____

                                              $ _____

Adjusted Bank Statement Balance $ _____

Ledger Balance of Cash $ _____

Add: $ _____

                                                             $ _____

Deduct:

Adjusted Ledger Balance of Cash $ _____

GENERAL JOURNAL   PAGE _____

	DATE	DESCRIPTION	POST. REF.	DEBIT	CREDIT	
1						1
2						2
3						3
4						4
5						5
6						6
7						7
8						8
9						9
10						10
11						11
12						12
13						13
14						14

Copyright © by Houghton Mifflin Company. All rights reserved.

NAME _____ DATE _____ CLASS _____

PROBLEM 7-2A or 7-2B

GENERAL JOURNAL   PAGE _____

	DATE	DESCRIPTION	POST. REF.	DEBIT	CREDIT	
1						1
2						2
3						3
4						4
5						5
6						6
7						7
8						8
9						9
10						10
11						11
12						12
13						13
14						14
15						15
16						16
17						17
18						18
19						19
20						20
21						21
22						22
23						23
24						24
25						25
26						26
27						27
28						28
29						29
30						30
31						31
32						32
33						33
34						34
35						35
36						36
37						37

Copyright © by Houghton Mifflin Company. All rights reserved.

PROBLEM 7-2A or 7-2B (concluded)

PETTY CASH PAYMENTS RECORD

DATE	VOU. NO.	EXPLANATION	PAYMENTS	DISTRIBUTION OF PAYMENTS			OTHER ACCOUNTS	
				OFFICE SUPPLIES	DELIVERY EXPENSE	MISCELLANEOUS EXPENSE	ACCOUNT	AMOUNT

Copyright © by Houghton Mifflin Company. All rights reserved.

PROBLEM 7-3A or 7-3B

GENERAL JOURNAL

	DATE	DESCRIPTION	POST. REF.	DEBIT	CREDIT	
1						1
2						2
3						3
4						4
5						5
6						6
7						7
8						8
9						9
10						10
11						11
12						12
13						13
14						14
15						15
16						16
17						17
18						18
19						19
20						20
21						21
22						22
23						23
24						24
25						25
26						26
27						27
28						28
29						29
30						30
31						31
32						32
33						33
34						34
35						35
36						36
37						37

Copyright © by Houghton Mifflin Company. All rights reserved.

PROBLEM 7-4A or 7-4B

Bank Reconciliation

Bank Statement Balance		$
Add:		
		$ ___
Deduct:		
	$	
Adjusted Bank Statement Balance		$ ___
Ledger Balance of Cash		$
Deduct:		$
Adjusted Ledger Balance of Cash		$ ___

GENERAL JOURNAL

PAGE _____

	DATE	DESCRIPTION	POST. REF.	DEBIT	CREDIT	
1						1
2						2
3						3
4						4
5						5
6						6
7						7
8						8
9						9
10						10
11						11
12						12
13						13
14						14
15						15
16						16

Copyright © by Houghton Mifflin Company. All rights reserved.

PROBLEM 7-4A or 7-4B (concluded)

THIS FORM IS PROVIDED TO HELP YOU BALANCE
YOUR BANK STATEMENT

CHECKS OUTSTANDING NOT CHARGED TO ACCOUNT		
No.	$	
TOTAL	$	

BEFORE YOU START

PLEASE BE SURE YOU HAVE ENTERED IN YOUR CHECK-BOOK ALL AUTOMATIC TRANSACTIONS SHOWN ON THE FRONT OF YOUR STATEMENT.

YOU SHOULD HAVE ADDED IF ANY OCCURRED:

1. Loan advances.
2. Credit memos.
3. Other automatic deposits.

YOU SHOULD HAVE SUB-TRACTED IF ANY OCCURRED:

1. Automatic loan payments.
2. Automatic savings transfers.
3. Service charges.
4. Debit memos.
5. Other automatic deductions and payments.

BANK BALANCE SHOWN ON THIS STATEMENT $ _____

ADD

DEPOSITS NOT SHOWN ON THIS STATEMENT *(IF ANY)* $ _____

_____

_____

TOTAL $ _____

SUBTRACT

CHECKS OUTSTANDING $ _____

BALANCE $ _____

SHOULD AGREE WITH YOUR CHECKBOOK BALANCE AFTER DEDUCTING SERVICE CHARGES (IF ANY) SHOWN ON THIS STATEMENT.

Please examine immediately and report if incorrect. If no reply is received within 15 days, the account will be considered correct.

IN CASE OF ERRORS OR INQUIRIES ABOUT YOUR BILL

Send your inquiry in writing on a separate sheet so that the creditor receives it within 60 days after the bill was mailed to you. Your written inquiry must include:

1. Your name and account number;
2. A description of the error and why (to the extent you can explain) you believe it is an error; and
3. The dollar amount of the suspected error.

If you have authorized your creditor to automatically pay your bill from your checking or savings account, you can stop or reverse payment on any amount you think is wrong by mailing your notice so that the creditor receives it within 16 days after the bill was sent to you.

You remain obligated to pay the parts of your bill not in dispute, but you do not have to pay any amount in dispute during the time the creditor is resolving the dispute. During that same time, the creditor may not take any action to collect disputed amounts or report disputed amounts as delinquent.

This is a summary of your rights; a full statement of your rights and the creditor's responsibilities under the Federal Fair Credit Billing Act will be sent to you both upon request and in response to a billing error notice.

Copyright © by Houghton Mifflin Company. All rights reserved.

PROBLEM B-1

GENERAL JOURNAL   PAGE ___17___

	DATE		DESCRIPTION	POST. REF.	DEBIT	CREDIT	
1							1
2							2
3							3
4							4
5							5
6							6
7							7
8							8
9							9
10							10
11							11
12							12
13							13
14							14

PROBLEM B-2

GENERAL JOURNAL   PAGE ___46___

	DATE		DESCRIPTION	POST. REF.	DEBIT	CREDIT	
1							1
2							2
3							3
4							4
5							5
6							6
7							7
8							8
9							9
10							10
11							11
12							12
13							13
14							14
15							15
16							16
17							17
18							18

Copyright © by Houghton Mifflin Company. All rights reserved.

NAME _____ DATE _____ CLASS _____

PROBLEM B-3

GENERAL JOURNAL

	DATE	DESCRIPTION	POST. REF.	DEBIT	CREDIT	
1						1
2						2
3						3
4						4
5						5
6						6
7						7
8						8
9						9
10						10
11						11
12						12
13						13
14						14
15						15
16						16
17						17
18						18
19						19
20						20
21						21
22						22
23						23
24						24
25						25
26						26
27						27
28						28
29						29
30						30
31						31
32						32
33						33
34						34
35						35
36						36
37						37

Copyright © by Houghton Mifflin Company. All rights reserved.

8

Employee Earnings and Deductions

PERFORMANCE OBJECTIVES

1. Calculate total earnings based on an hourly, piece-rate, or commission basis.
2. Determine deductions from tables of employees' income tax withholding.
3. Complete a payroll register.
4. Journalize the payroll entry from a payroll register.
5. Maintain employees' individual earnings records.

KEY TERMS

Calendar year
Employee
Employee's individual earnings record
Employee's Withholding Allowance
   Certificate (Form W-4)
Exemption
FICA taxes
Gross pay

Independent contractor
Medicare taxes
Net pay
Payroll bank account
Payroll register
Social Security taxes
Taxable earnings
Wage-bracket tax tables
Withholding allowance

STUDY GUIDE QUESTIONS

PART 1   True/False

For each of the following statements, circle T if the statement is true and F if the statement is false.

T   F   1. Social Security and Medicare taxes are paid by both the employer and the employee.

T   F   2. The difference between an employee's net pay and her take-home pay is the amount of her personal deductions.

T   F   3. Information for an employee's individual earnings record is taken directly from the general journal.

T   F   4. The payroll register is considered to be a book of original entry.

T   F   5. On a payroll register, an employee's net amount paid equals total earnings minus total individual deductions.

T   F   6. All employers should use a special payroll bank account.

T   F   7. Individual earnings records should be kept for salaried employees.

T   F   8. The basis for the payroll register is the payroll journal entry.

T   F   9. Employees are required by law to participate in the Social Security program provided by the FICA.

T   F   10. The fee paid by a company to a CPA for auditing its books is subject to income tax withholding.

Copyright © by Houghton Mifflin Company. All rights reserved.

PART 2 Completion—Language of Business

Complete each of the following statements by writing the appropriate word(s) in the spaces provided.

1. Total earnings for an employee are called the employee's _____.
2. A(n) _____ is one who works for compensation under the direction or control of an employer.
3. Another term having the same meaning as withholding allowance is _____ _____.
4. Another term having the same meaning as take-home pay is _____.
5. Someone who is engaged for a definite job and who chooses his or her own means of doing the work is a(n) _____.
6. Each employee's personal payroll information for the year is listed in the _____ _____.

PART 3 Calculation of Earnings

Henderson Company pays its employees time-and-a-half for all hours worked in excess of forty per week. For the first week of October, determine the total earnings for each of the following employees.

Employee's Name	Hours Worked	Regular Hourly Rate	Total Earnings
A. L. Gonzales	42	$ 9.60	
L. A. Lamar	46	8.40	
C. W. Nelson	51	10.20	

PART 4 Payroll Entry

Using the column totals for the week ended March 14 as listed in the payroll register, give the entry in general journal form to record the payroll. Number the page 79.

Total Earnings	$93,640.00
Federal Income Tax Deduction	9,300.00
Social Security Tax Deduction	5,805.68
Medicare Tax Deduction	1,357.78
U.S. Savings Bonds Deduction	900.00
Union Dues Deduction	1,200.00
Medical Insurance Deduction	2,000.00
Net Amount	73,076.54
Sales Salary Expense	72,000.00
Office Salary Expense	21,640.00

Copyright © by Houghton Mifflin Company. All rights reserved.

DEMONSTRATION PROBLEM

Kelsey Company's payroll register reveals the following information concerning its two employees for the month ended July 31 of this year:

D. C. Garcia		**T. C. Bennett**	
Total earnings	$2,000.00	Total earnings	$1,800.00
Federal income tax withheld	400.00	Federal income tax withheld	360.00
Social Security tax withheld	124.00	Social Security tax withheld	111.60
Medicare tax withheld	29.00	Medicare tax withheld	26.10
Medical insurance withheld	129.00	Medical insurance withheld	125.00
Net amount (Ck. No. 6701)	1,318.00	Net amount (Ck. No. 6702)	1,177.30

The employees are paid by checks issued on the firm's regular bank account.

Instructions

Record the payroll entry in a general journal.

SOLUTION

GENERAL JOURNAL   PAGE _____

DATE		DESCRIPTION	POST. REF.	DEBIT	CREDIT
20—					
July	31	Salary Expense		3 8 0 0 00	
		Employees' Federal Income Tax			
		Payable			7 6 0 00
		FICA Tax Payable			2 9 0 70
		Employees' Medical Insurance			
		Payable			2 5 4 00
		Cash			2 4 9 5 30
		Paid salaries for the month			
		(D.C. Garcia, $1,318, Ck.			
		No. 6701; T.C. Bennett,			
		$1,177.30, Ck. No. 6702).			

Copyright © by Houghton Mifflin Company. All rights reserved.

NAME _____ DATE _____ CLASS _____

PROBLEM 8-1A or 8-1B

_____

REGULAR PAY	OVERTIME PAY	GROSS PAY	NET PAY

Copyright © by Houghton Mifflin Company. All rights reserved.

NAME _____ DATE _____ CLASS _____

PROBLEM 8-2A or 8-2B

PAYROLL REGISTER FOR WEEK

	NAME	TOTAL HOURS	BEGINNING CUMULATIVE EARNINGS	EARNINGS			ENDING CUMULATIVE EARNINGS	TAXABLE	
				REGULAR	OVERTIME	TOTAL		UNEMPLOYMENT	SOCIAL SECURITY
1									
2									
3									
4									
5									
6									
7									
8									

GENERAL JOURNAL   PAGE _____

	DATE	DESCRIPTION	POST. REF.	DEBIT	CREDIT	
1						1
2						2
3						3
4						4
5						5
6						6
7						7
8						8
9						9
10						10
11						11
12						12
13						13
14						14
15						15
16						16
17						17
18						18
19						19
20						20
21						21
22						22
23						23
24						24

Copyright © by Houghton Mifflin Company. All rights reserved.

PROBLEM 8-2A or 8-2B (concluded)

ENDED _____   PAGE _____

EARNINGS	DEDUCTIONS				PAYMENTS			
MEDICARE	FEDERAL INCOME TAX	SOCIAL SECURITY TAX	MEDICARE TAX	TOTAL	NET AMOUNT	CK. NO.	WAGES EXPENSE DEBIT	
								1
								2
								3
								4
								5
								6
								7
								8

Copyright © by Houghton Mifflin Company. All rights reserved.

PROBLEM 8-3A or 8-3B

PAYROLL REGISTER FOR WEEK

	NAME	TOTAL HOURS	BEGINNING CUMULATIVE EARNINGS	EARNINGS			ENDING CUMULATIVE EARNINGS	TAXABLE	
				REGULAR	OVERTIME	TOTAL		UNEMPLOYMENT	SOCIAL SECURITY
1									
2									
3									
4									
5									
6									
7									
8									
9									
10									

GENERAL JOURNAL

PAGE _____

	DATE	DESCRIPTION	POST. REF.	DEBIT	CREDIT	
1						1
2						2
3						3
4						4
5						5
6						6
7						7
8						8
9						9
10						10
11						11
12						12
13						13
14						14
15						15
16						16
17						17
18						18
19						19
20						20
21						21
22						22
23						23
24						24

Copyright © by Houghton Mifflin Company. All rights reserved.

PROBLEM 8-3A or 8-3B (concluded)

ENDED _____   PAGE _____

EARNINGS	DEDUCTIONS				PAYMENTS			
MEDICARE	FEDERAL INCOME TAX	SOCIAL SECURITY TAX	MEDICARE TAX	TOTAL	NET AMOUNT	CK. NO.	WAGES EXPENSE DEBIT	
								1
								2
								3
								4
								5
								6
								7
								8
								9
								10

Copyright © by Houghton Mifflin Company. All rights reserved.

213

NAME _____ DATE _____ CLASS _____

PROBLEM 8-4A or 8-4B

PAYROLL REGISTER FOR WEEK

	NAME	TOTAL HOURS	BEGINNING CUMULATIVE EARNINGS	TOTAL EARNINGS	ENDING CUMULATIVE EARNINGS	TAXABLE EARNINGS		
						UNEMPLOYMENT	SOCIAL SECURITY	MEDICARE
1								
2								
3								
4								
5								
6								
7								
8								
9								
10								
11								
12								

GENERAL JOURNAL

PAGE _____

	DATE	DESCRIPTION	POST. REF.	DEBIT	CREDIT	
1						1
2						2
3						3
4						4
5						5
6						6
7						7
8						8
9						9
10						10
11						11
12						12
13						13
14						14
15						15
16						16
17						17
18						18
19						19
20						20
21						21
22						22

214

Copyright © by Houghton Mifflin Company. All rights reserved.

PROBLEM 8-4A or 8-4B (concluded)

ENDED _____   PAGE _____

			DEDUCTIONS						PAYMENTS		EXPENSE ACCOUNT DEBITED		
FEDERAL INCOME TAX	SOCIAL SECURITY TAX	MEDICARE TAX	OTHER CODE	AMOUNT		TOTAL		NET AMOUNT	CK. NO.	SALES SALARY EXPENSE		OFFICE SALARY EXPENSE		
														1
														2
														3
														4
														5
														6
														7
														8
														9
														10
														11
														12

Copyright © by Houghton Mifflin Company. All rights reserved.

9 | Employer Taxes, Payments, and Reports

PERFORMANCE OBJECTIVES

1. Calculate the amount of payroll tax expense and journalize the related entry.
2. Journalize the entry for the deposit of employees' federal income taxes withheld and FICA taxes (both employees' withheld and employer's matching share) and prepare the deposit coupon.
3. Journalize the entries for the payment of employer's state and federal unemployment taxes.
4. Journalize the entry for the deposit of employees' state income taxes withheld.
5. Complete Employer's Quarterly Federal Tax Return, Form 941.
6. Prepare W-2 and W-3 forms and Form 940.
7. Calculate the premium for workers' compensation insurance, and prepare the entry for payment in advance.
8. Determine the amount of the end-of-the-year adjustments for (a) workers' compensation insurance and (b) accrued salaries and wages, and record the adjustments.

KEY TERMS

Employer identification number
Federal unemployment tax (FUTA)
Form 940
Form 941
Form W-2

Form W-3
Payroll Tax Expense
Quarters
State unemployment tax (SUTA)
Workers' compensation insurance

STUDY GUIDE QUESTIONS

PART 1   True/False

For each of the following statements, circle T if the statement is true and F if the statement is false.

T F   1. Companies must furnish their employees with W-2 forms by April 15.

T F   2. The Payroll Tax Expense account handles the unemployment taxes as well as the employer's and employees' FICA taxes.

T F   3. Form 941 is completed four times a year.

T F   4. The times for making deposits of FICA taxes and employees' income taxes withheld depend strictly on the number of employees involved.

T F   5. Form 940 is an annual tax return that relates to federal unemployment tax.

T F   6. A premium for workers' compensation insurance is paid at the beginning of the year.

T F   7. The state unemployment tax is determined by multiplying the net amount as shown in the payroll register by the state unemployment tax rate.

T F   8. The federal unemployment tax is paid by the employer only.

Copyright © by Houghton Mifflin Company. All rights reserved.

T   F   9. If the Unemployment Taxable Earnings column of the payroll register is blank, this indicates that the employee has cumulative earnings for the calendar year of more than the maximum unemployment taxable income.

T   F   10. Form W-4 is submitted to the Internal Revenue Service along with copies of the employees' W-2 forms.

PART 2   Completion—Language of Business

Complete each of the following statements by writing the appropriate word(s) in the spaces provided.

1. The second _____ of the year consists of the months of April, May, and June.

2. _____ provides an employee with his or her total earnings and tax deductions.

3. Employers' reports submitted to the Internal Revenue Service all must contain the _____ _____ .

4. The _____ account is used to record the employer's matching portion of the FICA tax, the federal unemployment tax, and the state unemployment tax.

5. _____ is used to provide benefits for employees injured on the job.

6. Form _____ is submitted to the Social Security Administration accompanied by copies of W-2 forms.

7. _____ is the Employer's Quarterly Federal Tax Return.

PART 3   Completing Form W-2

Complete the Form W-2 provided for June Clara Perkins. Perkins is employed by Barclay Company, 1620 Hampton Place, Boston, Massachusetts 02116. Barclay Company's federal employer identification number is 72-1162127, and its state identification number is 42-6916. The following information is taken from Perkins's Individual Earnings Record. Her address is 2219 Henderson Street, Boston, Massachusetts 02121. Her Social Security number is 561-24-5229. During the year, Perkins earned $34,218.42. Her withholdings were as follows: federal income tax, $3,716.22; state income tax, $1,780.04; Social Security tax withheld, $2,121.54; Medicare tax withheld, $496.17.

a Control number 22222	Void ☐	For Official Use Only ▶ OMB No. 1545-0008	
b Employer's identification number		1 Wages, tips, other compensation	2 Federal income tax withheld
c Employer's name, address, and ZIP code		3 Social security wages	4 Social security tax withheld
		5 Medicare wages and tips	6 Medicare tax withheld
		7 Social security tips	8 Allocated tips
d Employee's social security number		9 Advance EIC payment	10 Dependent care benefits
e Employee's name (first, middle initial, last)		11 Nonqualified plans	12 Benefits included in box 1
		13 See Instrs. for box 13	14 Other
		15 Statutory employee ☐ Deceased ☐ Pension plan ☐ Legal rep. ☐ Hshld. emp. ☐ Subtotal ☐ Deferred compensation ☐	
f Employee's address and ZIP code			

16 State Employer's state I.D. No.	17 State wages, tips, etc.	18 State income tax	19 Locality name	20 Local wages, tips, etc.	21 Local income tax

41-852411   APR. I.R.S.   Department of the Treasury – Internal Revenue Service

Form **W-2** Wage and Tax Statement **2000**

For Paperwork Reduction Act Notice, see separate instructions.

Copy A For Social Security Administration

Copyright © by Houghton Mifflin Company. All rights reserved.

DEMONSTRATION PROBLEM

The totals of the payroll register for City-Wide Moving are given below. Assume the employment taxes are as follows:

State unemployment, 5.4 percent   Social Security, 6.2 percent
Federal unemployment, .8 percent   Medicare, 1.45 percent

Total Earnings	$86,000
State Unemployment Taxable Earnings	18,000
Federal Unemployment Taxable Earnings	18,000
Social Security Taxable Earnings	84,000
Medicare Taxable Earnings	86,000
Federal Income Tax Deduction	9,800
Social Security Tax Deduction	5,208
Medicare Tax Deduction	1,247
Union Dues Deduction	1,560
Medical Insurance Deduction	4,250
Total Deductions	22,065
Net Pay	63,935

Instructions

Journalize the following entries:

a. To record the payroll, assuming the use of a payroll bank account.
b. To record the payroll tax expense.
c. To pay the payroll.
d. To record the deposit of federal taxes that will be reported on the Employer's Quarterly Federal Tax Return (Form 941): employees' income taxes withheld, employees' FICA taxes withheld, and employer's share of FICA tax.
e. To record payment of state unemployment insurance that will be reported on the state unemployment insurance tax form.
f. To record the deposit of federal unemployment insurance that will be reported on the Employer's Annual Federal Unemployment Tax Return (Form 940).
g. To record payment of employees' union dues withheld.
h. To record payment of employees' medical insurance withheld.

Copyright © by Houghton Mifflin Company. All rights reserved.

SOLUTION

GENERAL JOURNAL

DATE		DESCRIPTION	POST. REF.	DEBIT	CREDIT
	a.	Wages Expense		86 0 0 0 00	
		Employees' Federal Income Tax Payable			9 8 0 0 00
		FICA Tax Payable			6 4 5 5 00
		Employees' Union Dues Payable			1 5 6 0 00
		Employees' Medical Insurance Payable			4 2 5 0 00
		Wages Payable			63 9 3 5 00
		To record wages as listed in the payroll register, page 73.			
	b.	Payroll Tax Expense		7 5 7 1 00	
		FICA Tax Payable			6 4 5 5 00
		State Unemployment Tax Payable			9 7 2 00
		Federal Unemployment Tax Payable			1 4 4 00
		To record employer's share of FICA tax and federal and state unemployment taxes. (FICA tax = Social Security tax + Medicare tax; Social Security tax = $84,000 × .062 = $5,208. Medicare tax = $86,000 × .0145 = $1,247. FICA tax = $5,208 + $1,247 = $6,455.) SUTA tax = $18,000 × .054 = $972. FUTA tax = $18,000 × .008 = $144.			
	c.	Wages Payable		63 9 3 5 00	
		Cash			63 9 3 5 00
		Paid wages.			

Copyright © by Houghton Mifflin Company. All rights reserved.

DATE	DESCRIPTION	POST. REF.	DEBIT	CREDIT
	d. Employees' Income Tax Payable		9 8 0 0 00	
	FICA Tax Payable		12 9 1 0 00	
	Cash			22 7 1 0 00
	Issued check to record deposit			
	of federal taxes.			
	e. State Unemployment Tax Payable		9 7 2 00	
	Cash			9 7 2 00
	To record payment of state			
	unemployment tax.			
	f. Federal Unemployment Tax Payable		1 4 4 00	
	Cash			1 4 4 00
	To record deposit of federal			
	unemployment tax.			
	g. Employees' Union Dues Payable		1 5 6 0 00	
	Cash			1 5 6 0 00
	To record payment of employees'			
	union dues withheld.			
	h. Employees' Medical Insurance			
	Payable		4 2 5 0 00	
	Cash			4 2 5 0 00
	To record payment of employees'			
	medical insurance premiums			
	withheld.			

Copyright © by Houghton Mifflin Company. All rights reserved.

NAME _____ DATE _____ CLASS _____

PROBLEM 9-1A or 9-1B

GENERAL JOURNAL   PAGE _____

	DATE	DESCRIPTION	POST. REF.	DEBIT	CREDIT	
1						1
2						2
3						3
4						4
5						5
6						6
7						7
8						8
9						9
10						10
11						11
12						12
13						13
14						14
15						15
16						16
17						17
18						18
19						19
20						20
21						21
22						22
23						23
24						24
25						25
26						26
27						27
28						28
29						29
30						30
31						31
32						32
33						33
34						34
35						35
36						36
37						37

Copyright © by Houghton Mifflin Company. All rights reserved.

NAME _____ DATE _____ CLASS _____

PROBLEM 9-2A or 9-2B

PAYROLL REGISTER FOR WEEK

	NAME	BEGINNING CUMULATIVE EARNINGS	TOTAL EARNINGS	ENDING CUMULATIVE EARNINGS	TAXABLE EARNINGS		
					UNEMPLOYMENT	SOCIAL SECURITY	MEDICARE
1							
2							
3							
4							
5							
6							
7							
8							
9							
10							
11							
12							
13							
14							
15							
16							
17							
18							
19							
20							
21							
22							
23							
24							
25							
26							
27							
28							
29							
30							
31							
32							
33							
34							
35							

222

Copyright © by Houghton Mifflin Company. All rights reserved.

PROBLEM 9-2A or 9-2B (continued)

ENDED _____   PAGE _____

FEDERAL INCOME TAX	STATE INCOME TAX	SOCIAL SECURITY TAX	MEDICARE TAX	TOTAL	NET AMOUNT	CK. NO.	SALARY EXPENSE DEBIT	
								1
								2
								3
								4
								5
								6
								7
								8
								9
								10
								11
								12
								13
								14
								15
								16
								17
								18
								19
								20
								21
								22
								23
								24
								25
								26
								27
								28
								29
								30
								31
								32
								33
								34
								35

DEDUCTIONS   PAYMENTS

Copyright © by Houghton Mifflin Company. All rights reserved.

PROBLEM 9-2A or 9-2B (concluded)

GENERAL JOURNAL

PAGE _____

	DATE		DESCRIPTION	POST. REF.	DEBIT	CREDIT	
1							1
2							2
3							3
4							4
5							5
6							6
7							7
8							8
9							9
10							10
11							11
12							12
13							13
14							14
15							15
16							16
17							17
18							18
19							19
20							20
21							21
22							22
23							23
24							24
25							25
26							26
27							27
28							28
29							29
30							30
31							31
32							32
33							33
34							34
35							35
36							36
37							37

Copyright © by Houghton Mifflin Company. All rights reserved.

PROBLEM 9-3A or 9-3B

Form 941
(Rev. January 1999)
Department of the Treasury
Internal Revenue Service

Employer's Quarterly Federal Tax Return

▶ See separate instructions for information on completing this return.
Please type or print.

Enter state code for state in which deposits were made ONLY if different from state in address to the right ▶ ☐ (see page 2 of instructions).

Name (as distinguished from trade name)	Date quarter ended
Trade name, if any	Employer identification number
Address (number and street)	City, state, and ZIP code

OMB No. 1545-0029

T
FF
FD
FP
I
T

If address is different from prior return, check here ▶ ☐

IRS Use

1	1	1	1	1	1	1	1	1	1		2		3	3	3	3	3	3	3		4	4	4		5	5	5
6	7	8	8	8	8	8	8	8		9	9	9	9	9		10	10	10	10	10	10	10	10	10	10		

If you do not have to file returns in the future, check here ▶ ☐ and enter date final wages paid ▶

If you are a seasonal employer, see **Seasonal employers** on page 1 of the instructions and check here ▶

1	Number of employees in the pay period that includes March 12th . ▶	1	
2	Total wages and tips, plus other compensation	2	
3	Total income tax withheld from wages, tips, and sick pay	3	
4	Adjustment of withheld income tax for preceding quarters of calendar year	4	
5	Adjusted total of income tax withheld (line 3 as adjusted by line 4—see instructions)	5	
6	Taxable social security wages	6a	× 12.4% (.124) =	6b	
	Taxable social security tips	6c	× 12.4% (.124) =	6d	
7	Taxable Medicare wages and tips . . .	7a	× 2.9% (.029) =	7b	
8	Total social security and Medicare taxes (add lines 6b, 6d, and 7b). Check here if wages are not subject to social security and/or Medicare tax . . . . ▶ ☐	8	
9	Adjustment of social security and Medicare taxes (see instructions for required explanation) Sick Pay $ _____ ± Fractions of Cents $ _____ ± Other $ _____ =	9	
10	Adjusted total of social security and Medicare taxes (line 8 as adjusted by line 9—see instructions)	10	
11	**Total taxes** (add lines 5 and 10)	11	
12	Advance earned income credit (EIC) payments made to employees	12	
13	Net taxes (subtract line 12 from line 11). **If $1,000 or more, this must equal line 17, column (d) below (or line D of Schedule B (Form 941))**	13	
14	Total deposits for quarter, including overpayment applied from a prior quarter	14	
15	**Balance due** (subtract line 14 from line 13). See instructions	15	
16	**Overpayment.** If line 14 is more than line 13, enter excess here ▶ $ _____		

and check if to be: ☐ Applied to next return **OR** ☐ Refunded.

- **All filers:** If line 13 is less than $1,000, you need not complete line 17 or Schedule B (Form 941).
- **Semiweekly schedule depositors:** Complete Schedule B (Form 941) and check here . . . . ▶ ☐
- **Monthly schedule depositors:** Complete line 17, columns (a) through (d), and check here . . . . ▶ ☐

17	Monthly Summary of Federal Tax Liability. Do not complete if you were a semiweekly schedule depositor.			
	(a) First month liability	**(b)** Second month liability	**(c)** Third month liability	**(d)** Total liability for quarter

Sign Here

Under penalties of perjury, I declare that I have examined this return, including accompanying schedules and statements, and to the best of my knowledge and belief, it is true, correct, and complete.

Signature ▶ _____ Print Your Name and Title ▶ _____ Date ▶ _____

For Privacy Act and Paperwork Reduction Act Notice, see back of form. Cat. No. 17001Z Form **941** (Rev. 1-99)

Copyright © by Houghton Mifflin Company. All rights reserved.

PROBLEM 9-4A or 9-4B

GENERAL JOURNAL

	DATE	DESCRIPTION	POST. REF.	DEBIT	CREDIT	
1						1
2						2
3						3
4						4
5						5
6						6
7						7
8						8
9						9
10						10
11						11
12						12
13						13
14						14
15						15
16						16
17						17
18						18
19						19
20						20
21						21
22						22
23						23
24						24
25						25
26						26
27						27
28						28
29						29
30						30
31						31
32						32
33						33
34						34
35						35
36						36
37						37

Copyright © by Houghton Mifflin Company. All rights reserved.

PROBLEM 9-4A or 9-4B (concluded)

GENERAL JOURNAL

	DATE		DESCRIPTION	POST. REF.	DEBIT	CREDIT	
1							1
2							2
3							3
4							4
5							5
6							6
7							7
8							8
9							9
10							10
11							11
12							12
13							13
14							14
15							15
16							16
17							17
18							18
19							19
20							20
21							21
22							22
23							23
24							24
25							25
26							26
27							27
28							28
29							29
30							30
31							31
32							32
33							33
34							34
35							35
36							36
37							37

Copyright © by Houghton Mifflin Company. All rights reserved.

GENERAL JOURNAL

PAGE _____

2.

	DATE		DESCRIPTION	POST. REF.	DEBIT	CREDIT	
1							1
2							2
3							3
4							4
5							5
6							6
7							7
8							8
9							9
10							10
11							11
12							12
13							13
14							14
15							15
16							16
17							17
18							18
19							19
20							20
21							21
22							22
23							23
24							24
25							25
26							26
27							27
28							28
29							29
30							30
31							31
32							32
33							33
34							34
35							35
36							36
37							37

Copyright © by Houghton Mifflin Company. All rights reserved.

3.

PAGE _____

	DATE		DESCRIPTION	POST. REF.	DEBIT	CREDIT	
1							1
2							2
3							3
4							4
5							5
6							6
7							7
8							8
9							9
10							10
11							11
12							12
13							13
14							14
15							15
16							16
17							17
18							18
19							19
20							20
21							21
22							22
23							23
24							24
25							25
26							26
27							27
28							28
29							29
30							30
31							31
32							32
33							33
34							34
35							35
36							36
37							37

Copyright © by Houghton Mifflin Company. All rights reserved.

10 The Sales Journal

PERFORMANCE OBJECTIVES

1. Describe the specific accounts used by a merchandising firm.
2. Record transactions in sales journals.
3. Post from sales journals to an accounts receivable ledger and a general ledger.
4. Prepare a schedule of accounts receivable.
5. Journalize sales returns and allowances, including credit memorandums and returns involving sales tax, and post to the ledger accounts.
6. Locate errors.
7. Post directly from sales invoices to an accounts receivable ledger and journalize and post a summarizing entry in the general journal.

KEY TERMS

Accounts receivable ledger   Sales
Controlling account   Sales Discount
Credit memorandum   Sales journal
Freight In   Sales Returns and Allowances
Merchandise inventory   Sales tax
Purchases   Special journals
Purchases Discount   Subsidiary ledger
Purchases Returns and Allowances   Summarizing entry

STUDY GUIDE QUESTIONS

PART 1   True/False

For each of the following statements, circle T if the statement is true and F if the statement is false.

T   F   1. Posting from the sales journal to the Accounts Receivable account in the general ledger takes place at the end of the month.

T   F   2. The sales journal is used to record all sales.

T   F   3. Businesses list customer accounts in alphabetical order in their accounts receivable ledger.

T   F   4. Increases in Sales Returns and Allowances are recorded on the credit side.

T   F   5. Check marks in the Post. Ref. column of the sales journal indicate that the amounts are not to be posted.

T   F   6. At the end of the month, after all posting is completed, the total of the schedule of accounts receivable should equal the balance of the Sales account in the general ledger.

T   F   7. The accounts receivable ledger contains a separate account for each sale.

T   F   8. In posting directly from a sales invoice, the invoice number rather than the journal page number is recorded in the Post. Ref. columns of customer accounts in the accounts receivable ledger.

Copyright © by Houghton Mifflin Company. All rights reserved.

T   F   9. When using a sales journal, you do not have to post to any accounts in the general ledger.

T   F   10. The schedule of accounts receivable lists the balances of all the charge customer accounts at the end of the month.

PART 2   Completion—Language of Business

Complete each of the following statements by writing the appropriate word(s) in the spaces provided.

1. The book of original entry used to record sales of merchandise on account is called a(n) _____ .

2. A stock of ready-made goods that a company buys and intends to resell at a profit is called _____ .

3. Books of original entry used to record specialized types of transactions are referred to as _____ .

4. The Accounts Receivable account in the general ledger is called a(n) _____ .

5. The accounts receivable ledger may be called a special ledger or a(n) _____ .

6. A document issued by the seller to a customer allowing a reduction from the price at which the goods were originally sold is called a(n) _____ .

7. The entry made at the end of the month when amounts are posted directly from sales invoices is referred to as the _____ .

PART 3   Posting

Post the following sales journal to the accounts in the general ledger.

SALES JOURNAL   PAGE 26

DATE		INV. NO.	CUSTOMER'S NAME	POST. REF.	ACCOUNTS RECEIVABLE DEBIT	SALES TAX PAYABLE CREDIT	SALES CREDIT
20—							
June	1	32	Calvin Parsons		1 4 5 60	5 60	1 4 0 00
	30	171	Clara Lambert		1 6 1 41	6 21	1 5 5 20
	30				3 1 6 8 07	1 2 1 85	3 0 4 6 22

GENERAL LEDGER

ACCOUNT Accounts Receivable   ACCOUNT NO. 113

DATE	ITEM	POST. REF.	DEBIT	CREDIT	BALANCE DEBIT	BALANCE CREDIT

Copyright © by Houghton Mifflin Company. All rights reserved.

ACCOUNT _Sales Tax Payable_   ACCOUNT NO. _214_

DATE	ITEM	POST. REF.	DEBIT	CREDIT	BALANCE	
					DEBIT	CREDIT

ACCOUNT _Sales_   ACCOUNT NO. _411_

DATE	ITEM	POST. REF.	DEBIT	CREDIT	BALANCE	
					DEBIT	CREDIT

DEMONSTRATION PROBLEM

The following selected transactions were completed by the Adams Company:

Sept.   16 Sold merchandise on account to the Foster Company, sales invoice no. 1032, $3,742.
       20 Sold merchandise on account to the King Company, sales invoice no. 1033, $8,950.
       25 Sold merchandise on account to Zimmer Company, sales invoice no. 1034, $173.
       27 King Company returned $982 of merchandise relating to sales invoice no. 1033; Adams Company issued credit memo no. 131.

Instructions

1. Record the transactions in either the sales journal or the general journal, as appropriate.
2. Immediately after recording each transaction, post to the accounts receivable ledger.
3. Post the entries from the general journal and the total of the sales journal to the general ledger.
4. Prepare a schedule of accounts receivable.
5. Compare the total of the schedule of accounts receivable with the September 30 balance of the Accounts Receivable (controlling) account.

SOLUTION

SALES JOURNAL   PAGE _134_

DATE		INV. NO.	CUSTOMER'S NAME	POST. REF.	ACCOUNTS RECEIVABLE DR. SALES CR.				
20—									
Sept.	16	1032	Foster Company	√	3	7	4	2	00
	20	1033	King Company	√	8	9	5	0	00
	25	1034	Zimmer Company	√		1	7	3	00
	30				12	8	6	5	00
					(113) (411)				

Copyright © by Houghton Mifflin Company. All rights reserved.

DATE		DESCRIPTION	POST. REF.	DEBIT	CREDIT
20—					
Sept.	27	Sales Returns and Allowances	412	9 8 2 00	
		Accounts Receivable, King Company	113/ √		9 8 2 00
		Credit memo no. 131 relating to invoice			
		no. 1033.			

GENERAL LEDGER

ACCOUNT __Accounts Receivable__   ACCOUNT NO. _113_

DATE		ITEM	POST. REF.	DEBIT	CREDIT	BALANCE DEBIT	BALANCE CREDIT
20—							
Sept.	1	Balance	√			5 3 9 0 00	
	27		J159		9 8 2 00	4 4 0 8 00	
	30		S134	12 8 6 5 00		17 2 7 3 00	

ACCOUNT __Sales__   ACCOUNT NO. _411_

DATE		ITEM	POST. REF.	DEBIT	CREDIT	BALANCE DEBIT	BALANCE CREDIT
20—							
Sept.	1	Balance	√				51 5 9 7 00
	30		S134		12 8 6 5 00		64 4 6 2 00

ACCOUNT __Sales Returns and Allowances__   ACCOUNT NO. _412_

DATE		ITEM	POST. REF.	DEBIT	CREDIT	BALANCE DEBIT	BALANCE CREDIT
20—							
Sept.	1	Balance	√			2 7 7 7 00	
	27		J159	9 8 2 00		3 7 5 9 00	

Copyright © by Houghton Mifflin Company. All rights reserved.

ACCOUNTS RECEIVABLE LEDGER

NAME **Foster Company**

ADDRESS **330 Wexler Road, S.W.**
Atlanta, GA 30305

DATE		ITEM	POST. REF.	DEBIT	CREDIT	BALANCE
20—						
Sept.	1	Balance	✓			5 3 9 0 00
	16		S134	3 7 4 2 00		9 1 3 2 00

NAME **King Company**

ADDRESS **1450 Myron Avenue, S.W.**
Atlanta, GA 30307

DATE		ITEM	POST. REF.	DEBIT	CREDIT	BALANCE
20—						
Sept.	20		S134	8 9 5 0 00		8 9 5 0 00
	27		J159		9 8 2 00	7 9 6 8 00

NAME **Zimmer Company**

ADDRESS **1226 Euclid Avenue, S.W.**
Atlanta, GA 30309

DATE		ITEM	POST. REF.	DEBIT	CREDIT	BALANCE
20—						
Sept.	25		S134	1 7 3 00		1 7 3 00

Adams Company
Schedule of Accounts Receivable
September 30, 20—

Foster Company	$ 9 1 3 2 00
King Company	7 9 6 8 00
Zimmer Company	1 7 3 00
	$17 2 7 3 00

Copyright © by Houghton Mifflin Company. All rights reserved.

NAME _____ DATE _____ CLASS _____

PROBLEM 10-1A or 10-1B

SALES JOURNAL

	DATE	INV. NO.	CUSTOMER'S NAME	POST. REF.	ACCOUNTS RECEIVABLE DR. SALES CR.	
1						1
2						2
3						3
4						4
5						5
6						6
7						7
8						8
9						9
10						10
11						11
12						12
13						13
14						14

GENERAL JOURNAL

	DATE	DESCRIPTION	POST. REF.	DEBIT	CREDIT	
1						1
2						2
3						3
4						4
5						5
6						6
7						7
8						8
9						9
10						10
11						11
12						12
13						13
14						14
15						15
16						16
17						17
18						18

Copyright © by Houghton Mifflin Company. All rights reserved.

PROBLEM 10-1A or 10-1B (continued)

GENERAL LEDGER

ACCOUNT _Accounts Receivable_   ACCOUNT NO. _113_

DATE		ITEM	POST. REF.	DEBIT	CREDIT	BALANCE DEBIT	BALANCE CREDIT
20—							
Nov.	1	Balance	✓			4 2 0 00	

ACCOUNT _Sales_   ACCOUNT NO. _411_

DATE		ITEM	POST. REF.	DEBIT	CREDIT	BALANCE DEBIT	BALANCE CREDIT
20—							
Nov.	1	Balance	✓				6 3 1 6 20

ACCOUNT _Sales Returns and Allowances_   ACCOUNT NO. _412_

DATE		ITEM	POST. REF.	DEBIT	CREDIT	BALANCE DEBIT	BALANCE CREDIT
20—							
Nov.	1	Balance	✓			2 7 6 00	

ACCOUNTS RECEIVABLE LEDGER

NAME _The Coiffure Center_

ADDRESS _____

DATE		ITEM	POST. REF.	DEBIT	CREDIT	BALANCE
20—						
Nov.	1		✓			4 2 0 00

Copyright © by Houghton Mifflin Company. All rights reserved.

PROBLEM 10-1A or 10-1B (concluded)

NAME *The Hair Stop*

ADDRESS

DATE		ITEM	POST. REF.	DEBIT	CREDIT	BALANCE

NAME *Lia's Hair Design*

ADDRESS

DATE		ITEM	POST. REF.	DEBIT	CREDIT	BALANCE

NAME *Shear Touch*

ADDRESS

DATE		ITEM	POST. REF.	DEBIT	CREDIT	BALANCE

Copyright © by Houghton Mifflin Company. All rights reserved.

PROBLEM 10-2A or 10-2B

SALES JOURNAL

	DATE	INV. NO.	CUSTOMER'S NAME	POST. REF.	ACCOUNTS RECEIVABLE DR., SALES CR.	
1						1
2						2
3						3
4						4
5						5
6						6
7						7
8						8
9						9
10						10
11						11
12						12
13						13
14						14

GENERAL JOURNAL

	DATE	DESCRIPTION	POST. REF.	DEBIT	CREDIT	
1						1
2						2
3						3
4						4
5						5
6						6
7						7
8						8
9						9
10						10
11						11
12						12
13						13
14						14
15						15
16						16
17						17
18						18
19						19

Copyright © by Houghton Mifflin Company. All rights reserved.

PROBLEM 10-2A or 10-2B (continued)

GENERAL LEDGER

ACCOUNT _Accounts Receivable_   ACCOUNT NO. **113**

DATE		ITEM	POST. REF.	DEBIT	CREDIT	BALANCE	
						DEBIT	CREDIT
20—							
Apr.	1	Balance	√			1 1 6 9 42	

ACCOUNT _Sales_   ACCOUNT NO. **411**

DATE		ITEM	POST. REF.	DEBIT	CREDIT	BALANCE	
						DEBIT	CREDIT
20—							
Apr.	1	Balance	√				11 2 6 0 44

ACCOUNT _Sales Returns and Allowances_   ACCOUNT NO. **412**

DATE		ITEM	POST. REF.	DEBIT	CREDIT	BALANCE	
						DEBIT	CREDIT
20—							
Apr.	1	Balance	√			3 9 6 42	

ACCOUNTS RECEIVABLE LEDGER

NAME _Benson Company_

ADDRESS _____

DATE		ITEM	POST. REF.	DEBIT	CREDIT	BALANCE
20—						
Apr.	1		√			9 2 7 76

Copyright © by Houghton Mifflin Company. All rights reserved.

PROBLEM 10-2A or 10-2B (continued)

NAME __*Danson Hardware*_____

ADDRESS _____

DATE		ITEM	POST. REF.	DEBIT	CREDIT	BALANCE

NAME __*L. R. Friedel Company*_____

ADDRESS _____

DATE		ITEM	POST. REF.	DEBIT	CREDIT	BALANCE

NAME __*Mayhew Company*_____

ADDRESS _____

DATE		ITEM	POST. REF.	DEBIT	CREDIT	BALANCE
20—						
Apr.	1		√			2 4 1 66

NAME __*Overall Company*_____

ADDRESS _____

DATE		ITEM	POST. REF.	DEBIT	CREDIT	BALANCE

Copyright © by Houghton Mifflin Company. All rights reserved.

PROBLEM 10-2A or 10-2B (concluded)

NAME _Porter Company_ _____

ADDRESS _____

DATE		ITEM	POST. REF.	DEBIT	CREDIT	BALANCE

Copyright © by Houghton Mifflin Company. All rights reserved.

NAME _____ DATE _____ CLASS _____

PROBLEM 10-3A or 10-3B

SALES JOURNAL

	DATE	INV. NO.	CUSTOMER'S NAME	POST. REF.	ACCOUNTS RECEIVABLE DEBIT	SALES TAX PAYABLE CREDIT	SALES CREDIT	
1								1
2								2
3								3
4								4
5								5
6								6
7								7
8								8
9								9
10								10
11								11
12								12
13								13
14								14
15								15

GENERAL JOURNAL

	DATE	DESCRIPTION	POST. REF.	DEBIT	CREDIT	
1						1
2						2
3						3
4						4
5						5
6						6
7						7
8						8
9						9
10						10
11						11
12						12
13						13
14						14
15						15
16						16
17						17

Copyright © by Houghton Mifflin Company. All rights reserved.

PROBLEM 10-3A or 10-3B (continued)

GENERAL LEDGER

ACCOUNT *Accounts Receivable* _____ ACCOUNT NO. ___113___

DATE		ITEM	POST. REF.	DEBIT	CREDIT	BALANCE	
						DEBIT	CREDIT
20—							
Mar.	1	Balance	√			1 3 8 22	

ACCOUNT *Sales Tax Payable* _____ ACCOUNT NO. ___214___

DATE		ITEM	POST. REF.	DEBIT	CREDIT	BALANCE	
						DEBIT	CREDIT
20—							
Mar.	1	Balance	√				7 2 84

ACCOUNT *Sales* _____ ACCOUNT NO. ___411___

DATE		ITEM	POST. REF.	DEBIT	CREDIT	BALANCE	
						DEBIT	CREDIT
20—							
Mar.	1	Balance	√				8 4 6 97

ACCOUNT *Sales Returns and Allowances* _____ ACCOUNT NO. ___412___

DATE		ITEM	POST. REF.	DEBIT	CREDIT	BALANCE	
						DEBIT	CREDIT

Copyright © by Houghton Mifflin Company. All rights reserved.

PROBLEM 10-3A or 10-3B (continued)

ACCOUNTS RECEIVABLE LEDGER

NAME _American Club_____

ADDRESS _____

DATE		ITEM	POST. REF.	DEBIT	CREDIT	BALANCE
20—						
Mar.	1		√			6 1 22

NAME _B. Carr_____

ADDRESS _____

DATE		ITEM	POST. REF.	DEBIT	CREDIT	BALANCE

NAME _R. Droy_____

ADDRESS _____

DATE		ITEM	POST. REF.	DEBIT	CREDIT	BALANCE

NAME _C. Milo_____

ADDRESS _____

DATE		ITEM	POST. REF.	DEBIT	CREDIT	BALANCE
20—						
Mar.	1		√			1 9 50

Copyright © by Houghton Mifflin Company. All rights reserved.

PROBLEM 10-3A or 10-3B (concluded)

NAME _Piedmont Savings and Loan Association_ _____

ADDRESS _____

DATE		ITEM	POST. REF.	DEBIT	CREDIT	BALANCE
20—						
Mar.	1		✓			5 7 50

NAME _Troy Funeral Home_ _____

ADDRESS _____

DATE		ITEM	POST. REF.	DEBIT	CREDIT	BALANCE

_____

_____

Copyright © by Houghton Mifflin Company. All rights reserved.

PROBLEM 10-4A or 10-4B

GENERAL JOURNAL

PAGE _____ 33

	DATE		DESCRIPTION	POST. REF.	DEBIT	CREDIT	
1							1
2							2
3							3
4							4
5							5

GENERAL LEDGER

ACCOUNT __Accounts Receivable__ ACCOUNT NO. __113__

DATE		ITEM	POST. REF.	DEBIT	CREDIT	BALANCE DEBIT	BALANCE CREDIT
20—							
Dec.	1	Balance	✓			779 00	

ACCOUNT __Sales__ ACCOUNT NO. __411__

DATE		ITEM	POST. REF.	DEBIT	CREDIT	BALANCE DEBIT	BALANCE CREDIT
20—							
Dec.	1	Balance	✓				11316 00

ACCOUNTS RECEIVABLE LEDGER

NAME __C.T. Baker__

ADDRESS _____

DATE		ITEM	POST. REF.	DEBIT	CREDIT	BALANCE
20—						
Dec.	1		✓			215 00

Copyright © by Houghton Mifflin Company. All rights reserved.

PROBLEM 10-4A or 10-4B (continued)

NAME **R. A. Finch Company**

ADDRESS _____

DATE		ITEM	POST. REF.	DEBIT	CREDIT	BALANCE

NAME **Jason Company**

ADDRESS _____

DATE		ITEM	POST. REF.	DEBIT	CREDIT	BALANCE

NAME **Matthew's, Inc.**

ADDRESS _____

DATE		ITEM	POST. REF.	DEBIT	CREDIT	BALANCE
20—						
Dec.	1		√			3 7 2 00

NAME **Richard and Company**

ADDRESS _____

DATE		ITEM	POST. REF.	DEBIT	CREDIT	BALANCE

Copyright © by Houghton Mifflin Company. All rights reserved.

PROBLEM 10-4A or 10-4B (concluded)

NAME _Soro Athletic Supply_ _____

ADDRESS _____

DATE		ITEM	POST. REF.	DEBIT	CREDIT	BALANCE
20—						
Dec.	1		√			1 9 2 00

NAME _Travalina Company_ _____

ADDRESS _____

DATE		ITEM	POST. REF.	DEBIT	CREDIT	BALANCE

Copyright © by Houghton Mifflin Company. All rights reserved.

11 | The Purchases Journal

PERFORMANCE OBJECTIVES

1. Journalize transactions in a three-column purchases journal.
2. Post from a three-column purchases journal to an accounts payable ledger and a general ledger.
3. Journalize transactions involving purchases returns and allowances in a general journal.
4. Prepare a schedule of accounts payable.
5. Journalize transactions in a multicolumn purchases journal.
6. Post from a multicolumn purchases journal to an accounts payable ledger and a general ledger.
7. Post directly from purchase invoices to an accounts payable ledger and journalize and post a summarizing entry in the general journal.

KEY TERMS

Accounts payable ledger
Credit memorandum
Crossfooting
FOB destination
FOB shipping point
Internal control

Invoice
Purchase order
Purchase requisition
Purchases discount
Purchases journal

STUDY GUIDE QUESTIONS

PART 1   True/False

For each of the following statements, circle T if the statement is true and F if the statement is false:

T   F   1. The purchase requisition is sent to the supplier.

T   F   2. The Purchases account is used to record the buying of merchandise only.

T   F   3. Increases in the Purchases Returns and Allowances account are recorded on the debit side.

T   F   4. If the freight charges are FOB shipping point, the buyer pays the transportation charges.

T   F   5. Posting from a multicolumn purchases journal to an accounts payable ledger is done at the end of the month.

T   F   6. The purchases journal is used for the buying of merchandise for cash and on account.

T   F   7. When you post directly from the purchases invoice, you eliminate the accounts payable ledger.

T   F   8. The purchases journal contains an Accounts Payable Credit column, a Freight In Debit column, and a Purchases Debit column.

Copyright © by Houghton Mifflin Company. All rights reserved.

T F 9. Check marks in the Post. Ref. column of the purchases journal indicate that the amounts in the Accounts Payable column have been posted to the accounts payable ledger.

T F 10. If the transportation terms are FOB destination, the cost of the freight charge is included in the selling price.

PART 2 Completion—Language of Business

Complete each of the following statements by writing the appropriate word(s) in the spaces provided:

1. The form sent to the supplier of merchandise is called a(n) _____ .
2. When the buyer pays the transportation charges on incoming merchandise, the terms are called _____ .
3. Plans and procedures built into the accounting system to promote efficiency and prevent fraud and waste are called _____ .
4. Proving that total debits equal total credits in a multicolumn purchases journal is called _____ .
5. From the buyer's viewpoint, the form prepared by the seller listing the items shipped, their costs, and the mode of shipment is called a(n) _____ .
6. A document sent by the seller to the buyer, indicating that the Accounts Receivable account is being reduced on the seller's books, is known as a(n) _____ .
7. A transportation arrangement in which the seller retains title to the goods in transit is called _____ .

DEMONSTRATION PROBLEM

The following transactions were completed by Brownfield Company. The company is located in San Diego, California.

Aug. 3 Bought merchandise on account from Keller Company, invoice no. 1998, $5,544; terms 2/10, n/30; dated August 1; FOB Los Angeles, freight prepaid and added to the invoice, $554 (total $6,098).

10 Bought supplies on account from Nichols Company, invoice no. A1120, $572; terms net 30 days; dated August 10; FOB San Diego.

12 Received credit memo no. 170 from Keller Company, $640, for merchandise returned.

15 Bought merchandise on account from Lopez Company, invoice no. 3567C, $3,977; terms 1/10, n/30; dated August 12; FOB Reno; freight prepaid and added to the invoice, $380 (total $4,357).

17 Received credit memo no. 435 from Nichols Company, $52, for allowance on damaged supplies purchased August 10.

Instructions

1. Record the transactions in either the three-column purchases journal or the general journal, as appropriate.
2. Post the entries to the accounts payable ledger daily.
3. Post the entries in the general journal immediately after you make each entry.
4. Post the totals from the three-column purchases journal at the end of the month.
5. Prepare a schedule of accounts payable.
6. Compare the total of the schedule of accounts payable with the balance of the controlling account.

Copyright © by Houghton Mifflin Company. All rights reserved.

SOLUTION

PURCHASES JOURNAL

DATE		SUPPLIER'S NAME	INV. NO.	INV. DATE	TERMS	POST. REF.	ACCOUNTS PAYABLE CREDIT	FREIGHT IN DEBIT	PURCHASES DEBIT
20—									
Aug.	3	Keller Company	1998	8/1	2/10, n/30	✓	6 0 9 8 00	5 5 4 00	5 5 4 4 00
	15	Lopez Company	3567C	8/12	1/10, n/30	✓	4 3 5 7 00	3 8 0 00	3 9 7 7 00
	31						10 4 5 5 00	9 3 4 00	9 5 2 1 00
							(2 2 1)	(5 1 4)	(5 1 1)

GENERAL JOURNAL

DATE		DESCRIPTION	POST. REF.	DEBIT	CREDIT
20—					
Aug.	10	Supplies	115	5 7 2 00	
		Accounts Payable, Nichols Company	221/✓		5 7 2 00
		Bought supplies on account, invoice			
		no. A1120, dated August 10, net			
		30 days.			
	12	Accounts Payable, Keller Company	221/✓	6 4 0 00	
		Purchases Returns and Allowances	512		6 4 0 00
		Credit memo no. 170 for merchandise			
		returned.			
	17	Accounts Payable, Nichols Company	221/✓	5 2 00	
		Supplies	115		5 2 00
		Credit memo no. 435 for allowance			
		on damaged supplies.			

GENERAL LEDGER

ACCOUNT Supplies   ACCOUNT NO. 115

DATE		ITEM	POST. REF.	DEBIT	CREDIT	BALANCE DEBIT	BALANCE CREDIT
20—							
Aug.	1	Balance	✓			5 7 9 0 00	
	10		J105	5 7 2 00		6 3 6 2 00	
	17		J105		5 2 00	6 3 1 0 00	

Copyright © by Houghton Mifflin Company. All rights reserved.

ACCOUNT _Accounts Payable_ _____ ACCOUNT NO. 221

DATE		ITEM	POST. REF.	DEBIT	CREDIT	BALANCE DEBIT	BALANCE CREDIT
20—							
Aug.	1	Balance	√				3 7 8 0 00
	10		J105		5 7 2 00		4 3 5 2 00
	12		J105	6 4 0 00			3 7 1 2 00
	17		J105	5 2 00			3 6 6 0 00
	31		P81		10 4 5 5 00		14 1 1 5 00

ACCOUNT _Purchases_ _____ ACCOUNT NO. 511

DATE		ITEM	POST. REF.	DEBIT	CREDIT	BALANCE DEBIT	BALANCE CREDIT
20—							
Aug.	1	Balance	√			73 1 8 5 00	
	31		P81	9 5 2 1 00		82 7 0 6 00	

ACCOUNT _Purchases Returns and Allowances_ _____ ACCOUNT NO. 512

DATE		ITEM	POST. REF.	DEBIT	CREDIT	BALANCE DEBIT	BALANCE CREDIT
20—							
Aug.	1	Balance	√				2 0 3 5 00
	12		J105		6 4 0 00		2 6 7 5 00

ACCOUNT _Freight In_ _____ ACCOUNT NO. 514

DATE		ITEM	POST. REF.	DEBIT	CREDIT	BALANCE DEBIT	BALANCE CREDIT
20—							
Aug.	1	Balance	√			7 4 5 9 00	
	31		P81	9 3 4 00		8 3 9 3 00	

ACCOUNTS PAYABLE LEDGER

NAME _Keller Company_

ADDRESS _679 Gurnard Ave._
Des Moines, IA 50371

DATE		ITEM	POST. REF.	DEBIT	CREDIT	BALANCE
20—						
Aug.	1	Balance	√			1 9 7 0 00
	3		P81		6 0 9 8 00	8 0 6 8 00
	12		J105	6 4 0 00		7 4 2 8 00

252

Copyright © by Houghton Mifflin Company. All rights reserved.

NAME   *Lopez Company*

ADDRESS   *482 Jeffries Way*
             Des Moines, IA 50372

DATE		ITEM	POST. REF.	DEBIT	CREDIT	BALANCE
20—						
Aug.	1	Balance	✓			1 8 1 0 00
	15		P81		4 3 5 7 00	6 1 6 7 00

NAME   *Nichols Company*

ADDRESS   *3864 Silva Ave.*
             Des Moines, IA 50372

DATE		ITEM	POST. REF.	DEBIT	CREDIT	BALANCE
20—						
Aug.	10		J105		5 7 2 00	5 7 2 00
	17		J105	5 2 00		5 2 0 00

Brownfield Company
Schedule of Accounts Payable
August 31, 20—

Keller Company	$ 7 4 2 8 00
Lopez Company	6 1 6 7 00
Nichols Company	5 2 0 00
Total Accounts Payable	$14 1 1 5 00

Copyright © by Houghton Mifflin Company. All rights reserved.

NAME _____ DATE _____ CLASS _____

PROBLEM 11-1A or 11-1B

PURCHASES JOURNAL

	DATE	SUPPLIER'S NAME	INV. NO.	INV. DATE	TERMS	POST. REF.	ACCOUNTS PAYABLE CREDIT	FREIGHT IN DEBIT	PURCHASES DEBIT	
1										1
2										2
3										3
4										4
5										5
6										6
7										7
8										8
9										9
10										10
11										11
12										12

GENERAL LEDGER

ACCOUNT _Accounts Payable_ _____ ACCOUNT NO. 221

DATE	ITEM	POST. REF.	DEBIT	CREDIT	BALANCE	
					DEBIT	CREDIT

ACCOUNT _Purchases_ _____ ACCOUNT NO. 511

DATE	ITEM	POST. REF.	DEBIT	CREDIT	BALANCE	
					DEBIT	CREDIT

ACCOUNT _Freight In_ _____ ACCOUNT NO. 514

DATE	ITEM	POST. REF.	DEBIT	CREDIT	BALANCE	
					DEBIT	CREDIT

Copyright © by Houghton Mifflin Company. All rights reserved.

PROBLEM 11-1A or 11-1B (continued)

ACCOUNTS PAYABLE LEDGER

NAME _____

ADDRESS _____

_____

	DATE	ITEM	POST. REF.	DEBIT	CREDIT	BALANCE

NAME _____

ADDRESS _____

_____

	DATE	ITEM	POST. REF.	DEBIT	CREDIT	BALANCE

NAME _____

ADDRESS _____

_____

	DATE	ITEM	POST. REF.	DEBIT	CREDIT	BALANCE

NAME _____

ADDRESS _____

_____

	DATE	ITEM	POST. REF.	DEBIT	CREDIT	BALANCE

Copyright © by Houghton Mifflin Company. All rights reserved.

PROBLEM II-IA or II-IB (concluded)

NAME _____

ADDRESS _____

_____

DATE		ITEM	POST. REF.	DEBIT	CREDIT	BALANCE	

NAME _____

ADDRESS _____

_____

DATE		ITEM	POST. REF.	DEBIT	CREDIT	BALANCE	

_____

_____

Copyright © by Houghton Mifflin Company. All rights reserved.

PROBLEM 11-2A

PURCHASES JOURNAL

PAGE _____

DATE	SUPPLIER'S NAME	INVOICE NUMBER	INVOICE DATE	TERMS	POST. REF.	ACCOUNTS PAYABLE CREDIT	PURCHASES DEBIT	FREIGHT IN DEBIT	STORE SUPPLIES DEBIT	OFFICE SUPPLIES DEBIT	OTHER ACCOUNTS DEBIT		
											ACCOUNT	POST. REF.	AMOUNT

Debit Totals

Purchases $ _____

Freight In

Store Supplies

Office Supplies $ _____

Accounts Payable

Credit Total

$ _____

Copyright © by Houghton Mifflin Company. All rights reserved.

PROBLEM 11-2A (continued)

GENERAL JOURNAL

PAGE _____

	DATE		DESCRIPTION	POST. REF.	DEBIT	CREDIT	
1							1
2							2
3							3
4							4
5							5
6							6
7							7
8							8
9							9
10							10
11							11
12							12
13							13
14							14
15							15
16							16
17							17
18							18
19							19
20							20
21							21
22							22
23							23
24							24
25							25
26							26
27							27
28							28
29							29
30							30
31							31
32							32
33							33
34							34
35							35
36							36
37							37

Copyright © by Houghton Mifflin Company. All rights reserved.

PROBLEM 11-2A (continued)

GENERAL LEDGER

ACCOUNT _____ ACCOUNT NO. _____

DATE	ITEM	POST. REF.	DEBIT	CREDIT	BALANCE	
					DEBIT	CREDIT

ACCOUNT _____ ACCOUNT NO. _____

DATE	ITEM	POST. REF.	DEBIT	CREDIT	BALANCE	
					DEBIT	CREDIT

ACCOUNT _____ ACCOUNT NO. _____

DATE	ITEM	POST. REF.	DEBIT	CREDIT	BALANCE	
					DEBIT	CREDIT

ACCOUNT _____ ACCOUNT NO. _____

DATE	ITEM	POST. REF.	DEBIT	CREDIT	BALANCE	
					DEBIT	CREDIT

Copyright © by Houghton Mifflin Company. All rights reserved.

PROBLEM II-2A (continued)

ACCOUNT _____ ACCOUNT NO. _____

DATE		ITEM	POST. REF.	DEBIT	CREDIT	BALANCE	
						DEBIT	CREDIT

ACCOUNT _____ ACCOUNT NO. _____

DATE		ITEM	POST. REF.	DEBIT	CREDIT	BALANCE	
						DEBIT	CREDIT

ACCOUNTS PAYABLE LEDGER

NAME _____

ADDRESS _____

DATE		ITEM	POST. REF.	DEBIT	CREDIT	BALANCE

NAME _____

ADDRESS _____

DATE		ITEM	POST. REF.	DEBIT	CREDIT	BALANCE

Copyright © by Houghton Mifflin Company. All rights reserved.

PROBLEM 11-2A (continued)

NAME _____

ADDRESS _____

_____

	DATE	ITEM	POST. REF.	DEBIT	CREDIT	BALANCE

NAME _____

ADDRESS _____

_____

	DATE	ITEM	POST. REF.	DEBIT	CREDIT	BALANCE

NAME _____

ADDRESS _____

_____

	DATE	ITEM	POST. REF.	DEBIT	CREDIT	BALANCE

NAME _____

ADDRESS _____

_____

	DATE	ITEM	POST. REF.	DEBIT	CREDIT	BALANCE

Copyright © by Houghton Mifflin Company. All rights reserved.

PROBLEM 11-2A (concluded)

NAME _____

ADDRESS _____

_____

DATE		ITEM	POST. REF.	DEBIT				CREDIT				BALANCE			

Copyright © by Houghton Mifflin Company. All rights reserved.

PROBLEM 11-2B

PURCHASES JOURNAL

DATE	SUPPLIER'S NAME	INVOICE NUMBER	INVOICE DATE	TERMS	POST. REF.	ACCOUNTS PAYABLE CREDIT	PURCHASES DEBIT	FREIGHT IN DEBIT	STORE SUPPLIES DEBIT	OFFICE SUPPLIES DEBIT	OTHER ACCOUNTS DEBIT		
											ACCOUNT	POST. REF.	AMOUNT

Debit Totals
$

Purchases
Freight In
Store Supplies _____
Office Supplies =======
Equipment

$
=======

Accounts Payable

Credit Total
$ _____
=======

Copyright © by Houghton Mifflin Company. All rights reserved.

PROBLEM 11-2B (continued)

GENERAL JOURNAL

PAGE _____

	DATE		DESCRIPTION	POST. REF.	DEBIT	CREDIT	
1							1
2							2
3							3
4							4
5							5
6							6
7							7
8							8
9							9
10							10
11							11
12							12
13							13
14							14
15							15
16							16
17							17
18							18
19							19
20							20
21							21
22							22
23							23
24							24
25							25
26							26
27							27
28							28
29							29
30							30
31							31
32							32
33							33
34							34
35							35
36							36
37							37

Copyright © by Houghton Mifflin Company. All rights reserved.

NAME _____ DATE _____ CLASS _____

PROBLEM 11-2B (continued)

GENERAL LEDGER

ACCOUNT _____ ACCOUNT NO. _____

DATE	ITEM	POST. REF.	DEBIT	CREDIT	BALANCE	
					DEBIT	CREDIT

ACCOUNT _____ ACCOUNT NO. _____

DATE	ITEM	POST. REF.	DEBIT	CREDIT	BALANCE	
					DEBIT	CREDIT

ACCOUNT _____ ACCOUNT NO. _____

DATE	ITEM	POST. REF.	DEBIT	CREDIT	BALANCE	
					DEBIT	CREDIT

ACCOUNT _____ ACCOUNT NO. _____

DATE	ITEM	POST. REF.	DEBIT	CREDIT	BALANCE	
					DEBIT	CREDIT

Copyright © by Houghton Mifflin Company. All rights reserved.

NAME _____ DATE _____ CLASS _____

PROBLEM II-2B (continued)

ACCOUNT _____ ACCOUNT NO. _____

DATE	ITEM	POST. REF.	DEBIT	CREDIT	BALANCE	
					DEBIT	CREDIT

ACCOUNT _____ ACCOUNT NO. _____

DATE	ITEM	POST. REF.	DEBIT	CREDIT	BALANCE	
					DEBIT	CREDIT

ACCOUNT _____ ACCOUNT NO. _____

DATE	ITEM	POST. REF.	DEBIT	CREDIT	BALANCE	
					DEBIT	CREDIT

ACCOUNTS PAYABLE LEDGER

NAME _____

ADDRESS _____

DATE	ITEM	POST. REF.	DEBIT	CREDIT	BALANCE

Copyright © by Houghton Mifflin Company. All rights reserved.

PROBLEM 11-2B (continued)

NAME _____

ADDRESS _____

DATE	ITEM	POST. REF.	DEBIT	CREDIT	BALANCE

NAME _____

ADDRESS _____

DATE	ITEM	POST. REF.	DEBIT	CREDIT	BALANCE

NAME _____

ADDRESS _____

DATE	ITEM	POST. REF.	DEBIT	CREDIT	BALANCE

NAME _____

ADDRESS _____

DATE	ITEM	POST. REF.	DEBIT	CREDIT	BALANCE

Copyright © by Houghton Mifflin Company. All rights reserved.

PROBLEM 11-2B (continued)

NAME _____

ADDRESS _____

DATE	ITEM	POST. REF.	DEBIT	CREDIT	BALANCE

NAME _____

ADDRESS _____

DATE	ITEM	POST. REF.	DEBIT	CREDIT	BALANCE

Copyright © by Houghton Mifflin Company. All rights reserved.

PROBLEM 11-2B (concluded)

Copyright © by Houghton Mifflin Company. All rights reserved.

NAME _____ DATE _____ CLASS _____

PROBLEM 11-3A or 11-3B

GENERAL JOURNAL

	DATE		DESCRIPTION	POST. REF.	DEBIT	CREDIT	
1							1
2							2
3							3
4							4
5							5
6							6
7							7
8							8
9							9
10							10
11							11
12							12
13							13
14							14
15							15
16							16
17							17
18							18
19							19
20							20
21							21
22							22
23							23
24							24
25							25
26							26
27							27
28							28
29							29
30							30
31							31
32							32
33							33
34							34
35							35
36							36
37							37

Copyright © by Houghton Mifflin Company. All rights reserved.

PROBLEM 11-4A or 11-4B

SALES JOURNAL

PAGE ___ 24

	DATE	INV. NO.	CUSTOMER'S NAME	POST. REF.	ACCOUNTS RECEIVABLE DR., SALES CR.	
1						1
2						2
3						3
4						4
5						5
6						6
7						7
8						8
9						9
10						10
11						11
12						12
13						13
14						14
15						15

PURCHASES JOURNAL

PAGE ___ 18

	DATE	SUPPLIER'S NAME	INV. NO.	INV. DATE	TERMS	POST. REF.	ACCOUNTS PAYABLE CREDIT	FREIGHT IN DEBIT	PURCHASES DEBIT	
1										1
2										2
3										3
4										4
5										5
6										6
7										7
8										8
9										9
10										10
11										11
12										12
13										13
14										14
15										15

Copyright © by Houghton Mifflin Company. All rights reserved.

PROBLEM II-4A or II-4B (continued)

GENERAL JOURNAL

	DATE		DESCRIPTION	POST. REF.	DEBIT	CREDIT	
1							1
2							2
3							3
4							4
5							5
6							6
7							7
8							8
9							9
10							10
11							11
12							12
13							13
14							14
15							15
16							16
17							17
18							18
19							19
20							20
21							21
22							22
23							23
24							24

Copyright © by Houghton Mifflin Company. All rights reserved.

PROBLEM II-4A or II-4B (continued)

GENERAL LEDGER

ACCOUNT **Accounts Receivable**   ACCOUNT NO. _113_

DATE	ITEM	POST. REF.	DEBIT	CREDIT	BALANCE DEBIT	BALANCE CREDIT

ACCOUNT **Office Supplies**   ACCOUNT NO. _115_

DATE	ITEM	POST. REF.	DEBIT	CREDIT	BALANCE DEBIT	BALANCE CREDIT
20—						
Apr. 1	Balance	√			2 2 0 00	

ACCOUNT **Accounts Payable**   ACCOUNT NO. _221_

DATE	ITEM	POST. REF.	DEBIT	CREDIT	BALANCE DEBIT	BALANCE CREDIT

ACCOUNT **Sales**   ACCOUNT NO. _411_

DATE	ITEM	POST. REF.	DEBIT	CREDIT	BALANCE DEBIT	BALANCE CREDIT
20—						
Apr. 1	Balance	√				11 0 0 0 00

Copyright © by Houghton Mifflin Company. All rights reserved.

PROBLEM 11-4A or 11-4B (continued)

ACCOUNT *Sales Returns and Allowances* — ACCOUNT NO. **412**

DATE		ITEM	POST. REF.	DEBIT	CREDIT	BALANCE	
						DEBIT	CREDIT
20—							
Apr.	1	Balance	√			4 1 0 00	

ACCOUNT *Purchases* — ACCOUNT NO. **511**

DATE		ITEM	POST. REF.	DEBIT	CREDIT	BALANCE	
						DEBIT	CREDIT
20—							
Apr.	1	Balance	√			9 6 0 0 00	

ACCOUNT *Purchases Returns and Allowances* — ACCOUNT NO. **512**

DATE		ITEM	POST. REF.	DEBIT	CREDIT	BALANCE	
						DEBIT	CREDIT
20—							
Apr.	1	Balance	√				6 0 00

ACCOUNT *Freight In* — ACCOUNT NO. **514**

DATE		ITEM	POST. REF.	DEBIT	CREDIT	BALANCE	
						DEBIT	CREDIT
20—							
Apr.	1	Balance	√			7 1 2 00	

Copyright © by Houghton Mifflin Company. All rights reserved.

PROBLEM II-4A or II-4B (continued)

ACCOUNTS RECEIVABLE LEDGER

NAME _____

ADDRESS _____

DATE		ITEM	POST. REF.	DEBIT	CREDIT	BALANCE

NAME _____

ADDRESS _____

DATE		ITEM	POST. REF.	DEBIT	CREDIT	BALANCE

NAME _____

ADDRESS _____

DATE		ITEM	POST. REF.	DEBIT	CREDIT	BALANCE

NAME _____

ADDRESS _____

DATE		ITEM	POST. REF.	DEBIT	CREDIT	BALANCE

Copyright © by Houghton Mifflin Company. All rights reserved.

PROBLEM II-4A or II-4B (continued)

ACCOUNTS PAYABLE LEDGER

NAME _____

ADDRESS _____

	DATE	ITEM	POST. REF.	DEBIT	CREDIT	BALANCE

NAME _____

ADDRESS _____

	DATE	ITEM	POST. REF.	DEBIT	CREDIT	BALANCE

NAME _____

ADDRESS _____

	DATE	ITEM	POST. REF.	DEBIT	CREDIT	BALANCE

NAME _____

ADDRESS _____

	DATE	ITEM	POST. REF.	DEBIT	CREDIT	BALANCE

Copyright © by Houghton Mifflin Company. All rights reserved.

PROBLEM II-4A or II-4B (concluded)

NAME _____

ADDRESS _____

_____

DATE		ITEM	POST. REF.	DEBIT	CREDIT	BALANCE

12 The Cash Receipts Journal and the Cash Payments Journal

PERFORMANCE OBJECTIVES

1. Journalize transactions for a retail merchandising business in a cash receipts journal.
2. Post from a cash receipts journal to a general ledger and an accounts receivable ledger.
3. Determine cash discounts according to credit terms, and record cash receipts from charge customers who are entitled to deduct the cash discount.
4. Journalize transactions in a cash payments journal for a service enterprise.
5. Post from a cash payments journal to a general ledger and an accounts payable ledger.
6. Journalize transactions involving cash discounts in a cash payments journal for a merchandising enterprise.
7. Journalize transactions in a check register.
8. Journalize transactions involving trade discounts.

KEY TERMS

Bank charge card
Cash discount
Cash payments journal
Cash receipts journal
Check register

Credit period
Notes Payable
Promissory note
Trade discount

STUDY GUIDE QUESTIONS

PART 1   True/False

For each of the following statements, circle T if the statement is true and F if the statement is false.

T F   1. The normal balance of the Sales Discount account is on the debit side.

T F   2. An investment of cash by the owner is always recorded in the general journal.

T F   3. In a cash receipts journal, the individual amounts in the Other Accounts credit column are posted at the end of the month.

T F   4. Entries in the Accounts Payable Debit column of a cash payments journal are posted daily to the accounts payable ledger.

T F   5. The Purchases Discount account is classified as a revenue account.

T F   6. Credit terms of 1/10, n/30 indicate that a discount of one-tenth may be deducted if the bill is paid in thirty days.

T F   7. The amount of the discount that the bank deducts for a credit card transaction is usually between 10 and 15 percent.

T F   8. The buyer records the purchases discount when payment is made.

T F   9. Trade discounts are not recorded on the books of either the buyer or the seller.

T F   10. A check register performs the same function as a cash payments journal.

Copyright © by Houghton Mifflin Company. All rights reserved.

PART 2 Completion—Language of Business

Complete each of the following statements by writing the appropriate word(s) in the spaces provided:

1. Large deductions from the list prices of merchandise are referred to as _____ .

2. The time the seller allows the buyer before full payment on a charge sale has to be made is called the _____ .

3. The _____ is the amount a customer may deduct for paying a bill within a specified period of time.

PART 3 Matching

For each numbered item, choose the appropriate journal and write the identifying letter.

_____ 1. Bought merchandise on account	S Sales journal
_____ 2. Sold merchandise for cash	P Purchases journal (3 columns)
_____ 3. Recorded supplies used	CR Cash receipts journal
_____ 4. Collected accounts receivable and allowed a cash discount	CP Cash payments journal
_____ 5. Bought store equipment on credit	J General journal
_____ 6. Recorded accrued wages	
_____ 7. Received credit memo for merchandise returned	
_____ 8. Paid freight bill on merchandise purchased	
_____ 9. Sold merchandise on account	
_____ 10. Paid state unemployment tax	

PART 4 Cash Receipts Journal

Label the money columns as Debit or Credit.

Other Accounts	Accounts Receivable	Sales	Sales Discount	Cash

Copyright © by Houghton Mifflin Company. All rights reserved.

DEMONSTRATION PROBLEM

Elegant Jewelry, a retail store, sells merchandise (1) for cash, (2) on charge accounts, and (3) on bank credit cards. The store uses a sales journal, a purchases journal, a cash receipts journal, a cash payments journal, and a general journal. The store engaged in the following selected transactions:

June 16 Sold merchandise on account to T. Morgan, sales ticket no. 1230, $9,757, plus $790.32 sales tax.

17 Sold merchandise paid by bank credit cards, $2,271, plus $183.95 sales tax. The bank charges 4 percent of the total sales plus sales tax.

18 Bought merchandise on account from Gem Central, invoice no. D109, dated June 16; $4,542; terms 1/10, n/30; FOB shipping point, freight prepaid and added to the invoice, $60 (total, $4,602).

19 Received credit memorandum no. 926 from Gem Central for merchandise return, $529.

22 Paid Gem Central, its invoice no. D109, Ck. No. 5901, $4,032.87. ($4,542 less $529 return and less 1 percent cash discount. Freight is not included in the amount to be discounted. $4,602 − $60 − $529 = $4,013; $4,013 × .01 = $40.13; $4,013 − $40.13 = $3,972.87; $3,972.87 + $60 freight = $4,032.87.)

24 Bought packaging supplies on account from The Box Company, its invoice no. 990, dated June 22; net 30 days; $459.

29 Paid rent for the month, Ck. No. 5902, $1,980.

30 Bought merchandise on account from Todd Company, its invoice no. 10002, dated June 29; list price $2,950, less 40 percent trade discount; terms 2/10, n/30; FOB shipping point.

30 Paid freight bill to Fast Freight, Ck. No. 5903, for merchandise received from Todd Company, $110.

30 Issued Ck. No. 5904 for $258.36 to customer L. O. Sherry, for merchandise returned, $239, plus $19.36 sales tax.

Instructions

1. Journalize the transactions.
2. Total and rule the journals.
3. Prove the equality of the debits and credits at the bottom of each journal.

Copyright © by Houghton Mifflin Company. All rights reserved.

SOLUTION

SALES JOURNAL

DATE		TKT. NO.	CUSTOMER'S NAME	POST. REF.	ACCOUNTS RECEIVABLE DEBIT	SALES TAX PAYABLE CREDIT	SALES CREDIT
20—							
June	16	1230	T. Morgan		10 5 4 7 32	7 9 0 32	9 7 5 7 00
	30				10 5 4 7 32	7 9 0 32	9 7 5 7 00

Debits	Credits
$10,547.32	$ 790.32
	9,757.00
$10,547.32	$10,547.32

PURCHASES JOURNAL

DATE		SUPPLIER'S NAME	INV. NO.	INV. DATE	TERMS	POST. REF.	ACCOUNTS PAYABLE CREDIT	FREIGHT IN DEBIT	PURCHASES DEBIT
20—									
June	18	Gem Central	D109	6/16	1/10, n/30		4 6 0 2 00	6 0 00	4 5 4 2 00
	30	Todd Company	10002	6/29	2/10, n/30		1 7 7 0 00		1 7 7 0 00
	30						6 3 7 2 00	6 0 00	6 3 1 2 00

Debits	Credits
$ 60.00	$6,372.00
6,312.00	
$6,372.00	$6,372.00

CASH RECEIPTS JOURNAL

DATE		ACCOUNT CREDITED	POST. REF.	OTHER ACCOUNTS CREDIT	ACCOUNTS RECEIVABLE CREDIT	SALES CREDIT	SALES TAX PAYABLE CREDIT	CREDIT CARD EXPENSE DEBIT	CASH DEBIT
20—									
June	17	Sales				2 2 7 1 00	1 8 3 95	9 8 20	2 3 5 6 75
	30					2 2 7 1 00	1 8 3 95	9 8 20	2 3 5 6 75

Debits	Credits
$ 98.20	$2,271.00
2,356.75	183.95
$2,454.95	$2,454.95

Copyright © by Houghton Mifflin Company. All rights reserved.

CASH PAYMENTS JOURNAL

DATE		CK. NO.	ACCOUNT DEBITED	POST. REF.	OTHER ACCOUNTS DEBIT	ACCOUNTS PAYABLE DEBIT	PURCHASES DISCOUNT CREDIT	CASH CREDIT
20—								
June	22	5901	Gem Central			4 0 7 3 00	4 0 13	4 0 3 2 87
	29	5902	Rent Expense		1 9 8 0 00			1 9 8 0 00
	30	5903	Freight In		1 1 0 00			1 1 0 00
	30	5904	Sales Returns and Allow.		2 3 9 00			2 5 8 36
			Sales Tax Payable		1 9 36			
	30				2 3 4 8 36	4 0 7 3 00	4 0 13	6 3 8 1 23

Debits	Credits
$2,348.36	$ 40.13
4,073.00	6,381.23
$6,421.36	$6,421.36

GENERAL JOURNAL

DATE		DESCRIPTION	POST. REF.	DEBIT	CREDIT
20—					
June	19	Accounts Payable, Gem Central		5 2 9 00	
		Purchases Returns and Allow.			5 2 9 00
		Credit memo no. 926.			
	24	Supplies		4 5 9 00	
		Accounts Payable, The Box Co.			4 5 9 00
		Packing supplies, invoice			
		no. 990, dated June 22,			
		net 30 days.			

Copyright © by Houghton Mifflin Company. All rights reserved.

PROBLEM 12-1A or 12-1B

PAGE _____

CASH RECEIPTS JOURNAL

DATE	ACCOUNT CREDITED	POST. REF.	OTHER ACCOUNTS CREDIT	ACCOUNTS RECEIVABLE CREDIT	SALES CREDIT	SALES TAX PAYABLE CREDIT	CREDIT CARD EXPENSE DEBIT	CASH DEBIT
1								
2								
3								
4								
5								
6								
7								
8								
9								
10								
11								
12								
13								
14								
15								
16								
17								
18								
19								
20								
21								

Equality of Debits and Credits

Debits	Credits
$	$
$	$

Copyright © by Houghton Mifflin Company. All rights reserved.

PROBLEM 12-1A or 12-1B (continued)

GENERAL LEDGER

ACCOUNT _Accounts Receivable_ _____ ACCOUNT NO. _113_

DATE	ITEM	POST. REF.	DEBIT	CREDIT	BALANCE	
					DEBIT	CREDIT

ACCOUNTS RECEIVABLE LEDGER

NAME _____

ADDRESS _____

_____

DATE	ITEM	POST. REF.	DEBIT	CREDIT	BALANCE

NAME _____

ADDRESS _____

_____

DATE	ITEM	POST. REF.	DEBIT	CREDIT	BALANCE

NAME _____

ADDRESS _____

_____

DATE	ITEM	POST. REF.	DEBIT	CREDIT	BALANCE

Copyright © by Houghton Mifflin Company. All rights reserved.

PROBLEM 12-1A or 12-1B (concluded)

NAME _____

ADDRESS _____

DATE		ITEM	POST. REF.	DEBIT	CREDIT	BALANCE

NAME _____

ADDRESS _____

DATE		ITEM	POST. REF.	DEBIT	CREDIT	BALANCE

NAME _____

ADDRESS _____

DATE		ITEM	POST. REF.	DEBIT	CREDIT	BALANCE

Copyright © by Houghton Mifflin Company. All rights reserved.

PROBLEM 12-2A or 12-2B

CASH RECEIPTS JOURNAL

PAGE ___ 71

DATE	ACCOUNT CREDITED	POST. REF.	OTHER ACCOUNTS CREDIT	ACCOUNTS RECEIVABLE CREDIT	SALES CREDIT	SALES DISCOUNT DEBIT	CASH DEBIT	
								1
								2
								3
								4
								5
								6
								7
								8
								9
								10
								11
								12
								13

Equality of Debits and Credits

Debits	Credits
$	$
$	$

SALES JOURNAL

PAGE ___ 43

DATE	INV. NO.	CUSTOMER'S NAME	POST. REF.	ACCOUNTS RECEIVABLE DR. SALES CR.	
					1
					2
					3
					4
					5
					6

286

Copyright © by Houghton Mifflin Company. All rights reserved.

PROBLEM 12-3A or 12-3B

CHECK REGISTER

DATE	CK. NO.	PAYEE	ACCOUNT DEBITED	POST. REF.	OTHER ACCOUNTS DEBIT	ACCOUNTS PAYABLE DEBIT	PURCHASES DISCOUNT CREDIT	FIRST NAT'L BANK CREDIT

Equality of Debits and Credits

Debits $ _____   Credits $ _____

$ _____ $ _____

Copyright © by Houghton Mifflin Company. All rights reserved.

PROBLEM 12-4A or 12-4B

SALES JOURNAL

PAGE _____

	DATE	INV. NO.	CUSTOMER'S NAME	POST. REF.	ACCOUNTS RECEIVABLE DR. SALES CR.	
1						1
2						2
3						3
4						4
5						5
6						6
7						7
8						8

PURCHASES JOURNAL

PAGE _____

	DATE	SUPPLIER'S NAME	INV. NO.	INV. DATE	TERMS	POST. REF.	ACCOUNTS PAYABLE CREDIT	FREIGHT IN DEBIT	PURCHASES DEBIT	
1										1
2										2
3										3
4										4
5										5
6										6

Equality of Debits and Credits

Debits	Credits
$	$
$	$

Copyright © by Houghton Mifflin Company. All rights reserved.

NAME _____ DATE _____ CLASS _____

PROBLEM 12-4A or 12-4B (continued)

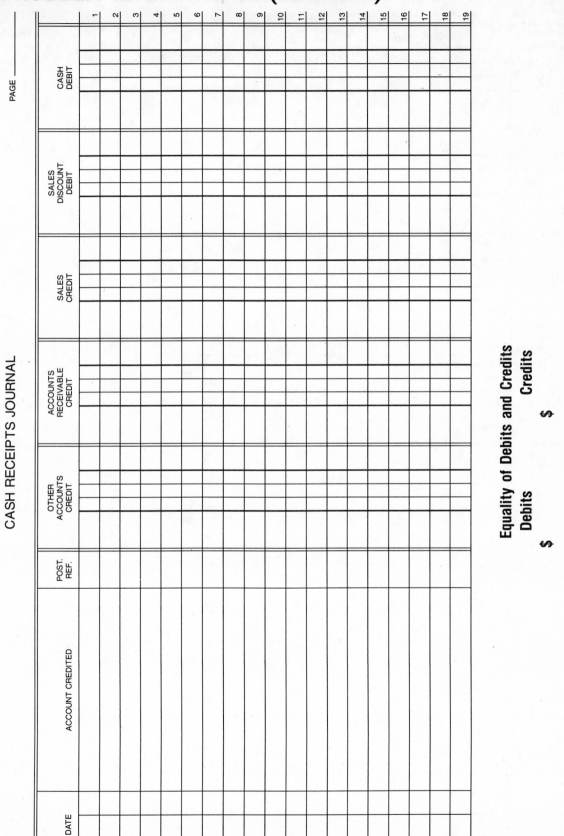

CASH RECEIPTS JOURNAL

PAGE _____

Equality of Debits and Credits

Debits   Credits

$ _____ $ _____

$ _____ $ _____

Copyright © by Houghton Mifflin Company. All rights reserved.

NAME _____ DATE _____ CLASS _____

PROBLEM 12-4A or 12-4B (continued)

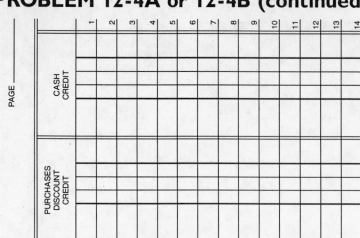

CASH PAYMENTS JOURNAL

PAGE _____

Equality of Debits and Credits

Debits	Credits
$	$
$	$

Copyright © by Houghton Mifflin Company. All rights reserved.

NAME _____ DATE _____ CLASS _____

PROBLEM 12-4A or 12-4B (continued)

GENERAL JOURNAL   PAGE _____

	DATE		DESCRIPTION	POST. REF.	DEBIT	CREDIT	
1							1
2							2
3							3
4							4
5							5
6							6
7							7
8							8
9							9
10							10
11							11
12							12
13							13
14							14
15							15
16							16
17							17
18							18
19							19
20							20
21							21
22							22
23							23
24							24
25							25
26							26
27							27
28							28
29							29
30							30
31							31
32							32
33							33
34							34
35							35
36							36
37							37

Copyright © by Houghton Mifflin Company. All rights reserved.

PROBLEM 12-4A or 12-4B (continued)

GENERAL LEDGER

ACCOUNT _Cash_ _____ ACCOUNT NO. _111_

DATE		ITEM	POST. REF.	DEBIT	CREDIT	BALANCE	
						DEBIT	CREDIT
20—							
Jan.	1	Balance	✓			8 5 4 0 00	

ACCOUNT _Accounts Receivable_ _____ ACCOUNT NO. _113_

DATE		ITEM	POST. REF.	DEBIT	CREDIT	BALANCE	
						DEBIT	CREDIT
20—							
Jan.	1	Balance	✓			1 9 5 0 00	

ACCOUNT _Merchandise Inventory_ _____ ACCOUNT NO. _114_

DATE		ITEM	POST. REF.	DEBIT	CREDIT	BALANCE	
						DEBIT	CREDIT
20—							
Jan.	1	Balance	✓			20 5 8 4 00	

292

Copyright © by Houghton Mifflin Company. All rights reserved.

PROBLEM 12-4A or 12-4B (continued)

ACCOUNT *Supplies*   ACCOUNT NO. **115**

DATE		ITEM	POST. REF.	DEBIT	CREDIT	BALANCE	
						DEBIT	CREDIT
20—							
Jan.	1	Balance	√			5 9 2 00	

ACCOUNT *Prepaid Insurance*   ACCOUNT NO. **116**

DATE		ITEM	POST. REF.	DEBIT	CREDIT	BALANCE	
						DEBIT	CREDIT
20—							
Jan.	1	Balance	√			3 9 0 00	

ACCOUNT *Equipment*   ACCOUNT NO. **121**

DATE		ITEM	POST. REF.	DEBIT	CREDIT	BALANCE	
						DEBIT	CREDIT
20—							
Jan.	1	Balance	√			3 6 4 4 00	

ACCOUNT *Salaries Payable*   ACCOUNT NO. **215**

DATE		ITEM	POST. REF.	DEBIT	CREDIT	BALANCE	
						DEBIT	CREDIT

Copyright © by Houghton Mifflin Company. All rights reserved.

PROBLEM 12-4A or 12-4B (continued)

ACCOUNT *Employees' Federal Income Tax Payable*   ACCOUNT NO. *216*

DATE	ITEM	POST. REF.	DEBIT	CREDIT	BALANCE	
					DEBIT	CREDIT

ACCOUNT *FICA Tax Payable*   ACCOUNT NO. *217*

DATE	ITEM	POST. REF.	DEBIT	CREDIT	BALANCE	
					DEBIT	CREDIT

ACCOUNT *State Unemployment Tax Payable*   ACCOUNT NO. *218*

DATE	ITEM	POST. REF.	DEBIT	CREDIT	BALANCE	
					DEBIT	CREDIT

ACCOUNT *Federal Unemployment Tax Payable*   ACCOUNT NO. *219*

DATE	ITEM	POST. REF.	DEBIT	CREDIT	BALANCE	
					DEBIT	CREDIT

Copyright © by Houghton Mifflin Company. All rights reserved.

PROBLEM 12-4A or 12-4B (continued)

ACCOUNT *Accounts Payable*   ACCOUNT NO. **221**

DATE		ITEM	POST. REF.	DEBIT	CREDIT	BALANCE DEBIT	BALANCE CREDIT
20—							
Jan.	1	Balance	✓				7 0 0 00

ACCOUNT _____ *, Capital*   ACCOUNT NO. **311**

DATE		ITEM	POST. REF.	DEBIT	CREDIT	BALANCE DEBIT	BALANCE CREDIT
20—							
Jan.	1	Balance	✓				35 0 0 0 00

ACCOUNT _____ *, Drawing*   ACCOUNT NO. **312**

DATE		ITEM	POST. REF.	DEBIT	CREDIT	BALANCE DEBIT	BALANCE CREDIT

ACCOUNT *Sales*   ACCOUNT NO. **411**

DATE		ITEM	POST. REF.	DEBIT	CREDIT	BALANCE DEBIT	BALANCE CREDIT

Copyright © by Houghton Mifflin Company. All rights reserved.

PROBLEM 12-4A or 12-4B (continued)

ACCOUNT _*Sales Returns and Allowances*_ _____ ACCOUNT NO. _412_

DATE	ITEM	POST. REF.	DEBIT	CREDIT	BALANCE	
					DEBIT	CREDIT

ACCOUNT _*Sales Discount*_ _____ ACCOUNT NO. _413_

DATE	ITEM	POST. REF.	DEBIT	CREDIT	BALANCE	
					DEBIT	CREDIT

ACCOUNT _*Purchases*_ _____ ACCOUNT NO. _511_

DATE	ITEM	POST. REF.	DEBIT	CREDIT	BALANCE	
					DEBIT	CREDIT

ACCOUNT _*Purchases Returns and Allowances*_ _____ ACCOUNT NO. _512_

DATE	ITEM	POST. REF.	DEBIT	CREDIT	BALANCE	
					DEBIT	CREDIT

Copyright © by Houghton Mifflin Company. All rights reserved.

PROBLEM 12-4A or 12-4B (continued)

ACCOUNT *Purchases Discount* _____ ACCOUNT NO. _____ 513 _____

DATE	ITEM	POST. REF.	DEBIT	CREDIT	BALANCE	
					DEBIT	CREDIT

ACCOUNT *Freight In* _____ ACCOUNT NO. _____ 514 _____

DATE	ITEM	POST. REF.	DEBIT	CREDIT	BALANCE	
					DEBIT	CREDIT

ACCOUNT *Salary Expense* _____ ACCOUNT NO. _____ 621 _____

DATE	ITEM	POST. REF.	DEBIT	CREDIT	BALANCE	
					DEBIT	CREDIT

ACCOUNT *Payroll Tax Expense* _____ ACCOUNT NO. _____ 622 _____

DATE	ITEM	POST. REF.	DEBIT	CREDIT	BALANCE	
					DEBIT	CREDIT

ACCOUNT *Rent Expense* _____ ACCOUNT NO. _____ 627 _____

DATE	ITEM	POST. REF.	DEBIT	CREDIT	BALANCE	
					DEBIT	CREDIT

Copyright © by Houghton Mifflin Company. All rights reserved.

PROBLEM 12-4A or 12-4B (continued)

ACCOUNT *Miscellaneous Expense* _____ ACCOUNT NO. *631*

DATE	ITEM	POST. REF.	DEBIT	CREDIT	BALANCE	
					DEBIT	CREDIT

ACCOUNTS RECEIVABLE LEDGER

NAME *Byron Supply* _____

ADDRESS _____

DATE	ITEM	POST. REF.	DEBIT	CREDIT	BALANCE

NAME *Engle Company* _____

ADDRESS _____

DATE	ITEM	POST. REF.	DEBIT	CREDIT	BALANCE

NAME *L. Parks* _____

ADDRESS _____

DATE	ITEM	POST. REF.	DEBIT	CREDIT	BALANCE

Copyright © by Houghton Mifflin Company. All rights reserved.

PROBLEM 12-4A or 12-4B (continued)

NAME *Peters, Inc.*

ADDRESS _____

_____

DATE		ITEM	POST. REF.	DEBIT	CREDIT	BALANCE
20—						
Jan.	1	Balance	√			7 5 0 00

NAME *Van Appliance*

ADDRESS _____

_____

DATE		ITEM	POST. REF.	DEBIT	CREDIT	BALANCE
20—						
Jan.	1	Balance	√			1 2 0 0 00

Copyright © by Houghton Mifflin Company. All rights reserved.

PROBLEM 12-4A or 12-4B (continued)

ACCOUNTS PAYABLE LEDGER

NAME *Cross Products*

ADDRESS _____

DATE		ITEM	POST. REF.	DEBIT	CREDIT	BALANCE

NAME *Dobson Office Supply*

ADDRESS _____

DATE		ITEM	POST. REF.	DEBIT	CREDIT	BALANCE

NAME *Franklin Company*

ADDRESS _____

DATE		ITEM	POST. REF.	DEBIT	CREDIT	BALANCE
20—						
Jan.	1	Balance	✓			7 0 0 00

NAME *Vicks and Company*

ADDRESS _____

DATE		ITEM	POST. REF.	DEBIT	CREDIT	BALANCE

Copyright © by Houghton Mifflin Company. All rights reserved.

PROBLEM 12-4A or 12-4B (continued)

ACCOUNT NAME	DEBIT	CREDIT

Copyright © by Houghton Mifflin Company. All rights reserved.

PROBLEM 12-4A or 12-4B (concluded)

Copyright © by Houghton Mifflin Company. All rights reserved.

<table>
<tr><td>**13**</td><td># Worksheet and Adjusting Entries</td></tr>
</table>

PERFORMANCE OBJECTIVES

1. Prepare an adjustment for merchandise inventory under the periodic inventory system.
2. Prepare an adjustment for unearned revenue.
3. Record the adjustment data in a work sheet (including merchandise inventory, unearned revenue, supplies used, expired insurance, depreciation, and accrued wages or salaries).
4. Complete the work sheet.
5. Journalize the adjusting entries for a merchandising business under the periodic inventory system.
6. Journalize the adjusting entry for merchandise inventory under the perpetual inventory system.

KEY TERMS

Periodic inventory system
Perpetual inventory system
Physical inventory
Unearned revenue

STUDY GUIDE QUESTIONS

PART 1   True/False

For each of the following statements, circle T if the statement is true and F if the statement is false.

T F 1. An actual count of a stock of goods on hand is called a physical inventory.

T F 2. The first adjustment for Merchandise Inventory is to debit Merchandise Inventory for the amount of the beginning inventory.

T F 3. The value of the ending Merchandise Inventory appears in the Balance Sheet Credit column of the work sheet.

T F 4. The balance of Sales Discount appears in the Income Statement Credit column.

T F 5. Under the periodic inventory system, entries are recorded in the Merchandise Inventory account at the end of the fiscal period only.

T F 6. When a business receives cash for a product or service that is to be delivered in the future, the Unearned Revenue account is credited.

T F 7. The balance of the Unearned Revenue account appears in the Balance Sheet Credit column.

T F 8. In the Balance Sheet columns of the work sheet, Income Summary is shown as two figures.

T F 9. The balance of Purchases Discount appears in the Income Statement Credit column.

T F 10. If Income Summary has a debit of $80,000 and a credit of $70,000 in the Adjustments columns of the work sheet, these will be combined into a debit of $10,000 in the Income Statement Debit column.

Copyright © by Houghton Mifflin Company. All rights reserved.

PART 2 Identifying Work Sheet Columns

Below is a list of selected accounts. Using a check mark, identify the columns in which the balance of each of the accounts would appear.

Account Name	Income Statement		Balance Sheet	
	Debit	Credit	Debit	Credit
Example: **0.** Rent Income		✓		
1. Sales Discount				
2. C. Carr, Drawing				
3. Supplies Expense				
4. Sales				
5. Merchandise Inventory				
6. Purchases Returns and Allowances				
7. Income Summary				
8. C. Carr, Capital				
9. Accumulated Depreciation, Equipment				
10. Purchases				
11. Sales Returns and Allowances				
12. Purchases Discount				
13. Unearned Rent				
14. Supplies				
15. Salaries Payable				

Copyright © by Houghton Mifflin Company. All rights reserved.

DEMONSTRATION PROBLEM

Office Specialists sells and services copiers and fax machines. The trial balance as of December 31, the end of its fiscal year, is as follows:

Office Specialists
Trial Balance
December 31, 20—

ACCOUNT NAME	DEBIT	CREDIT
Cash	4 000 00	
Merchandise Inventory	151 000 00	
Supplies	2 000 00	
Prepaid Insurance	1 000 00	
Store Equipment	26 000 00	
Accumulated Depreciation, Store Equipment		12 500 00
Accounts Payable		50 000 00
Employees' Income Tax Payable		3 000 00
Payroll Taxes and Employees' Withholding Taxes		
Payable		1 500 00
Unearned Service Contracts		15 000 00
L. Griswald, Capital		44 100 00
L. Griswald, Drawing	60 000 00	
Sales		453 000 00
Service Contract Income		56 000 00
Purchases	280 000 00	
Purchases Discount		3 800 00
Freight In	3 900 00	
Salary Expense	80 000 00	
Payroll Tax Expense	8 000 00	
Rent Expense	20 000 00	
Miscellaneous Expense	3 000 00	
	638 900 00	638 900 00

The earnings from short-term contracts completed during the year have been recorded in Service Contract Income. Amounts received in advance for longer-term service contracts have been recorded in Unearned Service Contracts. To save space by reducing the number of accounts, we use the account called Payroll Taxes and Employees' Withholding Taxes Payable for the FICA and unemployment tax liabilities. Data for the adjustments are as follows:

a–b. Merchandise inventory at December 31, $139,500.
 c. Supplies inventory, $1,700.
 d. Insurance expired, $600.
 e. Salaries accrued, $2,000.
 f. Depreciation of store equipment, $5,200.
 g. Unearned service contract income now earned, $4,800.

Instructions

Complete the work sheet.

Copyright © by Houghton Mifflin Company. All rights reserved.

SOLUTION

	ACCOUNT NAME	TRIAL BALANCE									
		DEBIT					CREDIT				
1	Cash		4	0	0	0	00				
2	Merchandise Inventory	151	0	0	0	00					
3	Supplies		2	0	0	0	00				
4	Prepaid Insurance		1	0	0	0	00				
5	Store Equipment	26	0	0	0	00					
6	Accumulated Depreciation, Store Equipment							12	5	0	0	00
7	Accounts Payable							50	0	0	0	00
8	Employees' Income Tax Payable							3	0	0	0	00
9	Payroll Taxes and Employees' Withholding Taxes Payable							1	5	0	0	00
10	Unearned Service Contracts							15	0	0	0	00
11	L. Griswald, Capital							44	1	0	0	00
12	L. Griswald, Drawing	60	0	0	0	00					
13	Sales							453	0	0	0	00
14	Service Contract Income							56	0	0	0	00
15	Purchases	280	0	0	0	00					
16	Purchases Discount							3	8	0	0	00
17	Freight In		3	9	0	0	00					
18	Salary Expense	80	0	0	0	00					
19	Payroll Tax Expense		8	0	0	0	00					
20	Rent Expense	20	0	0	0	00					
21	Miscellaneous Expense		3	0	0	0	00					
22		638	9	0	0	00	638	9	0	0	00	
23	Income Summary											
24	Supplies Expense											
25	Insurance Expense											
26	Salaries Payable											
27	Depreciation Expense, Store Equipment											
28												
29	Net Income											
30												
31												

Copyright © by Houghton Mifflin Company. All rights reserved.

| | ADJUSTMENTS | | INCOME STATEMENT | | BALANCE SHEET | | |
	DEBIT	CREDIT	DEBIT	CREDIT	DEBIT	CREDIT	
					4 0 0 0 00		1
	(b)139 5 0 0 00	(a)151 0 0 0 00			139 5 0 0 00		2
		(c) 3 0 0 00			1 7 0 0 00		3
		(d) 6 0 0 00			4 0 0 00		4
					26 0 0 0 00		5
		(f) 5 2 0 0 00				17 7 0 0 00	6
						50 0 0 0 00	7
						3 0 0 0 00	8
						1 5 0 0 00	9
	(g) 4 8 0 0 00					10 2 0 0 00	10
						44 1 0 0 00	11
					60 0 0 0 00		12
				453 0 0 0 00			13
		(g)4 8 0 0 00		60 8 0 0 00			14
			280 0 0 0 00				15
				3 8 0 0 00			16
			3 9 0 0 00				17
	(e) 2 0 0 0 00		82 0 0 0 00				18
			8 0 0 0 00				19
			20 0 0 0 00				20
			3 0 0 0 00				21
							22
	(a)151 0 0 0 00	(b)139 5 0 0 00	151 0 0 0 00	139 5 0 0 00			23
	(c) 3 0 0 00		3 0 0 00				24
	(d) 6 0 0 00		6 0 0 00				25
		(e) 2 0 0 0 00				2 0 0 0 00	26
	(f) 5 2 0 0 00		5 2 0 0 00				27
	303 4 0 0 00	303 4 0 0 00	554 0 0 0 00	657 1 0 0 00	231 6 0 0 00	128 5 0 0 00	28
			103 1 0 0 00			103 1 0 0 00	29
			657 1 0 0 00	657 1 0 0 00	231 6 0 0 00	231 6 0 0 00	30
							31

Copyright © by Houghton Mifflin Company. All rights reserved.

PROBLEM 13-1A or 13-1B

	ACCOUNT NAME	TRIAL BALANCE	
		DEBIT	CREDIT
1			
2			
3			
4			
5			
6			
7			
8			
9			
10			
11			
12			
13			
14			
15			
16			
17			
18			
19			
20			
21			
22			
23			
24			
25			
26			
27			
28			
29			
30			
31			
32			
33			

Copyright © by Houghton Mifflin Company. All rights reserved.

NAME _____ DATE _____ CLASS _____

PROBLEM 13-1A or 13-1B (concluded)

	ADJUSTMENTS		INCOME STATEMENT		BALANCE SHEET		
	DEBIT	CREDIT	DEBIT	CREDIT	DEBIT	CREDIT	
							1
							2
							3
							4
							5
							6
							7
							8
							9
							10
							11
							12
							13
							14
							15
							16
							17
							18
							19
							20
							21
							22
							23
							24
							25
							26
							27
							28
							29
							30
							31
							32
							33

Copyright © by Houghton Mifflin Company. All rights reserved.

NAME _____ DATE _____ CLASS _____

PROBLEM 13-2A or 13-2B

_____

_____

_____

	ACCOUNT NAME	TRIAL BALANCE	
		DEBIT	CREDIT
1			
2			
3			
4			
5			
6			
7			
8			
9			
10			
11			
12			
13			
14			
15			
16			
17			
18			
19			
20			
21			
22			
23			
24			
25			
26			
27			
28			
29			
30			
31			
32			
33			

310

Copyright © by Houghton Mifflin Company. All rights reserved.

PROBLEM 13-2A or 13-2B (continued)

ADJUSTMENTS		INCOME STATEMENT		BALANCE SHEET		
DEBIT	CREDIT	DEBIT	CREDIT	DEBIT	CREDIT	
						1
						2
						3
						4
						5
						6
						7
						8
						9
						10
						11
						12
						13
						14
						15
						16
						17
						18
						19
						20
						21
						22
						23
						24
						25
						26
						27
						28
						29
						30
						31
						32
						33

Copyright © by Houghton Mifflin Company. All rights reserved.

PROBLEM 13-2A or 13-2B (concluded)

GENERAL JOURNAL   PAGE ___16___

	DATE		DESCRIPTION	POST. REF.	DEBIT	CREDIT	
1							1
2							2
3							3
4							4
5							5
6							6
7							7
8							8
9							9
10							10
11							11
12							12
13							13
14							14
15							15
16							16
17							17
18							18
19							19
20							20
21							21
22							22
23							23
24							24
25							25
26							26
27							27
28							28
29							29
30							30
31							31
32							32
33							33

Copyright © by Houghton Mifflin Company. All rights reserved.

NAME _____ DATE _____ CLASS _____

EXTRA FORM

GENERAL JOURNAL   PAGE _____

	DATE		DESCRIPTION	POST. REF.	DEBIT	CREDIT	
1							1
2							2
3							3
4							4
5							5
6							6
7							7
8							8
9							9
10							10
11							11
12							12
13							13
14							14
15							15
16							16
17							17
18							18
19							19
20							20
21							21
22							22
23							23
24							24
25							25
26							26
27							27
28							28
29							29
30							30
31							31
32							32
33							33
34							34
35							35

Copyright © by Houghton Mifflin Company. All rights reserved.

NAME _____ DATE _____ CLASS _____

PROBLEM 13-3A or 13-3B

	ACCOUNT NAME	TRIAL BALANCE	
		DEBIT	CREDIT
1			
2			
3			
4			
5			
6			
7			
8			
9			
10			
11			
12			
13			
14			
15			
16			
17			
18			
19			
20			
21			
22			
23			
24			
25			
26			
27			
28			
29			
30			
31			
32			
33			
34			
35			
36			
37			
38			

Copyright © by Houghton Mifflin Company. All rights reserved.

PROBLEM 13-3A or 13-3B (continued)

ADJUSTMENTS		INCOME STATEMENT		BALANCE SHEET		
DEBIT	CREDIT	DEBIT	CREDIT	DEBIT	CREDIT	
						1
						2
						3
						4
						5
						6
						7
						8
						9
						10
						11
						12
						13
						14
						15
						16
						17
						18
						19
						20
						21
						22
						23
						24
						25
						26
						27
						28
						29
						30
						31
						32
						33
						34
						35
						36
						37
						38

Copyright © by Houghton Mifflin Company. All rights reserved.

PROBLEM 13-3A or 13-3B (concluded)

GENERAL JOURNAL

	DATE	DESCRIPTION	POST. REF.	DEBIT	CREDIT	
1						1
2						2
3						3
4						4
5						5
6						6
7						7
8						8
9						9
10						10
11						11
12						12
13						13
14						14
15						15
16						16
17						17
18						18
19						19
20						20
21						21
22						22
23						23
24						24
25						25
26						26
27						27
28						28
29						29
30						30
31						31
32						32
33						33
34						34
35						35

Copyright © by Houghton Mifflin Company. All rights reserved.

PROBLEM 13-4A or 13-4B

1.

GENERAL JOURNAL

	DATE		DESCRIPTION	POST. REF.	DEBIT	CREDIT	
1							1
2							2
3							3
4							4
5							5
6							6
7							7
8							8
9							9
10							10
11							11
12							12
13							13
14							14
15							15
16							16
17							17
18							18
19							19
20							20
21							21
22							22
23							23
24							24
25							25
26							26

2. Net Income: $

Total revenue (including ending inventory) $

— Total expenses (including beginning inventory)   _____

Net income $_____

3. , Capital: $

Beginning capital $

Net income $

— Withdrawals   _____

Increase in capital   _____

Ending capital $_____

Copyright © by Houghton Mifflin Company. All rights reserved.

Financial Statements, Closing Entries, and Reversing Entries

PERFORMANCE OBJECTIVES

1. Prepare a classified income statement for a merchandising firm.
2. Prepare a classified balance sheet for any type of business.
3. Compute working capital and current ratio.
4. Journalize the closing entries for a merchandising firm.
5. Determine which adjusting entries can be reversed, and journalize the reversing entries.

KEY TERMS

Cost of Goods Sold
Current Assets
Current liabilities
Current ratio
Delivered Cost of Purchases
General Expenses
Gross Profit
Liquidity
Long-term Liabilities

Net Income or Net Profit
Net Purchases
Net Sales
Notes Receivable (current)
Plant and Equipment
Reversing entries
Selling Expenses
Temporary-equity accounts
Working capital

STUDY GUIDE QUESTIONS

PART 1   True/False

For each of the following statements, circle T if the statement is true and F if the statement is false.

T F   1. The cost of goods sold is obtained by subtracting the goods available for sale from the net sales.

T F   2. An increase in Sales Returns and Allowances represents an increase in gross profit.

T F   3. Gross Profit is equal to Net Sales minus Cost of Goods Sold.

T F   4. Insurance Expense is classified in the Other Expenses section of an income statement.

T F   5. Freight In is classified in the Operating Expenses section of an income statement.

T F   6. In the Current Liabilities section of a balance sheet, Accounts Payable precedes Notes Payable.

T F   7. An unearned revenue account is classified as a current liability.

T F   8. Reversing entries are required for all adjusting entries.

T F   9. In a balance sheet, Prepaid Insurance is classified in the Plant and Equipment section.

T F   10. An increase in Rent Expense results in a decrease in Gross Profit.

Copyright © by Houghton Mifflin Company. All rights reserved.

PART 2   Completion—Language of Business

Complete each of the following statements by writing the appropriate word(s) in the spaces provided:

1. Current Assets minus Current Liabilities equals _____ .
2. Net Sales minus Cost of Goods Sold is _____ .
3. Goods Available for Sale minus ending Merchandise Inventory is called _____
    _____ .
4. Gross Profit minus Operating Expenses is called _____ .
5. Gross Purchases minus Purchases Returns and Allowances minus Purchases Discount
    plus _____ equals Delivered Cost of Purchases.

PART 3   Financial Statement Classifications

Classify the following accounts according to the title of the financial statement and the statement classification. The first two accounts are provided as examples.

Account Name	Financial Statement	Classification
0. Wages Expense	Income Statement	Operating Expenses
0. Accounts Payable	Balance Sheet	Current Liabilities
1. Purchases		
2. Accounts Receivable		
3. Building		
4. Freight In		
5. Interest Expense		
6. Supplies		
7. Sales Discount		
8. Unearned Subscriptions		
9. Accumulated Depreciation, Equipment		
10. Purchases Returns and Allowances		

Copyright © by Houghton Mifflin Company. All rights reserved.

DEMONSTRATION PROBLEM

Ben's Outdoor Store has a fiscal year extending from January 1 through December 31. Its account balances after adjustments are presented below in random order. The beginning merchandise inventory amounts to $35,870. With regard to the outstanding mortgage, $2,000 is due within the next twelve months.

Notes Receivable	$ 7,000	Freight In	$ 7,040
Interest Income	5,362	Office Salary Expense	11,119
Building	45,400	Accounts Receivable	46,627
Accounts Payable	25,245	Store Supplies	1,094
Prepaid Insurance	1,090	Interest Expense	2,100
Insurance Expense	2,505	Cash	3,305
Accumulated Depreciation,		Depreciation Expense,	
Building	15,133	Office Equipment	1,775
Notes Payable	10,250	Purchases Discount	1,335
Sales	267,111	Accumulated Depreciation,	
Sales Salary Expense	60,377	Store Equipment	10,750
Rent Income	2,400	Salaries Payable	3,420
Store Equipment	21,500	C. P. Bennett, Drawing	60,000
Mortgage Payable (current portion		Office Equipment	8,875
is $2,000)	31,000	Taxes Expense	4,006
Land	10,000	Accumulated Depreciation,	
Sales Commission Expense	6,400	Office Equipment	4,438
Sales Discount	2,671	Miscellaneous General Expense	1,750
Merchandise Inventory,		Store Supplies Expense	1,918
Dec. 31, 20—	41,998	C. P. Bennett, Capital,	
Purchases	133,556	Jan. 1, 20—	110,980
Advertising Expense	5,342	Depreciation Expense, Building	1,297
Sales Returns and Allowances	3,149	Depreciation Expense,	
Purchases Returns and		Store Equipment	4,300
Allowances	2,642		

Copyright © by Houghton Mifflin Company. All rights reserved.

Instructions

1. Prepare a classified income statement and subdivide operating expenses.
2. Prepare a statement of owner's equity.
3. Prepare a balance sheet.
4. Determine the amount of working capital and the current ratio.

SOLUTION

1.

Ben's Outdoor Store

Income Statement

For Year Ended December 31, 20—

Revenue from Sales:				
Sales		$267 1 1 1 00		
Less: Sales Returns and Allowances	$ 3 1 4 9 00			
Sales Discount	2 6 7 1 00	5 8 2 0 00		
Net Sales			$261 2 9 1 00	
Cost of Goods Sold:				
Merchandise Inventory, January 1, 20—		$ 35 8 7 0 00		
Purchases	$133 5 5 6 00			
Less: Purchases Returns and				
Allowances $2,642.00				
Purchases Discount 1,335.00	3 9 7 7 00			
Net Purchases	$129 5 7 9 00			
Add Freight In	7 0 4 0 00			
Delivered Cost of Purchases		136 6 1 9 00		
Goods Available for Sale		$172 4 8 9 00		
Less Merchandise Inventory,				
December 31, 20—		41 9 9 8 00		
Cost of Goods Sold			130 4 9 1 00	
Gross Profit			$130 8 0 0 00	
Operating Expenses:				
Selling Expenses:				
Sales Salary Expense	$ 60 3 7 7 00			
Sales Commission Expense	6 4 0 0 00			
Advertising Expense	5 3 4 2 00			
Depreciation Expense, Store Equipment	4 3 0 0 00			
Store Supplies Expense	1 9 1 8 00			
Total Selling Expenses		$ 78 3 3 7 00		
General Expenses:				
Office Salary Expense	$ 11 1 1 9 00			
Taxes Expense	4 0 0 6 00			
Depreciation Expense, Building	1 2 9 7 00			
Depreciation Expense, Office Equipment	1 7 7 5 00			
Insurance Expense	2 5 0 5 00			
Miscellaneous General Expense	1 7 5 0 00			
Total General Expenses		22 4 5 2 00		
Total Operating Expenses			100 7 8 9 00	
Income from Operations			$ 30 0 1 1 00	
Other Income:				
Rent Income		$ 2 4 0 0 00		
Interest Income		5 3 6 2 00		
Total Other Income		$ 7 7 6 2 00		
Other Expenses:				
Interest Expense		2 1 0 0 00	5 6 6 2 00	
Net Income			$ 35 6 7 3 00	

Copyright © by Houghton Mifflin Company. All rights reserved.

2.

Ben's Outdoor Store
Statement of Owner's Equity
For Year Ended December 31, 20—

C. P. Bennett, Capital, January 1, 20—		$110 980 00
Net Income for the Year	$35 673 00	
Less Withdrawals for the Year	60 000 00	
Decrease in Capital		24 327 00
C. P. Bennett, Capital, December 31, 20—		$ 86 653 00

3.

Ben's Outdoor Store
Balance Sheet
December 31, 20—

Assets			
Current Assets:			
Cash		$ 3 305 00	
Notes Receivable		7 000 00	
Accounts Receivable		46 627 00	
Merchandise Inventory		41 998 00	
Store Supplies		1 094 00	
Prepaid Insurance		1 090 00	
Total Current Assets			$101 114 00
Plant and Equipment:			
Land		$10 000 00	
Building	$45 400 00		
Less Accumulated Depreciation	15 133 00	30 267 00	
Office Equipment	$ 8 875 00		
Less Accumulated Depreciation	4 438 00	4 437 00	
Store Equipment	$21 500 00		
Less Accumulated Depreciation	10 750 00	10 750 00	
Total Plant and Equipment			55 454 00
Total Assets			$156 568 00
Liabilities			
Current Liabilities:			
Mortgage Payable (current portion)		$ 2 000 00	
Accounts Payable		25 245 00	
Notes Payable		10 250 00	
Salaries Payable		3 420 00	
Total Current Liabilities			$40 915 00
Long-Term Liabilities:			
Mortgage Payable			29 000 00
Total Liabilities			$ 69 915 00
Owner's Equity			
C. P. Bennett, Capital			86 653 00
Total Liabilities and Owner's Equity			$156 568 00

4. Working Capital = Current Assets − Current Liabilities
= $101,114 − $40,915 = $60,199

$$\text{Current Ratio} = \frac{\text{Current Assets}}{\text{Current Liabilities}} = \frac{\$101,114}{\$40,915} = 2.47 : 1$$

Copyright © by Houghton Mifflin Company. All rights reserved.

NAME _____ DATE _____ CLASS _____

PROBLEM 14-1A or 14-1B

Copyright © by Houghton Mifflin Company. All rights reserved.

PROBLEM 14-1A or 14-1B (concluded)

GENERAL JOURNAL

	DATE		DESCRIPTION	POST. REF.	DEBIT	CREDIT	
1							1
2							2
3							3
4							4
5							5
6							6
7							7
8							8
9							9
10							10
11							11
12							12
13							13
14							14
15							15
16							16
17							17
18							18
19							19
20							20
21							21
22							22
23							23
24							24
25							25
26							26
27							27
28							28
29							29
30							30
31							31
32							32
33							33
34							34
35							35
36							36
37							37

Copyright © by Houghton Mifflin Company. All rights reserved.

PROBLEM 14-2A or 14-2B

Copyright © by Houghton Mifflin Company. All rights reserved.

PROBLEM 14-2A or 14-2B (continued)

Copyright © by Houghton Mifflin Company. All rights reserved.

PROBLEM 14-2A or 14-2B (concluded)

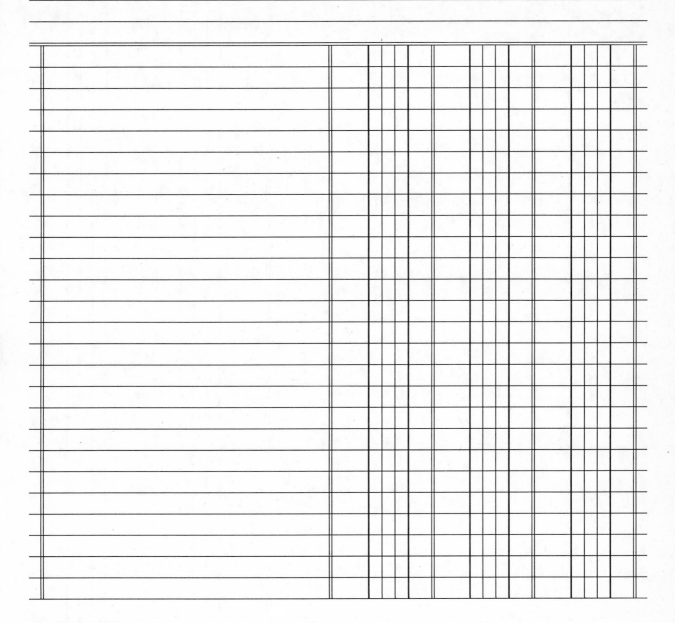

Working Capital = _____ $-$ _____

= $ _____ $-$ $ _____ = $ _____

Current Ratio = _____ = $\dfrac{\$ \text{\_\_\_\_\_}}{\$ \text{\_\_\_\_\_}}$ = ____ : ____

Copyright © by Houghton Mifflin Company. All rights reserved.

PROBLEM 14-3A or 14-3B

GENERAL JOURNAL

	DATE		DESCRIPTION	POST. REF.	DEBIT	CREDIT	
1							1
2							2
3							3
4							4
5							5
6							6
7							7
8							8
9							9
10							10
11							11
12							12
13							13
14							14
15							15
16							16
17							17
18							18
19							19
20							20
21							21
22							22
23							23
24							24
25							25
26							26
27							27
28							28
29							29
30							30
31							31
32							32
33							33
34							34
35							35
36							36
37							37

Copyright © by Houghton Mifflin Company. All rights reserved.

PROBLEM 14-3A or 14-3B (concluded)

GENERAL JOURNAL

PAGE _____ *82*

	DATE		DESCRIPTION	POST. REF.	DEBIT	CREDIT	
1							1
2							2
3							3
4							4
5							5
6							6
7							7
8							8
9							9
10							10
11							11
12							12
13							13
14							14
15							15
16							16
17							17
18							18
19							19
20							20
21							21
22							22
23							23
24							24
25							25
26							26
27							27
28							28
29							29
30							30
31							31
32							32
33							33
34							34
35							35
36							36
37							37

Copyright © by Houghton Mifflin Company. All rights reserved.

NAME _____ DATE _____ CLASS _____

PROBLEM 14-4A or 14-4B

_____

_____

_____

	ACCOUNT NAME	TRIAL BALANCE	
		DEBIT	CREDIT
1			
2			
3			
4			
5			
6			
7			
8			
9			
10			
11			
12			
13			
14			
15			
16			
17			
18			
19			
20			
21			
22			
23			
24			
25			
26			
27			
28			
29			
30			
31			
32			
33			

Copyright © by Houghton Mifflin Company. All rights reserved.

NAME _____ DATE _____ CLASS _____

PROBLEM 14-4A or 14-4B (continued)

| ADJUSTMENTS | | INCOME STATEMENT | | BALANCE SHEET | | |
DEBIT	CREDIT	DEBIT	CREDIT	DEBIT	CREDIT	
						1
						2
						3
						4
						5
						6
						7
						8
						9
						10
						11
						12
						13
						14
						15
						16
						17
						18
						19
						20
						21
						22
						23
						24
						25
						26
						27
						28
						29
						30
						31
						32
						33

Copyright © by Houghton Mifflin Company. All rights reserved.

PROBLEM 14-4A or 14-4B (continued)

Copyright © by Houghton Mifflin Company. All rights reserved.

PROBLEM 14-4A or 14-4B (continued)

Copyright © by Houghton Mifflin Company. All rights reserved.

PROBLEM 14-4A or 14-4B (continued)

Copyright © by Houghton Mifflin Company. All rights reserved.

PROBLEM 14-4A or 14-4B (continued)

GENERAL JOURNAL

	DATE		DESCRIPTION	POST. REF.	DEBIT	CREDIT	
1							1
2							2
3							3
4							4
5							5
6							6
7							7
8							8
9							9
10							10
11							11
12							12
13							13
14							14
15							15
16							16
17							17
18							18
19							19
20							20
21							21
22							22
23							23
24							24
25							25
26							26
27							27
28							28
29							29
30							30
31							31
32							32
33							33
34							34
35							35
36							36
37							37

Copyright © by Houghton Mifflin Company. All rights reserved.

PROBLEM 14-4A or 14-4B (concluded)

GENERAL JOURNAL

	DATE		DESCRIPTION	POST. REF.	DEBIT	CREDIT	
1							1
2							2
3							3
4							4
5							5
6							6
7							7
8							8
9							9
10							10
11							11
12							12
13							13
14							14
15							15
16							16
17							17
18							18
19							19
20							20
21							21
22							22
23							23
24							24
25							25
26							26
27							27
28							28
29							29
30							30
31							31
32							32
33							33
34							34
35							35
36							36
37							37

Copyright © by Houghton Mifflin Company. All rights reserved.

CUMULATIVE SELF-CHECK SOLUTIONS: Chapters 13–14

Part III

1.

GENERAL JOURNAL

PAGE _____

	DATE		DESCRIPTION	POST. REF.	DEBIT	CREDIT	
1							1
2							2
3							3
4							4
5							5
6							6

2.

GENERAL JOURNAL

PAGE _____

	DATE		DESCRIPTION	POST. REF.	DEBIT	CREDIT	
1							1
2							2
3							3
4							4
5							5
6							6

Copyright © by Houghton Mifflin Company. All rights reserved.

CUMULATIVE SELF-CHECK (continued)

3.

GENERAL JOURNAL

PAGE _____

	DATE		DESCRIPTION	POST. REF.	DEBIT	CREDIT	
1							1
2							2
3							3
4							4
5							5
6							6
7							7
8							8
9							9
10							10
11							11

Copyright © by Houghton Mifflin Company. All rights reserved.

COMPREHENSIVE REVIEW PROBLEM

SALES JOURNAL

	DATE	INV. NO.	CUSTOMER'S NAME	POST. REF.	ACCOUNTS RECEIVABLE DR., SALES CR.	
1						1
2						2
3						3
4						4
5						5
6						6
7						7

PURCHASES JOURNAL

	DATE	SUPPLIER'S NAME	INV. NO.	INV. DATE	TERMS	POST. REF.	ACCOUNTS PAYABLE CREDIT	FREIGHT IN DEBIT	PURCHASES DEBIT	
1										1
2										2
3										3
4										4
5										5
6										6
7										7

Copyright © by Houghton Mifflin Company. All rights reserved.

COMPREHENSIVE REVIEW PROBLEM (continued)

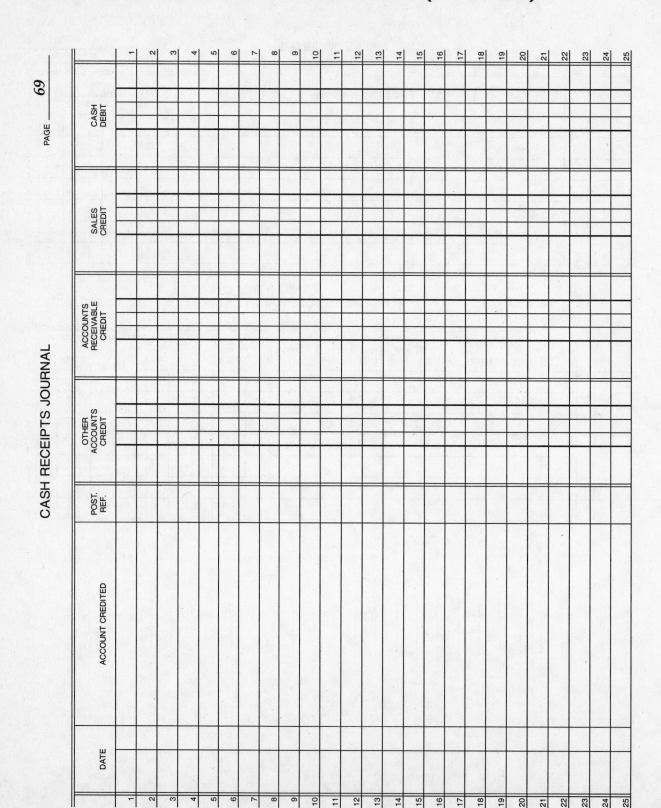

CASH RECEIPTS JOURNAL

PAGE ___ 69

Copyright © by Houghton Mifflin Company. All rights reserved.

COMPREHENSIVE REVIEW PROBLEM (continued)

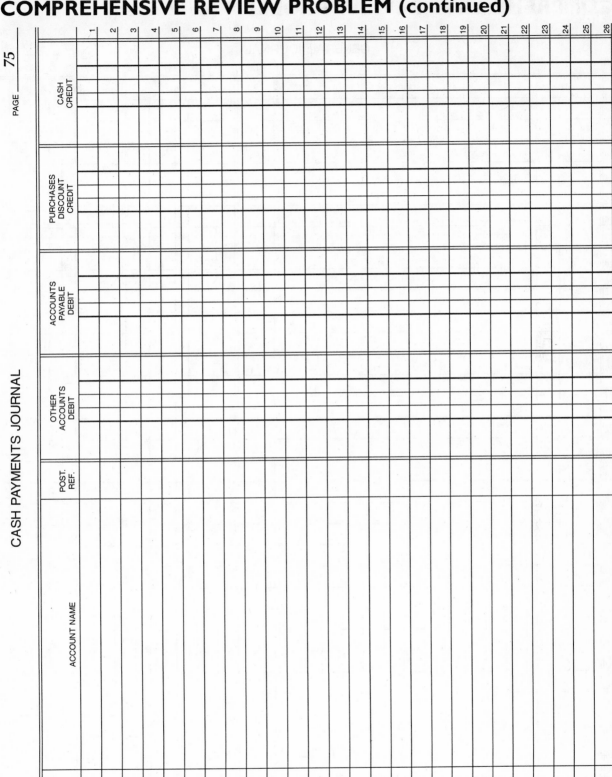

CASH PAYMENTS JOURNAL

PAGE 75

Copyright © by Houghton Mifflin Company. All rights reserved.

COMPREHENSIVE REVIEW PROBLEM (continued)

GENERAL JOURNAL

	DATE	DESCRIPTION	POST. REF.	DEBIT	CREDIT	
1						1
2						2
3						3
4						4
5						5
6						6
7						7
8						8
9						9
10						10
11						11
12						12
13						13
14						14
15						15
16						16
17						17
18						18
19						19
20						20
21						21
22						22
23						23
24						24
25						25
26						26
27						27
28						28
29						29
30						30
31						31
32						32
33						33
34						34
35						35
36						36
37						37

Copyright © by Houghton Mifflin Company. All rights reserved.

NAME _____ DATE _____ CLASS _____

COMPREHENSIVE REVIEW PROBLEM (continued)

GENERAL JOURNAL

PAGE ___*90*___

	DATE	DESCRIPTION	POST. REF.	DEBIT	CREDIT	
1						1
2						2
3						3
4						4
5						5
6						6
7						7
8						8
9						9
10						10
11						11
12						12
13						13
14						14
15						15

GENERAL JOURNAL

PAGE ___*91*___

	DATE	DESCRIPTION	POST. REF.	DEBIT	CREDIT	
1						1
2						2
3						3
4						4
5						5
6						6
7						7
8						8
9						9
10						10
11						11
12						12
13						13
14						14
15						15
16						16
17						17
18						18
19						19

Copyright © by Houghton Mifflin Company. All rights reserved.

COMPREHENSIVE REVIEW PROBLEM (continued)

GENERAL JOURNAL

	DATE		DESCRIPTION	POST. REF.	DEBIT	CREDIT	
1							1
2							2
3							3
4							4
5							5
6							6
7							7
8							8
9							9
10							10
11							11
12							12
13							13
14							14
15							15
16							16
17							17
18							18
19							19
20							20
21							21
22							22
23							23
24							24
25							25
26							26
27							27
28							28
29							29
30							30
31							31
32							32
33							33
34							34
35							35
36							36
37							37

Copyright © by Houghton Mifflin Company. All rights reserved.

COMPREHENSIVE REVIEW PROBLEM (continued)

ACCOUNTS RECEIVABLE LEDGER

NAME *Hotel Bentnor*

ADDRESS *4600 Beaumont Drive*

Dallas, TX 75294

DATE	ITEM	POST. REF.	DEBIT	CREDIT	BALANCE

NAME *Jerome and Woods*

ADDRESS *1420 Favela Road*

Dallas, TX 75294

DATE		ITEM	POST. REF.	DEBIT	CREDIT	BALANCE
20—						
Feb.	1	Balance	✓			11 6 1 9 50

NAME *Wilkes Decorators*

ADDRESS *642 Guthrie St.*

Dallas, TX 75294

DATE		ITEM	POST. REF.	DEBIT	CREDIT	BALANCE
20—						
Feb.	1	Balance	✓			4 9 2 0 14

Copyright © by Houghton Mifflin Company. All rights reserved.

COMPREHENSIVE REVIEW PROBLEM (continued)

ACCOUNTS PAYABLE LEDGER

NAME __Byran, Inc.__

ADDRESS __400 W. Tatum St.__

__Amarillo, TX 79177__

DATE	ITEM	POST. REF.	DEBIT	CREDIT	BALANCE

NAME __Keller Textiles__

ADDRESS __1464 Harding Drive__

__Dallas, TX 75294__

DATE		ITEM	POST. REF.	DEBIT	CREDIT	BALANCE
20—						
Feb.	1	Balance	✓			17 6 2 4 10

NAME __Meldon Fabrics__

ADDRESS __620 W. Huber St.__

__Corpus Christi, TX 78487__

DATE		ITEM	POST. REF.	DEBIT	CREDIT	BALANCE
20—						
Feb.	1	Balance	✓			9 6 1 6 00

Copyright © by Houghton Mifflin Company. All rights reserved.

NAME _____ DATE _____ CLASS _____

COMPREHENSIVE REVIEW PROBLEM (continued)

ACCOUNTS PAYABLE LEDGER

NAME _Taylor Manufacturing Company_

ADDRESS _842 N. Howard Ave._

Fort Worth, TX 76196

DATE		ITEM	POST. REF.	DEBIT	CREDIT	BALANCE
20—						
Feb.	1	Balance	✓			12 7 1 0 00

Copyright © by Houghton Mifflin Company. All rights reserved.

COMPREHENSIVE REVIEW PROBLEM (continued)

GENERAL LEDGER

ACCOUNT *Cash*   ACCOUNT NO. *111*

DATE		ITEM	POST. REF.	DEBIT	CREDIT	BALANCE	
						DEBIT	CREDIT
20—							
Feb.	1	Balance	✓			35 9 9 4 00	

ACCOUNT *Petty Cash Fund*   ACCOUNT NO. *112*

DATE		ITEM	POST. REF.	DEBIT	CREDIT	BALANCE	
						DEBIT	CREDIT
20—							
Feb.	1	Balance	✓			7 0 00	

ACCOUNT *Accounts Receivable*   ACCOUNT NO. *113*

DATE		ITEM	POST. REF.	DEBIT	CREDIT	BALANCE	
						DEBIT	CREDIT
20—							
Feb.	1	Balance	✓			16 5 3 9 64	

Copyright © by Houghton Mifflin Company. All rights reserved.

COMPREHENSIVE REVIEW PROBLEM (continued)

GENERAL LEDGER

ACCOUNT _Merchandise Inventory_   ACCOUNT NO. __114__

DATE		ITEM	POST. REF.	DEBIT	CREDIT	BALANCE	
						DEBIT	CREDIT
20—							
Feb.	1	Balance	✓			52 640 00	

ACCOUNT _Supplies_   ACCOUNT NO. __117__

DATE		ITEM	POST. REF.	DEBIT	CREDIT	BALANCE	
						DEBIT	CREDIT
20—							
Feb.	1	Balance	✓			5 16 50	

ACCOUNT _Prepaid Insurance_   ACCOUNT NO. __118__

DATE		ITEM	POST. REF.	DEBIT	CREDIT	BALANCE	
						DEBIT	CREDIT
20—							
Feb.	1	Balance	✓			4 80 00	

Copyright © by Houghton Mifflin Company. All rights reserved.

COMPREHENSIVE REVIEW PROBLEM (continued)

GENERAL LEDGER

ACCOUNT **Equipment**   ACCOUNT NO. **122**

DATE		ITEM	POST. REF.	DEBIT	CREDIT	BALANCE	
						DEBIT	CREDIT
20—							
Feb.	1	Balance	√			9 3 2 4 00	

ACCOUNT **Accumulated Depreciation, Equipment**   ACCOUNT NO. **123**

DATE		ITEM	POST. REF.	DEBIT	CREDIT	BALANCE	
						DEBIT	CREDIT
20—							
Feb.	1	Balance	√				5 3 2 8 00

ACCOUNT **Accounts Payable**   ACCOUNT NO. **221**

DATE		ITEM	POST. REF.	DEBIT	CREDIT	BALANCE	
						DEBIT	CREDIT
20—							
Feb.	1	Balance	√				39 9 5 0 10

Copyright © by Houghton Mifflin Company. All rights reserved.

COMPREHENSIVE REVIEW PROBLEM (continued)

GENERAL LEDGER

ACCOUNT _Employees' Income Tax Payable_   ACCOUNT NO. ___226___

DATE		ITEM	POST. REF.	DEBIT	CREDIT	BALANCE DEBIT	BALANCE CREDIT
20—							
Feb.	1	Balance	✓				1 3 9 1 60

ACCOUNT _FICA Tax Payable_   ACCOUNT NO. ___227___

DATE		ITEM	POST. REF.	DEBIT	CREDIT	BALANCE DEBIT	BALANCE CREDIT
20—							
Feb.	1	Balance	✓				1 5 2 0 84

ACCOUNT _State Unemployment Tax Payable_   ACCOUNT NO. ___228___

DATE		ITEM	POST. REF.	DEBIT	CREDIT	BALANCE DEBIT	BALANCE CREDIT
20—							
Feb.	1	Balance	✓				5 3 6 76

Copyright © by Houghton Mifflin Company. All rights reserved.

COMPREHENSIVE REVIEW PROBLEM (continued)

GENERAL LEDGER

ACCOUNT *Federal Unemployment Tax Payable*   ACCOUNT NO. 229

DATE		ITEM	POST. REF.	DEBIT	CREDIT	BALANCE	
						DEBIT	CREDIT
20—							
Feb.	1	Balance	✓				79 52

ACCOUNT *Salaries Payable*   ACCOUNT NO. 230

DATE		ITEM	POST. REF.	DEBIT	CREDIT	BALANCE	
						DEBIT	CREDIT
20—							
Feb.	1	Balance	✓				710 00

ACCOUNT *J. L. Fisher, Capital*   ACCOUNT NO. 311

DATE		ITEM	POST. REF.	DEBIT	CREDIT	BALANCE	
						DEBIT	CREDIT
20—							
Feb.	1	Balance	✓				66 047 32

Copyright © by Houghton Mifflin Company. All rights reserved.

COMPREHENSIVE REVIEW PROBLEM (continued)

GENERAL LEDGER

ACCOUNT _J. L. Fisher, Drawing_ _____ ACCOUNT NO. _312_

DATE	ITEM	POST. REF.	DEBIT	CREDIT	BALANCE	
					DEBIT	CREDIT

ACCOUNT _Income Summary_ _____ ACCOUNT NO. _399_

DATE	ITEM	POST. REF.	DEBIT	CREDIT	BALANCE	
					DEBIT	CREDIT

ACCOUNT _Sales_ _____ ACCOUNT NO. _411_

DATE	ITEM	POST. REF.	DEBIT	CREDIT	BALANCE	
					DEBIT	CREDIT

Copyright © by Houghton Mifflin Company. All rights reserved.

COMPREHENSIVE REVIEW PROBLEM (continued)

GENERAL LEDGER

ACCOUNT *Sales Returns and Allowances* _____ ACCOUNT NO. _412_

DATE		ITEM	POST. REF.	DEBIT	CREDIT	BALANCE	
						DEBIT	CREDIT

ACCOUNT *Purchases* _____ ACCOUNT NO. _511_

DATE		ITEM	POST. REF.	DEBIT	CREDIT	BALANCE	
						DEBIT	CREDIT

ACCOUNT *Purchases Returns and Allowances* _____ ACCOUNT NO. _512_

DATE		ITEM	POST. REF.	DEBIT	CREDIT	BALANCE	
						DEBIT	CREDIT

ACCOUNT *Purchases Discount* _____ ACCOUNT NO. _513_

DATE		ITEM	POST. REF.	DEBIT	CREDIT	BALANCE	
						DEBIT	CREDIT

Copyright © by Houghton Mifflin Company. All rights reserved.

COMPREHENSIVE REVIEW PROBLEM (continued)

GENERAL LEDGER

ACCOUNT _Freight In_ _____ ACCOUNT NO. _514_

DATE	ITEM	POST. REF.	DEBIT	CREDIT	BALANCE	
					DEBIT	CREDIT

ACCOUNT _Salary Expense_ _____ ACCOUNT NO. _611_

DATE	ITEM	POST. REF.	DEBIT	CREDIT	BALANCE	
					DEBIT	CREDIT

ACCOUNT _Payroll Tax Expense_ _____ ACCOUNT NO. _612_

DATE	ITEM	POST. REF.	DEBIT	CREDIT	BALANCE	
					DEBIT	CREDIT

Copyright © by Houghton Mifflin Company. All rights reserved.

COMPREHENSIVE REVIEW PROBLEM (continued)

GENERAL LEDGER

ACCOUNT *Rent Expense*   ACCOUNT NO. *613*

DATE	ITEM	POST. REF.	DEBIT	CREDIT	BALANCE DEBIT	BALANCE CREDIT

ACCOUNT *Utilities Expense*   ACCOUNT NO. *614*

DATE	ITEM	POST. REF.	DEBIT	CREDIT	BALANCE DEBIT	BALANCE CREDIT

ACCOUNT *Supplies Expense*   ACCOUNT NO. *616*

DATE	ITEM	POST. REF.	DEBIT	CREDIT	BALANCE DEBIT	BALANCE CREDIT

Copyright © by Houghton Mifflin Company. All rights reserved.

COMPREHENSIVE REVIEW PROBLEM (continued)

GENERAL LEDGER

ACCOUNT *Insurance Expense*   ACCOUNT NO. *617*

DATE	ITEM	POST. REF.	DEBIT	CREDIT	BALANCE	
					DEBIT	CREDIT

ACCOUNT *Depreciation Expense, Equipment*   ACCOUNT NO. *618*

DATE	ITEM	POST. REF.	DEBIT	CREDIT	BALANCE	
					DEBIT	CREDIT

ACCOUNT *Miscellaneous Expense*   ACCOUNT NO. *619*

DATE	ITEM	POST. REF.	DEBIT	CREDIT	BALANCE	
					DEBIT	CREDIT

Copyright © by Houghton Mifflin Company. All rights reserved.

COMPREHENSIVE REVIEW PROBLEM (continued)

Fine Fabrics

Schedule of Accounts Receivable

February 28, 20—

Copyright © by Houghton Mifflin Company. All rights reserved.

COMPREHENSIVE REVIEW PROBLEM (continued)

Fine Fabrics

Schedule of Accounts Payable

February 28, 20—

Copyright © by Houghton Mifflin Company. All rights reserved.

COMPREHENSIVE REVIEW PROBLEM (continued)

	ACCOUNT NAME	TRIAL BALANCE	
		DEBIT	CREDIT
1	Cash		
2	Petty Cash Fund		
3	Accounts Receivable		
4	Merchandise Inventory		
5	Supplies		
6	Prepaid Insurance		
7	Equipment		
8	Accumulated Depreciation, Equipment		
9	Accounts Payable		
10	Employees' Income Tax Payable		
11	FICA Tax Payable		
12	State Unemployment Tax Payable		
13	Federal Unemployment Tax Payable		
14	J. L. Fisher, Capital		
15	J. L. Fisher, Drawing		
16	Sales		
17	Sales Returns and Allowances		
18	Purchases		
19	Purchases Returns and Allowances		
20	Purchases Discount		
21	Freight In		
22	Salary Expense		
23	Payroll Tax Expense		
24	Rent Expense		
25	Utilities Expense		
26	Miscellaneous Expense		
27			
28			
29			
30			
31			
32			
33			
34			
35			
36			

Copyright © by Houghton Mifflin Company. All rights reserved.

COMPREHENSIVE REVIEW PROBLEM (continued)

| ADJUSTMENTS | | INCOME STATEMENT | | BALANCE SHEET | | |
DEBIT	CREDIT	DEBIT	CREDIT	DEBIT	CREDIT	
						1
						2
						3
						4
						5
						6
						7
						8
						9
						10
						11
						12
						13
						14
						15
						16
						17
						18
						19
						20
						21
						22
						23
						24
						25
						26
						27
						28
						29
						30
						31
						32
						33
						34
						35
						36

Copyright © by Houghton Mifflin Company. All rights reserved.

COMPREHENSIVE REVIEW PROBLEM (continued)

Fine Fabrics

Income Statement

For Month Ended February 28, 20—

Copyright © by Houghton Mifflin Company. All rights reserved.

COMPREHENSIVE REVIEW PROBLEM (continued)

Fine Fabrics

Statement of Owner's Equity

For Month Ended February 28, 20—

Copyright © by Houghton Mifflin Company. All rights reserved.

COMPREHENSIVE REVIEW PROBLEM (continued)

Fine Fabrics

Balance Sheet

February 28, 20—

Copyright © by Houghton Mifflin Company. All rights reserved.

COMPREHENSIVE REVIEW PROBLEM (continued)

Fine Fabrics

Post-Closing Trial Balance

February 28, 20—

ACCOUNT NAME	DEBIT	CREDIT
Cash		
Petty Cash Fund		
Accounts Receivable		
Merchandise Inventory		
Supplies		
Prepaid Insurance		
Equipment		
Accumulated Depreciation, Equipment		
Accounts Payable		
Employees' Income Tax Payable		
FICA Tax Payable		
State Unemployment Tax Payable		
Federal Unemployment Tax Payable		
Salaries Payable		
J. L. Fisher, Capital		

Copyright © by Houghton Mifflin Company. All rights reserved.

COMPREHENSIVE REVIEW PROBLEM (continued)

PAYROLL REGISTER FOR SEMIMONTHLY PERIOD ENDED

	NAME	TOTAL HOURS	BEGINNING CUMULATIVE EARNINGS	TOTAL EARNINGS	ENDING CUMULATIVE EARNINGS	TAXABLE EARNINGS		
						UNEMPLOYMENT	SOCIAL SECURITY	MEDICARE
1		40	5 4 6 0 00					
2		40	4 4 8 0 00					
3			9 9 4 0 00					
4								

PAYROLL REGISTER FOR SEMIMONTHLY PERIOD ENDED

	NAME	TOTAL HOURS	BEGINNING CUMULATIVE EARNINGS	TOTAL EARNINGS	ENDING CUMULATIVE EARNINGS	TAXABLE EARNINGS		
						UNEMPLOYMENT	SOCIAL SECURITY	MEDICARE
1		40						
2		40						
3								
4								

366

Copyright © by Houghton Mifflin Company. All rights reserved.

COMPREHENSIVE REVIEW PROBLEM (concluded)

_____

DEDUCTIONS				PAYMENTS		SALARY EXPENSE	
INCOME TAX	SOCIAL SECURITY TAX	MEDICARE TAX	TOTAL	NET AMOUNT	CK. NO.	DEBIT	
							1
							2
							3
							4

_____

DEDUCTIONS				PAYMENTS		SALARY EXPENSE	
INCOME TAX	SOCIAL SECURITY TAX	MEDICARE TAX	TOTAL	NET AMOUNT	CK. NO.	DEBIT	
							1
							2
							3
							4

Copyright © by Houghton Mifflin Company. All rights reserved.

APPENDIX C

PROBLEM C-1

Beginning inventory   cu. yds. @ $ per cu. yd. = $

First purchase   cu. yds. @ $ per cu. yd. =

Second purchase   cu. yds. @ $ per cu. yd. =

Third purchase   _____ cu. yds. @ $ per cu. yd. = _____

Total units available _____ $_____

$$\text{cu. yds.} \overline{)\,\$ } \quad \frac{\$}{} \text{ average cost per cu. yd.}$$

cu. yds. × $ = $_____

PROBLEM C-2

cu. yds. @ $ per cu. yd. = $

_____ cu. yds. @ $ per cu. yd. = _____

_____ cu. yds. $_____

PROBLEM C-3

cu. yds. @ $ per cu. yd. = $_____

Copyright © by Houghton Mifflin Company. All rights reserved.

NAME _____ DATE _____ CLASS _____

APPENDIX D
PROBLEM D-1

_____

_____

_____

Copyright © by Houghton Mifflin Company. All rights reserved.

NAME _____ DATE _____ CLASS _____

PROBLEM D-2

Copyright © by Houghton Mifflin Company. All rights reserved.

NAME _____ DATE _____ CLASS _____

PROBLEM D-3

Copyright © by Houghton Mifflin Company. All rights reserved.

APPENDIX E
PROBLEM E-1

1. Gross Profit % (2001) = $\dfrac{\$}{\$}$ _____ = _____ = _____ %

   Gross Profit % (2000) = $\dfrac{\$}{\$}$ _____ = _____ = _____ %

2. Net Income % (2001) = $\dfrac{\$}{\$}$ _____ = _____ = _____ %

   Net Income % (2000) = $\dfrac{\$}{\$}$ _____ = _____ = _____ %

PROBLEM E-2

Average Merchandise Inventory (2001) = $\dfrac{\$ \quad + \$}{}$ _____ = \$ _____

Merchandise Inventory Turnover (2001) = $\dfrac{\$}{\$}$ _____ = _____ times per year

Average Merchandise Inventory (2000) = $\dfrac{\$ \quad + \$}{}$ _____ = \$ _____

Merchandise Inventory Turnover (2000) = $\dfrac{\$}{\$}$ _____ = _____ times per year

PROBLEM E-3

Average Capital (2001) = $\dfrac{\$ \quad + \$}{}$ _____ = \$ _____

Return on Investment (2001) = $\dfrac{\$}{\$}$ _____ = _____ = _____ %

Average Capital (2000) = $\dfrac{\$ \quad + \$}{}$ _____ = \$ _____

Return on Investment (2000) = $\dfrac{\$}{\$}$ _____ = _____ = _____ %

Copyright © by Houghton Mifflin Company. All rights reserved.

Answers to Study Guide Questions

CHAPTER 1

PART 1 True/False

1. T
2. F
3. F
4. T
5. T
6. T
7. T
8. T
9. T
10. T

PART 2 Completion—Language of Business

1. sole proprietorship
2. liabilities
3. creditor
4. accounts
5. transaction
6. capital
7. fundamental accounting equation
8. chart of accounts
9. equity
10. Revenue
11. withdrawal
12. Accounts Receivable
13. Expenses

PART 3 Classifying Accounts

Assets
Office Equipment
Supplies
Building
Cash
Land
Prepaid Insurance
Neon Sign

Liabilities
Accounts Payable
Mortgage Payable

Owner's Equity
M. A. Dailey, Capital
M. A. Dailey, Drawing

Revenue
Income from Services

Expenses
Rent Expense
Wages Expense

PART 4 Analyzing Transactions

	A	L	OE	R	E
0. *Example:* Owner invested cash	+		+		
1. Payment of rent	−				+
2. Sales of services for cash	+			+	
3. Investment of equipment by owner	+		+		
4. Payment of insurance premium for two years	+ −				
5. Payment of wages	−				+
6. Sales of services on account	+			+	
7. Withdrawal of cash by owner	−		−		
8. Purchase of supplies on account	+	+			
9. Collection from charge customer previously billed	+ −				
10. Payment made to creditor on account	−	−			

Copyright © by Houghton Mifflin Company. All rights reserved.

CHAPTER 2

PART 1   True/False

1.	T	6.	F
2.	T	7.	T
3.	T	8.	T
4.	F	9.	T
5.	F	10.	T

PART 2   Completion—Language of Business

1. debit
2. footings
3. transposition
4. trial balance
5. compound entry
6. credit

PART 3   Accounting Entries

Professional Equipment		Accounts Payable	
+	−	−	+
(a) 760			(a) 760

Accounts Receivable		Professional Fees	
+	−	−	+
(b) 764			(b) 764

Rent Expense		Cash	
+	−	+	−
(c) 950			(c) 950

Supplies		Accounts Payable	
+	−	−	+
(d) 410			(d) 410

Utilities Expense		Cash	
+	−	+	−
(e) 76			(e) 76

Cash		Accounts Receivable	
+	−	+	−
(f) 610			(f) 610

Accounts Payable		Cash	
−	+	+	−
(g) 500			(g) 500

Salary Expense		Cash	
+	−	+	−
(h) 990			(h) 990

Office Equipment		Cash	
+	−	+	−
(i) 342			(i) 342

Accounts Payable		Supplies	
−	+	+	−
(j) 200			(j) 200

Copyright © by Houghton Mifflin Company. All rights reserved.

CHAPTER 3

PART 1   True/False

1. F   6. T
2. F   7. F
3. F   8. F
4. F   9. T
5. T   10. F

PART 2   Completion—Language of Business

1. general ledger
2. posting
3. source documents
4. cost principle
5. journalizing
6. Post. Ref. column of the journal
7. account numbers

PART 3   Completing a Journal Entry

GENERAL JOURNAL   PAGE ___33___

	DATE		DESCRIPTION	POST. REF.	DEBIT	CREDIT	
1	20—						1
2	Oct.	29	Cash	111	1 1 0 0 00		2
3			Accounts Receivable	113	6 0 0 00		3
4			Income from Services	411		1 7 0 0 00	4
5			Received partial payment for				5
6			services performed.				6
7							7
8							8

1. $600 ($1,700 − $1,100)
2. $2,800 ($600 + $1,100 + $1,100)
3. $1,300 ($700 + $400 + $200)
4. compound

Copyright © by Houghton Mifflin Company. All rights reserved.

CHAPTER 4

PART 1   True/False

1.	T	6.	T
2.	F	7.	T
3.	T	8.	F
4.	T	9.	T
5.	T	10.	F

PART 2   Completion—Language of Business

1. book value
2. fiscal period
3. contra
4. adjustments
5. accrued wages
6. accounting cycle
7. mixed accounts
8. matching principle
9. depreciation

PART 3   Adjusting Entries

1.

Prepaid Insurance				Insurance Expense	
Bal.	950	Adj.	510	Adj.	510

2.

Supplies				Supplies Expense	
Bal.	1,100	Adj.	520	Adj.	520

3.

Accumulated Depreciation, Equipment				Depreciation Expense, Equipment	
		Bal.	7,500	Adj.	2,500
		Adj.	2,500		

4.

Wages Expense				Wages Payable	
Bal.	8,100			Adj.	470
Adj.	470				

Copyright © by Houghton Mifflin Company. All rights reserved.

PART 4 Analyzing the Work Sheet

Account Name	Trial Balance		Adjustments		Adj. Trial Balance		Income Statement		Balance Sheet	
	Debit	Credit	Debit	Credit	Debit	Credit	Debit	Credit	Debit	Credit
0. Equipment	X				X				X	
0. Supplies Expense			X		X		X			
1. Cash	X				X				X	
2. C. Tumi, Capital		X				X				X
3. Advertising Expense	X				X		X			
4. Accounts Receivable	X				X				X	
5. Wages Expense	X		X		X		X			
6. Accumulated Depreciation, Equipment		X		X		X				X
7. Wages Payable				X		X				X
8. Supplies	X			X	X				X	
9. C. Tumi, Drawing	X				X				X	
10. Service Revenue		X				X		X		

CHAPTER 5

PART 1 True/False

1.	F	6.	F
2.	T	7.	T
3.	T	8.	F
4.	F	9.	T
5.	F	10.	T

PART 2 Completion—Language of Business

1. post-closing trial balance
2. real or permanent
3. interim
4. Income Summary
5. closing
6. nominal or temporary-equity
7. accrual basis
8. modified cash basis

PART 3 Closing Entries

	Debit	Credit
1.	b	d
2.	d	a, f
3.	d	e
4.	e	c

Copyright © by Houghton Mifflin Company. All rights reserved.

PART 4   Posting Closing Entries

1. $41,000
2. $46,000
3. $5,000 net loss ($46,000 − $41,000)
4. $22,000
5. J. See, Capital; Income Summary
6. J. See, Capital; J. See, Drawing
7. $27,000 decrease ($22,000 + $5,000 net loss)
8. $123,000 ($150,000 − $22,000 − $5,000)

CHAPTER 6

PART 1   True/False

1. T   6. F
2. F   7. F
3. F   8. T
4. T   9. T
5. T   10. F

PART 2   Chart of Accounts

Assets
Cash
Supplies
Prepaid Insurance
Equipment
Accumulated Depreciation, Equipment
Truck
Accumulated Depreciation, Truck

Liabilities
Accounts Payable

Owner's Equity
L. Barnes, Capital
L. Barnes, Drawing
Income Summary

Revenue
Income from Services

Expenses
Salary Expense
Rent Expense
Advertising Expense
Utilities Expense
Supplies Expense
Insurance Expense
Depreciation Expense, Equipment
Depreciation Expense, Truck
Miscellaneous Expense

PART 3

Cash Debit and Credit
Sundry Debit and Credit
Income from Services Credit
Accounts Payable Debit and Credit
Advertising Expense Debit
Miscellaneous Expense Debit

Copyright © by Houghton Mifflin Company. All rights reserved.

CHAPTER 7

PART 1 True/False

1. F   6. T
2. F   7. T
3. F   8. F
4. F   9. F
5. T   10. F

PART 2 Completion—Language of Business

1. payee
2. service charge
3. endorsement
4. denominations
5. canceled checks
6. restrictive endorsement
7. drawer
8. ledger balance of cash
9. deposit in transit
10. change fund
11. qualified endorsement
12. bank reconciliation
13. Outstanding checks
14. blank endorsement

PART 3 Reimbursing the Petty Cash Fund

Balance of the Petty Cash Fund, $60

GENERAL JOURNAL
PAGE _____

	DATE		DESCRIPTION	POST. REF.	DEBIT	CREDIT	
1	20—						1
2	June	30	Repair Expense		7 10		2
3			Delivery Expense		4 20		3
4			Miscellaneous Expense		16 48		4
5			H. Ball, Drawing		11 50		5
6			Cash			39 28	6
7			Issued Ck. No. 711 to reimburse				7
8			the petty cash fund.				8
9							9
10							10
11							11
12							12
13							13

Copyright © by Houghton Mifflin Company. All rights reserved.

CHAPTER 8

PART 1 True/False

1. T	6. F
2. F	7. T
3. F	8. F
4. F	9. T
5. T	10. F

PART 2 Completion—Language of Business

1. gross pay
2. employee
3. exemption
4. net pay
5. independent contractor
6. employee's individual earnings record

PART 3 Calculation of Earnings

Employee's Name	Hours Worked	Regular Hourly Rate	Total Earnings
A. L. Gonzales	42	$ 9.60	$412.80
L. A. Lamar	46	8.40	411.60
C. W. Nelson	51	10.20	576.30

PART 4 Payroll Entry

GENERAL JOURNAL   PAGE ___79___

	DATE		DESCRIPTION	POST. REF.	DEBIT	CREDIT	
1	20—						1
2	Mar.	14	Sales Salary Expense		72 0 0 0 00		2
3			Office Salary Expense		21 6 4 0 00		3
4			Employees' Federal Income Tax				4
5			Payable			9 3 0 0 00	5
6			FICA Tax Payable			7 1 6 3 46	6
7			Employees' Bond Deductions				7
8			Payable			9 0 0 00	8
9			Employees' Union Dues Payable			1 2 0 0 00	9
10			Employees' Medical Insurance				10
11			Payable			2 0 0 00	11
12			Salaries Payable			73 0 7 6 54	12
13			To record payroll for the week				13
14			ended March 14.				14
15							15

Copyright © by Houghton Mifflin Company. All rights reserved.

CHAPTER 9

PART 1   True/False

1.	F	6.	T
2.	F	7.	F
3.	T	8.	T
4.	F	9.	T
5.	T	10.	F

PART 2   Completion—Language of Business

1. quarter
2. Form W-2
3. employer identification number
4. Payroll Tax Expense
5. Workers' compensation insurance
6. W-3
7. Form 941

PART 3   Completing Form W-2

a Control number 22222	Void ☐	For Official Use Only ▶ OMB No. 1545-0008		
b Employer's identification number 72-1162127		1 Wages, tips, other compensation 34,218.42	2 Federal income tax withheld 3,716.22	
c Employer's name, address, and ZIP code Barclay Company 1620 Hampton Place Boston, MA 02116		3 Social security wages 34,218.42	4 Social security tax withheld 2,121.54	
		5 Medicare wages and tips 34,218.42	6 Medicare tax withheld 496.17	
		7 Social security tips 0	8 Allocated tips 0	
d Employee's social security number 561-24-5229		9 Advance EIC payment 0	10 Dependent care benefits	
e Employee's name (first, middle initial, last) June Clara Perkins 2219 Henderson Street Boston, MA 02121		11 Nonqualified plans	12 Benefits included in box 1	
		13 See Instrs. for box 13	14 Other	
		15 Statutory employee ☐ Deceased ☐ Pension plan ☐ Legal rep. ☐ Hshld. emp. ☐ Subtotal ☐ Deferred compensation ☐		
f Employee's address and ZIP code				

16 State	Employer's state I.D. No.	17 State wages, tips, etc.	18 State income tax	19 Locality name	20 Local wages, tips, etc.	21 Local income tax
MA	42-6916	34,218.42	1,780.04			

41-852411   APR. I.R.S.   Department of the Treasury – Internal Revenue Service

Form W-2 Wage and Tax Statement **2000**

Copy A For Social Security Administration

For Paperwork Reduction Act Notice, see separate instructions.

Copyright © by Houghton Mifflin Company. All rights reserved.

CHAPTER 10

PART 1   True/False

1.	T	6.	F
2.	F	7.	F
3.	T	8.	T
4.	F	9.	F
5.	F	10.	T

PART 2   Completion—Language of Business

1. sales journal
2. merchandise inventory
3. special journals
4. controlling account
5. subsidiary ledger
6. credit memorandum
7. summarizing entry

PART 3   Posting

SALES JOURNAL   PAGE _____26_____

DATE		INV. NO.	CUSTOMER'S NAME	POST. REF.	ACCOUNTS RECEIVABLE DEBIT	SALES TAX PAYABLE CREDIT	SALES CREDIT
20—							
June	1	32	Calvin Parsons		1 4 5 60	5 60	1 4 0 00
	30	171	Clara Lambert		1 6 1 41	6 21	1 5 5 20
	30				3 1 6 8 07	1 2 1 85	3 0 4 6 22
					(1 1 3)	(2 1 4)	(4 1 1)

GENERAL LEDGER

ACCOUNT _Accounts Receivable_ _____ ACCOUNT NO. ____113____

DATE		ITEM	POST. REF.	DEBIT	CREDIT	BALANCE	
						DEBIT	CREDIT
20—							
June	30		S26	3 1 6 8 07		3 1 6 8 07	

ACCOUNT _Sales Tax Payable_ _____ ACCOUNT NO. ____214____

DATE		ITEM	POST. REF.	DEBIT	CREDIT	BALANCE	
						DEBIT	CREDIT
20—							
June	30		S26		1 2 1 85		1 2 1 85

Copyright © by Houghton Mifflin Company. All rights reserved.

ACCOUNT _Sales_								ACCOUNT NO. _411_

DATE		ITEM	POST. REF.	DEBIT	CREDIT	BALANCE	
						DEBIT	CREDIT
20—							
June	30		S26		3 0 4 6 22		3 0 4 6 22

CHAPTER 11

PART 1   True/False

1. F
2. T
3. F
4. T
5. F
6. F
7. F
8. T
9. T
10. T

PART 2   Completion—Language of Business

1. purchase order
2. FOB shipping point
3. internal control
4. crossfooting
5. purchase invoice
6. credit memorandum
7. FOB destination

CHAPTER 12

PART 1   True/False

1. T
2. F
3. F
4. T
5. F
6. F
7. F
8. T
9. T
10. T

PART 2   Completion—Language of Business

1. trade discounts
2. credit period
3. cash discount

PART 3   Matching

1. P
2. CR
3. J
4. CR
5. J
6. J
7. J
8. CP
9. S
10. CP

Copyright © by Houghton Mifflin Company. All rights reserved.

PART 4 Cash Receipts Journal

Other Accounts Credit
Accounts Receivable Credit
Sales Credit
Sales Discount Debit
Cash Debit

CHAPTER 13

PART 1 True/False

1.	T	6.	T
2.	F	7.	T
3.	F	8.	F
4.	F	9.	T
5.	T	10.	F

PART 2 Identifying Work Sheet Columns

Account Name	Income Statement		Balance Sheet	
	Debit	Credit	Debit	Credit
Example: 0. Rent Income		✓		
1. Sales Discount	✓			
2. C. Carr, Drawing			✓	
3. Supplies Expense	✓			
4. Sales		✓		
5. Merchandise Inventory			✓	
6. Purchases Returns and Allowances		✓		
7. Income Summary	✓	✓		
8. C. Carr, Capital				✓
9. Accumulated Depreciation, Equipment				✓
10. Purchases	✓			
11. Sales Returns and Allowances	✓			
12. Purchases Discount		✓		
13. Unearned Rent				✓
14. Supplies			✓	
15. Salaries Payable				✓

Copyright © by Houghton Mifflin Company. All rights reserved.

CHAPTER 14

PART 1   True/False

1.	F	6.	T
2.	F	7.	T
3.	T	8.	F
4.	F	9.	F
5.	F	10.	F

PART 2   Completion—Language of Business

1. Working Capital
2. Gross Profit
3. Cost of Goods Sold
4. Income from Operations
5. Freight In

PART 3   Financial Statement Classifications

Account Name	Financial Statement	Classification
0. Wages Expense	Income Statement	Operating Expenses
0. Accounts Payable	Balance Sheet	Current Liabilities
1. Purchases	Income Statement	Cost of Goods Sold
2. Accounts Receivable	Balance Sheet	Current Assets
3. Building	Balance Sheet	Plant and Equipment
4. Freight In	Income Statement	Cost of Goods Sold
5. Interest Expense	Income Statement	Other Expenses
6. Supplies	Balance Sheet	Current Assets
7. Sales Discount	Income Statement	Revenue from Sales
8. Unearned Subscriptions	Balance Sheet	Current Liabilities
9. Accumulated Depreciation, Equipment	Balance Sheet	Plant and Equipment
10. Purchases Returns and Allowances	Income Statement	Cost of Goods Sold

PROBLEM

GENERAL JOURNAL

PAGE _____

	DATE	DESCRIPTION	POST. REF.	DEBIT	CREDIT	
1						1
2						2
3						3
4						4
5						5
6						6
7						7
8						8
9						9
10						10
11						11
12						12
13						13
14						14
15						15
16						16
17						17
18						18
19						19
20						20
21						21
22						22
23						23
24						24
25						25
26						26
27						27
28						28
29						29
30						30
31						31
32						32
33						33
34						34
35						35
36						36
37						37

Copyright © by Houghton Mifflin Company. All rights reserved.

NAME _____ DATE _____ CLASS _____

PROBLEM

GENERAL JOURNAL

	DATE		DESCRIPTION	POST. REF.	DEBIT	CREDIT	
1							1
2							2
3							3
4							4
5							5
6							6
7							7
8							8
9							9
10							10
11							11
12							12
13							13
14							14
15							15
16							16
17							17
18							18
19							19
20							20
21							21
22							22
23							23
24							24
25							25
26							26
27							27
28							28
29							29
30							30
31							31
32							32
33							33
34							34
35							35
36							36
37							37

Copyright © by Houghton Mifflin Company. All rights reserved.

PROBLEM

GENERAL JOURNAL

	DATE	DESCRIPTION	POST. REF.	DEBIT	CREDIT	
1						1
2						2
3						3
4						4
5						5
6						6
7						7
8						8
9						9
10						10
11						11
12						12
13						13
14						14
15						15
16						16
17						17
18						18
19						19
20						20
21						21
22						22
23						23
24						24
25						25
26						26
27						27
28						28
29						29
30						30
31						31
32						32
33						33
34						34
35						35
36						36
37						37

Copyright © by Houghton Mifflin Company. All rights reserved.

NAME _____ DATE _____ CLASS _____

PROBLEM

GENERAL JOURNAL

PAGE _____

	DATE		DESCRIPTION	POST. REF.	DEBIT	CREDIT	
1							1
2							2
3							3
4							4
5							5
6							6
7							7
8							8
9							9
10							10
11							11
12							12
13							13
14							14
15							15
16							16
17							17
18							18
19							19
20							20
21							21
22							22
23							23
24							24
25							25
26							26
27							27
28							28
29							29
30							30
31							31
32							32
33							33
34							34
35							35
36							36
37							37

Copyright © by Houghton Mifflin Company. All rights reserved.

PROBLEM

GENERAL JOURNAL

	DATE		DESCRIPTION	POST. REF.	DEBIT	CREDIT	
1							1
2							2
3							3
4							4
5							5
6							6
7							7
8							8
9							9
10							10
11							11
12							12
13							13
14							14
15							15
16							16
17							17
18							18
19							19
20							20
21							21
22							22
23							23
24							24
25							25
26							26
27							27
28							28
29							29
30							30
31							31
32							32
33							33
34							34
35							35
36							36
37							37

Copyright © by Houghton Mifflin Company. All rights reserved.

NAME _____ DATE _____ CLASS _____

PROBLEM

GENERAL JOURNAL

	DATE	DESCRIPTION	POST. REF.	DEBIT	CREDIT	
1						1
2						2
3						3
4						4
5						5
6						6
7						7
8						8
9						9
10						10
11						11
12						12
13						13
14						14
15						15
16						16
17						17
18						18
19						19
20						20
21						21
22						22
23						23
24						24
25						25
26						26
27						27
28						28
29						29
30						30
31						31
32						32
33						33
34						34
35						35
36						36
37						37

Copyright © by Houghton Mifflin Company. All rights reserved.

NAME _____ DATE _____ CLASS _____

PROBLEM

GENERAL JOURNAL

	DATE	DESCRIPTION	POST. REF.	DEBIT	CREDIT	
1						1
2						2
3						3
4						4
5						5
6						6
7						7
8						8
9						9
10						10
11						11
12						12
13						13
14						14
15						15
16						16
17						17
18						18
19						19
20						20
21						21
22						22
23						23
24						24
25						25
26						26
27						27
28						28
29						29
30						30
31						31
32						32
33						33
34						34
35						35
36						36
37						37

Copyright © by Houghton Mifflin Company. All rights reserved.

PROBLEM

CASH RECEIPTS JOURNAL

DATE	ACCOUNT NAME	POST. REF.	OTHER ACCOUNTS DEBIT	OTHER ACCOUNTS CREDIT	SALES CREDIT	SALES DISCOUNT DEBIT	CASH DEBIT

CASH PAYMENTS JOURNAL

DATE	CK. NO.	ACCOUNT NAME	POST. REF.	OTHER ACCOUNTS DEBIT	ACCOUNTS PAYABLE DEBIT	PURCHASES DISCOUNT CREDIT	CASH CREDIT

Copyright © by Houghton Mifflin Company. All rights reserved.

PROBLEM

CASH RECEIPTS JOURNAL

PAGE _____

DATE	ACCOUNT NAME	POST. REF.	OTHER ACCOUNTS DEBIT	OTHER ACCOUNTS CREDIT	SALES CREDIT	SALES DISCOUNT DEBIT	CASH DEBIT
							1
							2
							3
							4
							5
							6
							7
							8
							9

CASH PAYMENTS JOURNAL

PAGE _____

DATE	CK. NO.	ACCOUNT NAME	POST. REF.	OTHER ACCOUNTS DEBIT	ACCOUNTS PAYABLE DEBIT	PURCHASES DISCOUNT CREDIT	CASH CREDIT
							1
							2
							3
							4
							5
							6
							7
							8
							9
							10

394

Copyright © by Houghton Mifflin Company. All rights reserved.

PROBLEM

PAGE _____

CASH RECEIPTS JOURNAL

| DATE | ACCOUNT NAME | POST. REF. | OTHER ACCOUNTS | | SALES CREDIT | SALES DISCOUNT DEBIT | CASH DEBIT |
			DEBIT	CREDIT			

PAGE _____

CASH PAYMENTS JOURNAL

DATE	CK. NO.	ACCOUNT NAME	POST. REF.	OTHER ACCOUNTS DEBIT	ACCOUNTS PAYABLE DEBIT	PURCHASES DISCOUNT CREDIT	CASH CREDIT

Copyright © by Houghton Mifflin Company. All rights reserved.

PROBLEM

CASH RECEIPTS JOURNAL

DATE	ACCOUNT NAME	POST. REF.	OTHER ACCOUNTS DEBIT	OTHER ACCOUNTS CREDIT	SALES CREDIT	SALES DISCOUNT DEBIT	CASH DEBIT

CASH PAYMENTS JOURNAL

DATE	CK. NO.	ACCOUNT NAME	POST. REF.	OTHER ACCOUNTS DEBIT	ACCOUNTS PAYABLE DEBIT	PURCHASES DISCOUNT CREDIT	CASH CREDIT

Copyright © by Houghton Mifflin Company. All rights reserved.

PROBLEM

CASH RECEIPTS JOURNAL

PAGE _____

DATE	ACCOUNT NAME	POST. REF.	OTHER ACCOUNTS		SALES CREDIT	SALES DISCOUNT DEBIT	CASH DEBIT
			DEBIT	CREDIT			

CASH PAYMENTS JOURNAL

PAGE _____

DATE	CK. NO.	ACCOUNT NAME	POST. REF.	OTHER ACCOUNTS DEBIT	ACCOUNTS PAYABLE DEBIT	PURCHASES DISCOUNT CREDIT	CASH CREDIT

Copyright © by Houghton Mifflin Company. All rights reserved.

PROBLEM

PAGE _____

CASH RECEIPTS JOURNAL

DATE	ACCOUNT NAME	POST. REF.	OTHER ACCOUNTS DEBIT	OTHER ACCOUNTS CREDIT	SALES CREDIT	SALES DISCOUNT DEBIT	CASH DEBIT
1							
2							
3							
4							
5							
6							
7							
8							
9							

PAGE _____

CASH PAYMENTS JOURNAL

DATE	CK. NO.	ACCOUNT NAME	POST. REF.	OTHER ACCOUNTS DEBIT	ACCOUNTS PAYABLE DEBIT	PURCHASES DISCOUNT CREDIT	CASH CREDIT
1							
2							
3							
4							
5							
6							
7							
8							
9							
10							

Copyright © by Houghton Mifflin Company. All rights reserved.

NAME _____ DATE _____ CLASS _____

PROBLEM

CASH RECEIPTS JOURNAL

DATE	ACCOUNT NAME	POST. REF.	OTHER ACCOUNTS DEBIT	OTHER ACCOUNTS CREDIT	SALES CREDIT	SALES DISCOUNT DEBIT	CASH DEBIT
1							
2							
3							
4							
5							
6							
7							
8							
9							

CASH PAYMENTS JOURNAL

DATE	CK. NO.	ACCOUNT NAME	POST. REF.	OTHER ACCOUNTS DEBIT	ACCOUNTS PAYABLE DEBIT	PURCHASES DISCOUNT CREDIT	CASH CREDIT
1							
2							
3							
4							
5							
6							
7							
8							
9							
10							

Copyright © by Houghton Mifflin Company. All rights reserved.

PROBLEM

CASH RECEIPTS JOURNAL

PAGE _____

DATE	ACCOUNT NAME	POST. REF.	OTHER ACCOUNTS DEBIT	OTHER ACCOUNTS CREDIT	SALES CREDIT	SALES DISCOUNT DEBIT	CASH DEBIT
1							
2							
3							
4							
5							
6							
7							
8							
9							

CASH PAYMENTS JOURNAL

PAGE _____

DATE	CK. NO.	ACCOUNT NAME	POST. REF.	OTHER ACCOUNTS DEBIT	ACCOUNTS PAYABLE DEBIT	PURCHASES DISCOUNT CREDIT	CASH CREDIT
1							
2							
3							
4							
5							
6							
7							
8							
9							
10							

Copyright © by Houghton Mifflin Company. All rights reserved.